To all those who want to go beyond indignation

Michel Laloux

Detoxify the economy

Volume 1

A revolution in thinking about money

Translated from French by Raymond Aitken

Démocratie Évolutive
www.democratie-evolutive.fr

Table of contents

Abbreviations :

AB :   Throughout the text, [AB] refers to the Additionnal
        Bibliography, at the end of the book.

TG :   Throughout the text, [TG] refers to the Translator's
        Glossary, at the end of the book.

For more abreviations, acronyms and symbols used in
this book, see p. 359

Forward by the translator

"Monetary economics has traditionally been dominated by the question of how the quantity of money, or the growth rate of that quantity, affects prices and quantities of goods. My reasoning here suggests that this focus is misplaced. Money is a record-keeping device; hence, monetary policy should be designed so that record-keeping is performed in the most efficient way possible. How do we do that? Currently, we do not know. But searching for the answers should lead to a more satisfactory (and robust) understanding of optimal monetary policy." (Kocherlakota, 1998)[AB].

The above is quoted from a 1998 paper, by Narayana Kocherlakota, a former President of the Federal Reserve Bank of Minneapolis, who was named one of the top 100 Global Thinkers by Foreign Policy magazine. In my opinion, this book by Michel Laloux, which I have had the privilege to translate from the original French, answers the challenge posed some 18 years ago, by Narayana Kocherlakota.

However, what Michel Laloux proposes in this book might seem "unthinkable" to Kocherlakota, as well as to other economists whose livelihood is embedded in the paradigm of money being a financial commodity. When one considers this paradigm, whereby money can be "manufactured" as the ultimate economic "good", through a convoluted process of public and private sector interest-bearing indebtment, administered by the central banking cartel, one can ask: hasn't this paradigm now reached its apocalyptic End Time ?

In the words of Dirk J Bezemer, the approach Michel Laloux is based on *"the role of banks and credit in our socio-economic system using the metaphor of banks as social accountants, introduced by Stiglitz and Weiss (1988). It highlights the credit nature of money, and thus the fact that money is an accounting construct."* (Bezemer, 2009)[AB].

Neither human society, nor the planet, can afford the moribund concept that money can be traded in financial markets, or rented out at an exponential rate of compounding interest.

Well-being is the root meaning of "wealth", which gives the connotation of a living evolutionary dynamic, rather than the mummified stasis of materialistic accumulation. An etymological understanding of the words we use in economic and monetary discourse, reveals how far we have deviated from the original significance of economy and money. Economy is derived from the ancient Greek words "oikos" (eco), meaning household (society), and "nomos" (law). As Aristotle declared, money[1] "exists not

---

1   Money is a Latin word, which comes from ancient Rome, where coins were minted under the temple of the goddess Juno Moneta, who was the protectress of funds.

by nature (as a commodity) but by law (nomos).". Law is about human rights and obligations.

Today we live in a competitive frenzy to accumulate and store commodified records of transacted value, which serve as purchasing rights, supposedly backed by reciprocal obligations to produce new well-being. However, most of these "record-keeping devices" only account for value transactions that have been fictitiously generated in the *unreal economy*, through the speculative asset inflation-deflation arbitrage of financialization. As such, this mass of metastatic financial capital represents counterfeit purchasing power on natural and intellectual resources, as well as an illegitimate control over the ends and means of *real economy* production. So spellbound are we with the chrematistic glitter of the value of money, that we are failing to respond effectively, to the consequential austerity-driven collapse in the production of *real* value. But even worse, we are failing to arrest the accumulative catastrophic hollowing out of the natural and cultural capital on which human life depends.

Prof. Ismael Hossein-Zadeh, eruditely summaries the "irrational exuberance" exhibited by leading economic and monetary policymakers:

"Portraying asset-price inflation as a monetary tool of economic stimulation, policymakers in the United States and other core capitalist countries are no longer averse to creating financial bubbles; as such bubbles are viewed and depicted as fueling the economy through demand enhancement effects of asset-price appreciation. Instead of regulating or containing the disruptive speculative activities of the financial sector, economic policy makers,

spearheaded by the Federal Reserve Bank since the days of Alan Greenspan, have been actively promoting asset-price or financial bubbles—in effect, also further enriching the rich and exacerbating inequality.

Aside from issues such as social justice and economic security for the masses of people, the idea of creating asset-price bubbles as vehicles of economic stimulation is also unsustainable—indeed, destructive—in the long run: financial bubbles, no matter how long or how much they may expand, are ultimately bound by the amount of real values that are produced (by human labor) in an economy.

Champions of the policy of asset-price bubbles as economic stimuli do not seem to be worried about the destabilizing effects of the bubbles they help create, as they tend to believe (or hope) that the likely disturbances and losses from the potential bursting of one bubble could be offset by creating another bubble. In other words, they seem to believe that they have discovered an insurance policy for bubbles that burst by blowing new ones." (Hossein-Zadeh, 2014)[AB].

Furthermore, a great proportion of the monetised purchasing rights that we call money, which transit the *unreal economy* of QE[TG] finance, into the *real economy*, are not being spent for the production of human well-being (wealth), but its antithesis; or what John Ruskin called "illth"; meaning the production of a global matrix of human and earthly ill-being.

Not only does Michel Laloux present the unthinkable, in terms of an international monetary system without any need of any kind of financial market. Furthermore, his unthinkable decommodification approach liberates the commonwealth factors of production presently captured by shareholder capital, and the privatisation of natural resources (especially land), thereby upholding the sanctity of human work.

The author's approach is in line with that of Karl Polanyi[2], which Gary Flomenhoft has recently and eruditely brought to our attention:

"[Karl Polanyi] made the observation that land, capital, and labor are "fictitious" commodities, since they are not "produced for sale on the market" (Polanyi, p. 72), and therefore their prices are not equilibrated by supply and demand. He pointed out that the attempt to commodify these factors would demolish people, business, and nature if some mitigating steps were not taken.". And therefore: "It is the attempt to commodify land, money, and human labor which is at the root of many economic problems ...".

"In the neo-liberal dominance and globalization of the last few decades, deregulation of all three factors has taken place to a great extent. What Polanyi thought could never actually be realized has come closer to reality. The treatment of land and money as commodities for generation of unearned income[3] through asset bubbles has become sacred. "Flexible" labor markets are also

---

2   Karl Paul Polanyi, 1886 - 1964, was a Hungarian-American economic historian, economic anthropologist, political economist, historical sociologist and social philosopher. He is known for his opposition to traditional economic thought and for his book, The Great Transformation, which showed how the emergence of market-based societies in modern Europe was not inevitable but historically contingent. (Source: Wikipedia).

3   Unearned income is a synonym for "economic rent", which means income that is received without any reciprocal contribution in terms of work, or the added value product of human work.

promoted in the neo-liberal ideology of our time because they are good for business, but not necessarily for human beings who comprise labor.".

"Commodification of land, money, and labor are not necessary for a functioning market economy, and in fact are detrimental to it. For example, land can be placed in trusts, money can be administered as a public utility, and people can reclaim sovereignty over their own labor.".

"The concepts of socially responsible business, green economics, sustainable economics, the creative economy, natural capital, steady-state economics, caring economy, solidarity economy, cooperative economy, or any other suggested solutions, have no chance of succeeding in creating widespread prosperity or sustainability, unless the operating system of the economy can be reformed in these three crucial systemic ways." (Flomenhoft, 2016)[AB].

Michel Laloux's book is not about moralising on these issues, nor castigating bankers and politicians. Instead the author invites us to think in a new way about the economy, money and democracy, so that as Civil Society, we can empower ourselves to take appropriate and sufficient action. Michel Laloux proposes a transparent and accountable institutional framework of Civil Society Organisations (CSOs), for the operation of an interest-free international monetary system, as a non-partisan public service, democratically governed by and for all the Peoples.

The author's approach exemplifies the wise advice of Buckminster Fuller: *"In order to change an existing paradigm you do not struggle to try and change the problematic model. You create a new model and make the old one obsolete. That, in essence, is the higher service to which we are all being called."*

Let us have no doubt that the incumbent paradigm of money as a commodity is obsolete, and that the institutions which manage it are anachronisms[4]. Their continuance is predicated on our ignorance, on our not daring to question established dogma, on us not thinking outside the box of an orthodoxy, which is driven by irrational self-interest, spuriously justified through a distorted interpretation of Adam Smith's *Wealth of Nations*.

Here for example, is the witness of a former governor of the Bank of England, Lord King, extracted from a speech he gave in 1999, to top level bankers, which was sponsored by the Federal Reserve Bank of Kansas City:

"At present, central banks are the monopoly supplier of base money – cash and bank reserves. Because base money is the ultimate medium of exchange and of final settlement, central banks have enormous leverage over the value of transactions in the economy, even though the size of their balance sheet is very small in relation to those of the private sector. Is it possible that advances in technology will mean that the arbitrary assumptions necessary to introduce money into rigorous theoretical models will become redundant, and that the world may come to resemble a pure exchange economy? Electronic transactions in real time hold out that possibility. There is no reason, in principle, why final settlements could not be carried out by the private sector without the need for clearing through the central bank. Financial assets and real goods and services would be priced in terms of a unit of account. The choice of a unit of account (...) would

---

4   See chapter 17: The central bank, an anachronism.

held and handed over to someone else as a means of payment. There are only accounts inside the (imagined) digital social balance sheet. Any change in one account must have its exact balancing changes in one or more other accounts. All that occurs is transfer of rights. The reality of money as a species of rights practically forces itself into the mind of the economist. All the mysteries that have surrounded money throughout its long history disappear for good.".

"Money is not a thing but a species of credit, and hence a social relation involving rights and obligations." (Moini, 2001)[AB].

Recovering the health of the economy, and thereby its inherent fraternity and sustainability, depends on recovering our ability to think the "unthinkable" about money. We need to divest ourselves of a toxic legacy of intellectual sleights of hand, which have over centuries, colonised the corpus of economic and legal theory. Certain economic researchers, like Norbert Häring, are even convinced that we have been *"intentionally and systematically mislead about the nature of money and about the role of central banks and commercial banks in the monetary system."* (Häring, 2013)[AB]. As Einstein once put it: *"No problem can be solved by the same kind of thinking that created it.".*

Reading this book by Michel Laloux, can help us to learn how to think lucidly for ourselves. I can personally witness that my own capacity to think and communicate clearly about economic phenomena, and about the monetary system, has vastly improved as a result of reading and translating this book.

Michel Laloux repeatedly urges us to *"think the unthinkable"*. I have therefore extracted all instances where he describes and demonstrates the method he uses to analyse the economy. For the convenience of the reader, I have compiled them as a postscript: *"A phenomenological approach to analysing the economy"*. My hope is that this will serve as a useful learning resource and reminder for readers. I have also contributed another two resources: an Additional Bibliography and a Translator's glossary.

The Additional Bibliography complements the References of sources that were cited in the original French edition. It comprises a list of papers and other works in English, which is intended to provide the reader with a context and background, relative to the contents of this book.

The Translator's glossary is my present attempt to help the reader deal with the chronic problem of semantic obfuscation in economic discourse. Obfuscation is a longstanding problem, as was witnessed by early economists, like Thomas Robert Malthus (1766 – 1834), who remarked that: *"... one of the principal causes [of intractable differences of opinion among economists]* *"may be traced to the different meanings in which the same terms have been used."*[AB].

The first social institution is language, and the words we use, whether by conscious choice or careless ignorance, expand or contract our critical thinking capacity. The ancient Chinese political philosopher, Confucius, believed that social disorder can stem from the failure to call things by their proper names, because it results in a collective failure to perceive, understand, and deal with reality.

One person addressing this serious problem is Michael Hudson, a research professor of economics and one of the founding members of the World Economics Association, who has created the *"Insider's Economic Dictionary - telling it how it is, one definition at a time"*. This valuable resource can be consulted on-line[AB]. On the first page of Hudson's dictionary is a quotation from George Orwell, which succinctly describes the problem we face regarding meaningful economic analysis and discourse:

"Now, it is clear that the decline of a language must ultimately have political and economic causes . . . . It becomes ugly and inaccurate because our thoughts are foolish, but the slovenliness of our language makes it easier for us to have foolish thoughts. The point is that the process is reversible. . . . If one gets rid of these habits one can think more clearly, and to think clearly is a necessary first step toward political regeneration. George Orwell, "Politics and the English Language" (1946)

My more humble attempt in the form of a Translator's glossary, is limited to helping the reader to gain maximum benefit from the content of Michel Laloux's book.

Here I end, with a message from Max Planck, addressed to the next generation of economists, who I hope will dedicate themselves to not only thinking the unthinkable, but actually realising it: *"When you change the way you look at things the things you look at change"*.

Raymond Aitken

Preface by the author

When the fiasco of subprime crisis broke out, I said to myself : the point has been reached where civil society has to rethink the whole economy. This might appear to be a foolish pretension, especially when so many competent economists have already written so many books on the subject. Yet, their competence resides within the framework of what is usually considered to be the economy. Within this domain, they include certain elements such as money markets, central banking, base rates, stock exchanges, budget deficits, labour markets, and so on.

Since they were students, these economists learned that these elements are part of economy. From my point of view they are not, but have emerged as symptoms of a deep economic malaise. In the following chapters, I intend to show that these elements contribute to making the economy sick. And, I dare us to ask the essential question: do we know what a healthy economy looks like?

Considering what has happened since the subprime crisis, the answer to this question is obviously "No!". We continue to conflate the remedy with the pathogen.

But the *real economy* never lies to us. It always shows, even if it is in the long term, all the imbalances that have been introduced into it. We have to learn how to decipher the causes of economic disequilibrium. If we don't do it, then, one day or another, we have to pay for it. Nowadays, the bill is getting higher and higher in terms of the environment, unemployment, poverty, diseases, and so on.

Although the *real economy* never lies, the financial economy masks the reality for a time. In the end, the *real economy* will make reality evident. One way that the *real economy* chooses to open our eyes is by the autoinhibition of the pathogen itself.

For example, interest rates. Interest is the first step in making money out of money. The problem will be fully discussed in chapter 15. Today, the economy is so sick that interest rates are decreasing down to zero and even less. This is because huge amounts of hot money[TG] are looking for safe havens, and their owners are ready to pay for a protective harbour ... at a negative rate!

Fifty years ago, had a university taught that negative rates could be proposed as a healing measure in economy, the students would have laughed, as if it was a joke.

Central banking itself is showing its limits; having arrived at a point of zero effectiveness. The unbelievable Quantitative Easing technique confirms what I say in chapter 17; that central banking is anachronistic, and its continuancereveals that we are still stuck in a redundant paradigm of money as a commodity.

Quantitative Easing signals the autoinhibition of central banking itself. In reality, the concept of money as a financial commodity is falling into an abyss.

After 2008, another symptom of the malfunction of the modern economy came to the foreground : the Eurozone sovereign debt crisis. Although it seems to have reached a hiatus, it will continue to exacerbate, for as long as we do not tackle its root causes. The case of Greece is representative of how mainstream economic thinking drives countries into disastrous situations.

In a video, *4 measures for saving Greece*[5], I proposed a new approach to this issue. One will see how my concept for three monetary circuits, as described all along this book, addresses the root causes of the sovereign debt crisis.

But to have a complete overview of the challenge at hand, I should mention two critical issues:

1. Restoration of economic health implies a transformation in our approach to State administration and the State budget. This is a huge issue that would need a whole book. As an outline, I refer the reader to chapters 23 and 24, where I describe a new approach to public services, arising out of the monetary system architecture that I propose. Beyond the monetary aspect, it engenders a new type of democracy which I sketch out. I name it *Evolutive Democracy*, whereby organised civil society emerges to replace the worn out political system, which blocks or avoids all urgent changes that our world needs.

---

5   Published on Youtube, 6 July 2015, and subtitled in English at: https://www.youtube.com/watch?v=-kwXy5rLMuo&feature=youtu.be

2. The financial economy does not have its feet on the ground of reality. It floats in the air of speculation. The *real economy* has to land back, on the ground of reality, which is the locus of livelihood for billions of women and men. To do so, we have to develop a renewed capacity to follow the development and consequences of each phenomenon, which is introduced into the *real economy*. This capacity requires that we consider earth, society and the human being as a whole; with the economy functioning as a nexus of interconnection that maintains the whole.

From the perspective of money, one cannot say that we have acquired this new capacity, as long as we continue to deal with currencies and balances of payments in the way we do it today. As we will see in chapter 14, we have to dare a tremendous conceptual leap. To take an example, when a firm located in the Eurozone exports goods to Japan, it receives payment in Yen. The firm then exchanges these Yen for Euros in a money market. Clearly the purchasing rights, demoninated both in Yen and the Euros are treated like commodities, and they therefore coexist simultaneously, thereby doubling the money supply, (until the central bank of Japan buys the Yen back, in order to cancel this financial market money creation). This is the way we deal with currencies when we consider money as a commodity. It is economic nonsense. In the *real economy*, where money should only be considered as a unit of account, the purchasing rights expressed in the Yen unit of account, would be cancelled upon their conversion into Euros.

I consider what I wrote in chapter 14 as the most important part of the book. One can say that he has integrated the notion of money as accountancy, only if he can consider the translation of monetary purchasing rights, from one currency unit to another, as a pure conversion between units of account; not as an exchange between two simultaneously existing financial commodities. Of course, one question remains : how do we determine conversion rates? The reader will find a proposal in chapter 25, where I elaborate from a global perspective, a new International Monetary System that serves the *real economy*.

When I look back on what has happened since the 2008 subprime crisis, both to the *real economy*, as well as unreal financial economy; I have the impression that the ideas and proposals described in this book are becoming more topical every year. But it is up to the reader to decide whether this is correct or not. In any case, if the book can contribute to a new way of thinking about the *real economy*, it will have achieved its purpose.

Michel Laloux

be a matter for public choice and regulation, along the lines of existing weights and measures inspectors. The need to limit excessive money creation would be replaced by a concern to ensure the integrity of the computer systems used for settlement purposes. A regulatory body to monitor such systems would be required. Moreover, in just the same way as the Internet is unaware of national boundaries, settlement facilities would become international. There would be no unique role for base money, and hence the central bank monopoly of base money issue would have no value. Central banks would lose their ability to implement monetary policy. The successors to Bill Gates would have put the successors to Alan Greenspan out of business." (King, 1999)[AB].

The foresight that Mervyn King communicated to his central banking colleagues is the "unthinkable" that Michel Laloux proposes. In 2001, the late Mostafa Moini corroborated King's "unthinkable" foresight:

"Information Technology and deregulation are changing the meaning of the terms "bank", "banking" and "money". As money is increasingly recorded and transmitted in the form of digitally coded information, one is led to believe that perhaps money is not, and has never been a thing at all, as suggested by the medium-of-exchange concept. Rather it is a certain type of social relation about which the relevant information may be recorded and transmitted by a variety of means. This line of thought leads to a fresh investigation into the nature and origin of money.".

"In the context of the electronic model of the payment system noted there is no room for misunderstanding the nature of money, because there is no thing to be

1

The polluted economy

The beginning of the 21st century reveals two domains that are victimised by the thoughtless actions of humans. In the case of nature, we are talking about pollution. Can we use this same term for the economy? Let us try to draw a parallel with the aid of a few examples:

▷ The economy also produces its toxic waste which it does not know what to do with. During the 1980's, the expression *"junk bonds"* appeared. With the subprime crisis, there was talk about toxic products eroding the balance sheets of banks, investment funds and even of local and regional authorities.

▷ Just as nuclear waste is the most toxic pollutant, likewise, derivatives have proven to be extremely dangerous for the economy. Similarly, we destroyed the nucleus of what usually constitutes a financial product. We no longer sold a definite good or title deeds, as in the case of shares. We instead sold debts! But we had gone even farther, because we assembled fractions of different debts, to fabricate a title (a claim), which was gutted of all substance in relation to what is called the *real economy*. These derivative products originate from an atomization of debt securities. They have therefore, quite naturally, caused an uncontrollable chain reaction.There has been talk of tsunami ; but one could also call it a financial Chernobyl.

▷ Noting the toxicity of financial transactions for the *real economy*, it is proposed to tax them... like are carbon emissions. One must then wonder whether this will lead to the equivalent of pollution permits. They could be called transaction permits, traded on a transaction market. A hedge fund which would not have reached its quota of financial transactions could resell the unused part to another fund.

▷ In agriculture, the soil appears to be a "problem". It takes a lot of work and it is subject to the vagaries of the weather. Soilless culture was therefore invented. In industry, this is called offshoring. You transplant a factory outside the economic context and social conditions in which it was born. In this case, the wage bill is regarded as a problem. It is said to be a burden for the enterprise.

▷ Formerly, seeds were part of the natural agricultural cycle. The farmer would put aside a part of his harvest in order to resow his fields. Today seeds are patented. If the farmer wants to resow the seeds of his harvest, he will be required to pay a royalty to the enterprise that sold him the original seeds.

The loan is a seed for enterprises and institutions.

Currently, seed money is predominantly in the private hands of the commercial banks and of investment funds. To be able to borrow, the State must turn to these agencies and not to the central bank. On one side, the ancestral agricultural cycle has been diverted towards enterprises that produce patented seeds; on the other side, the public service of seed money provision became debt service paid to private financial institutions.

▷ In the economy too, one can see the emergence of organisations that are *"Genetically Modified Organisations"*. Little by little, the European Central Bank (ECB) sees its statute being transformed. In contradiction with EU treaties, the ECB comes to the rescue of over-indebted States, as well as of private banks who have strayed into risky speculation. The ECB has started to practice what the Federal Reserve Bank called by the palatable term: Quantitative Easing[6]. It is less embarrassing than talking about *"running the money printing press"*!

▷ We can characterize a weed by the fact that it seeks to take the place of the good crop (like wheat), which would enable us *"to make bread"*[7]. The weed and crop are therefore competitors. Herbicide will resolve this confrontation to the advantage of the crop. Likewise, in economics, if the usual rules

---

6   See the presentation of this concept: ch. 17 / Parag. 4

7   Translator's note: the original French text of "faire du blé" (to grow wheat) has a double meaning, in that it is also an idiomatic expression that means "to make money". This therefore has been transliterated in English as "to make bread", which likewise, also has the idiomatic meaning of "to make money".

of fair competition are not enough, there is recourse either to merger, or to acquisition, whether the acquisition is consensual or hostile (i.e. in the form of a "*takeover*"). In both senses, whether environmental or social, the collateral damage is consequential.

▷ During the 20th century, the productive yield of soils was pushed to extremes. Basically, behind all pollution is the notion of maximum yield. Chemical fertilizers have played an important role in the gradual elimination of the humus, resulting in a sterile soil. In economics, ways have also been found to increase yields beyond what is healthy for maintenance of the social soil.

What is a chemical fertilizer? An alien and synthetic element that nature cannot absorb without being damaged, to one degree or another. In the same way, something that has been introduced into the economic terrain, to intensify economic yields, also plays a role similar to that of chemical fertilizer. It is called speculation. It is also as alien to the *real economy* as chemical fertilizers are to nature.

Fertilizer acts in specific ways relative to elements that determine the productive potential of the crop (nitrogen, phosphorus, potassium,etc.); likewise, speculation also acts on specific areas, which can be reduced in total to four elements. These four elements have become commodities in themselves, whereas originally, they emerged only to facilitate the production and exchange of commodities.

The four economic elements are: money, financial capital, land/real estate, and labour. Speculation mainly causes growth in the first three of these elements and contraction in the element of labour.

In reality, speculation is the very first form of pollution of the economy. Speculation promotes and even generates the other forms of pollution. It is for this reason that we should pay attention to the detoxification of the four elements that we have just mentioned.

In this first volume, we will see how money has become a financial commodity. But more importantly, we will see how we can return money to its original station, by measures affecting the banking system as well as the determination of foreign currency[TG8] exchange rates. This will be the first component of a method for detoxification of the economy. The other three will be the subject of the second volume.

For each of these four elements, we will seek to identify fundamental laws inherent within the economy itself. And then we shall propose evolutive solutions, i.e. solutions that can be implemented through civil society initiatives, in order to be tested and improved. Thereby, the new can gradually take the place of the old.

Let us just clarify what I mean by an evolutive solution. It is not a lukewarm compromise in which nothing of substance can be discerned. Those who opt for evolutive solutions will take a real step forward, even a leap forward. Here again, a comparison with the environment will help us to grasp its principle.

---

8   Throughout the text, [TG] refers to the Translator's Glossary, at the end of the book.

When a farmer decides to change from conventional to organic production, this requires a few years of transition. During this time, it is said that the farm is in a process of conversion. But the farmer's choice is clear, and the methods he employs are well defined: so during the conversion period, the farm is already practicing organic cultivation.

In response to the increasing demand for this type of agricultural production, a compromise solution was invented: the concept of *"integrated agriculture"*. In economics, the same is done through ethical investment, which still remains an investment[9]. Like in the case of integrated agriculture, a qualitative leap is not carried out, and therefore I would not call ethical investment an evolutive solution.

These few examples illustrate the fact that nature and the economy passed through analogous processes of pollution. Both of them have reached a stage of acute crisis. We could sink a little deeper. We might believe in freeing ourselves of these crises by trivial political measures that play on appearances.

But if we decipher events with attention, we can only see the urgency for a change of direction, simultaneously in both these domains of nature and the economy. However, one of these domains conditions the other. In fact, pollution of the economy precedes that of the environment, and is one of its root causes. If the financial capital structure of firms had been different, and if labour had been considered otherwise, pollution

---

9   In the sense of "making money with money", especially through interest bearing debt as a financial commodity.

of the environment would not have taken its present magnitude. The measures to correct this, demanded by environmentalists from the outset, could have been adopted much sooner.

Pollution of the economy has therefore played a determining role in the pollution of the environment. Tackling economic pollution, means to work in the surest way to restore the health of nature.

Detoxification of the economy will not be without a revolution in our present understanding of it. But we must first consider the necessary conditions to ensure that this revolution is sustainable.

2

Sustainable Revolution

2011 will be remembered as the year when speculation openly took power.

Since a long time, speculative finance had already seized power, but it was acting in the background, hidden behind economic theories and political systems.

Today it is on the front stage, imposing changes of Prime Ministers and austerity plans. With unprecedented brutality, speculative finance dictates the behaviour of EU governments, the ECB and the European Commission.

It has a formidable weapon: interest rates. Should one Prime Minister propose to consult the people by referendum, or another one might delay cuts in social spending, immediately the interest rates at which speculative finance will lend to a State will rise, increasing the cost of repaying the public debt, and thereby nullifying the efforts of any previous austerity plan.

The European people are dazed, stunned. They helplessly watch the realisation of what Naomi Klein calls the Shock Doctrine (Klein, 2008), which enables the implementation of structural reforms, based on techniques similar to the interrogative torture of prisoners, and described in a CIA manual as follows: *"There is an interval — which may be extremely brief— of suspended animation, a kind of shock or paralysis. It is caused by a traumatic or sub-traumatic experience which explodes, as it were, the world that is familiar to the subject as well as his image of himself within that world. Experienced interrogators recognize this effect when it appears and know that at this moment the source is far more open to suggestion, far likelier to comply, than he was just before he experienced the shock."*[10]

Naomi Klein adds: *"The shock doctrine mimics this process precisely, attempting to achieve on a mass scale what torture does one on one in the interrogation cell. (...). Like the terrorized prisoner who gives up the names of comrades and renounces his faith, shocked societies often give up things they would otherwise fiercely protect."*[11]

Yet, the shock strategy we experience at the European level did not stun everyone. Youth, in particular, are manifesting capacities of resistance. Stéphane Hessel's exhortation encouraged it[12], as well as the protests in Tunisia and Egypt. We can expect anti-austerity movements to flourish in several European countries,

---

10 Blanton and Kornbluh, (no date)

11 Klein, (2008)

12 Hessel, (2011) - which 35 page track became a bestseller in France and other countries, advocating that citizens become outraged, and take direct nonviolent action for a peaceful uprising against the powers of finance capitalism.

including France. We can only hope so, because resignation would be the worst scenario.

But what can the anti-austerity movements in Europe achieve? They don't have to fight against a tyrant embodied in a person. The tyranny of the financial markets is more insidious, more indirect. It operates on the *real economy*, which then goes into crisis, with all the consequences that we suffer in terms of employment and cuts in socio-cultural budgets.

We cannot do as happened in Tunis, Cairo or Tripoli. There is nobody to depose. The financial dictatorship is exercised mainly through investment funds, in which, by the way, are included the pension funds and insurance companies of the victims of the crisis, as well as those of local authority employees, where all have invested their money, both of the political right and left. These hedge funds are based in different parts of the world. They are not reachable through demonstrations in the public places of European cities.

Certainly, proposals exist that could temporarily loosen the grip of speculation. For example, many demand that the ECB has the right to lend directly to States, although its statute prohibits it. A strong popular pressure could repeal the articles of the Treaties of Maastricht and Lisbon which govern these provisions. The States would then be able to borrow money from the ECB at a rate much lower than that of the markets. Public debt service would thereby be significantly reduced. The amounts thus released would contribute to the reduction of the nominal amounts of State debt.

This seems to be a common sense solution!

In the current circumstance, it would be an improvement. But at the same time, it would only displace the problem a notch. In fact, where would the money come from that the ECB would lend to the States? The ECB does not have funds similar to those of investors. It would therefore have to create that money, that is to say, to run the money printing presses. After some time, the consequences will be felt on the value[TG] of the Euro, and therefore on consumer prices, which would eventually increase, with all the consequences for the domestic economy and exports.

In other words, monetary creation by the central bank is tantamount to a form of loan "granted" by the citizens, who, without seeming to, pay a part of the monthly debt service payments through their purchases.

In reality, speculation would be taken away from the front-stage, but would continue to act on the money markets, where the Euro is exchanged for other currencies.

This example shows that we must look beyond the apparent causes. The state of economic chaos today, makes it urgent to go further, to go back to root causes.

Going directly from justified and well intentioned outrage, to a concrete strategy, would mean bypassing steps that we absolutely need to make, if we want to implement a sustainable revolution in economy.

As far as I know, no revolution triggered by the outrage that injustice creates, has ever prevented the restoration of the old powers, or the emergence of new forms of domination.

We need an in-depth diagnosis on such things as interest, money and financial capital. This will give birth to new concepts and evolutive change processes. Only then can we look at the strategy and its implementation.

It is also possible to consider the situation from a different angle.

Let's look at how the *real economy* is under the yoke of the *unreal economy* of financialization. If an individual suffered such abuse, and we did nothing, we would be accused of failing to assist a person in danger. Here we are dealing with a social body that is being tyrannised, which we must set free.

We introduce therefore a fundamental distinction in the way that we look at the economy. Injustice, lack of solidarity, poverty and misery do not originate in the *real economy*. We will show that if the *real economy* stands on its own foundations, it does not create these ills. It is the action on it, by the *unreal economy*[TG], of financial markets, which must be to blame.

Let us not fight the wrong battle. Let us mobilise ourselves for the one that is truly worthwhile, the one which will prevent the *unreal economy* from manifesting wherever it wants to. To this end, we must develop a methodology and concrete concepts that will overturn our conceptions of what we believe to be the economy.

In fact, we must think the unthinkable.

3

Thinking the Unthinkable

In the editorial of "Le Monde Diplomatique" of November 2008, Serge Halimi wrote: *"During decades of Keynesianism, the liberal right has thought the unthinkable and has used a great crisis to impose it"* (Halimi, 2008). The unthinkable of which he was speaking, is the economic doctrine of Milton Friedman, which his disciples, known as the Chicago boys, have implemented in many countries. The principle of this doctrine is to take advantage of a crisis, eventually deliberately caused, to impose ultra-liberal measures on an entire country.

But the Chicago boys didn't just think the unthinkable. They realised it, provoking immeasurable damage, in the economy in general, and also in the daily lives of billions of people, both in poorer countries as well as in the so called developed countries.

Serge Halimi then asks the following question: *"Who will propose to question the very heart of the system (...)?"* If he formulates the question in this way, it means that he notices that the reforms proposed by the different currents of society, be they from the right or from the left, do not touch the core of the system. According to Halimi, even the *"alternative left"* should not simply make do with *"dusting off its most modest projects, useful but rather timid, such as the Tobin taxes, an increase in the minimum wage, a new Bretton Woods, and some wind turbine farms."* (Halimi, 2008).

The economic and social crisis, which erupted in 2008, and which extended into the national debt of States, shows this clearly: it is about going much further, to attain what we dare not approach any more, for fear of being considered a dreamer, a Utopian, indeed an idealist. Today, going to the heart of the economic system means to think the unthinkable. We can't back off any more. We have to dare, as the crises urges us to do so every day.

But what is this *"unthinkable"*? We will get closer to it if we revisit, from the ground up, four domains from which issue the problems that pervade the economy: money, financial capital, labour and real estate. They constitute what I call the *"Economic Cross"*. It seems to me that repositioning these notions, as they should be in the life of Society, is the basis of an in depth transformation. For this transformation to take shape in daily life, it will require from us to go a step further, by providing tools, that is to say concrete measures, which promote a new way for humankind to relate to these four domains.

The image of the Economic Cross enables us to see, in summary form, the causes of the economic malady. It is the result of thirty five years of observation and research. I presented it for the first time in my book *La*

Démocratie Évolutive[13] (Evolutive Democracy). For each of these four domains, I proposed forms of remedy.

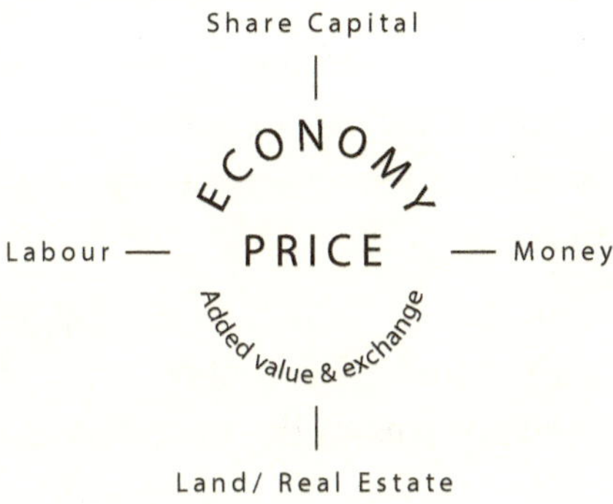

Diag. 1 - The economic cross

When the subprime crisis occurred, resulting in the crisis of capitalization of the banks, followed by a scarcity of bank loans and, finally, the closures of factories and firms, with subsequent considerable unemployment, the four domains of the Economic Cross were successively affected. I could thereby see an illustration of what I had written about in my previous book.

In conferences and seminars that I gave since the outbreak of the crisis, I found a real interest in this approach and especially in the fact that ways out of the crisis were seen as possible. For most people, the economy functions as a system which seems beyond the grasp of citizens. They experience the system with a kind of fatalism that seems to generate anxiety and a deep malaise.

---

13 Laloux, M. (2007)

The perspective of a citizen being able to exercise a decisive influence on the orientation of the economy, quickly generates enthusiasm to work on these issues, even if one is not necessarily an expert.

By exploring the Economic Cross, we discover the conditions of what I call an *Economy of Human Added Value*TG, that is to say an economy designed and organized for the human being.

There is one thing, which is indispensable to be asserted and instituted: the enslavement of the human being to the mechanisms of the economy is by no means inevitable. Such enslavement ceases to be, the moment we conceive, in a radically new way, the four domains of the Economic Cross.

We will firstly lay the foundation for a monetary system that is entirely at the service of the *real economy*. We will see how, for money to be healthy, it must lose its commodity character, and become only an instrument to measure exchange. We will then be able to distinguish between three types of money: Purchasing Money, Financing Money and Contribution Money. All three types of money would be denominated in the same unit of account (the euro, for example), but would flow in separate circuits. We will thus have a Purchasing Money that will accurately reflect the exchange of goods and services; thus a stable money, which will influence our way of thinking about notions of the balance of payments and foreign-exchange reserves, in the context of economic exchanges between countries and their monetary counterparts. This will lead us to an entirely new perspective on how to determine the conversion rates[TG] (between monetary units) that are no longer subject to the forces of supply and demand. We shall discover a method that will lead to an integration of social, wage and environmental policies of countries, and will increase the export price for those who practice dumping in these areas. This approach has the merit of including, in the economic process itself, incentives to justice and equity, instead of imposing them from the outside, through the unpractical crutches that are social taxes, environmental taxes.

We will then be able to turn our attention to Financing Money which, as we will see, shall scarcely come from savings, but from monetary creation by a Financing Institute of an entirely new type. Indeed, the value of that money thus created, will be based on criteria other than those that usually apply, such as the coverage ratios for financial capital and liquidity, recently redefined by the Basel III Accords.

To have a Financing Money entirely at the service of the *real economy*, we must remove from it anything that could lead it into the *unreal economy*[TG] of financialization, that is to say, which allows money to be made with money. The primary instrument that leads to this is interest. We will perceive the damage it causes in the *real economy*, and propose the means to forgo it.

As soon as we design an economy without interest rates, the utility of the central bank, whose main weapon is precisely the change in the base rate, it means that this utility collapses upon itself. We will therefore arrive at a new unthinkable: a monetary system without a central bank.

To understand the third form of money, we will have to expand the notion of taxation, by remembering its former name [in France]: Contributions. Looking at taxes in this light, means to consider that society can function only if the flows of money go from the commercial circuit of the economy[TG] to the noncommercial circuit. This therefore introduces the concept of contribution in the sense of gift (donation), as an indispensable factor in the health of the economy. We hence envisage a third monetary circuit: Contribution Money. Which will be added to that of Purchasing Money and that of Financing Money.

For each of these moneys, we shall describe monetary institutions to manage them in very distinctive ways: Banks of Purchasing Money, Financing Institutes, and Funds of Contribution Money.

It will be clear that these new monetary institutions offer a service that is in the public interest, a public service. In fact, shouldn't the administration of money be considered as a public service? But to put it that way might suggest a form of nationalization of commercial banks and of the central bank. Thus we must, beforehand, avoid all ambiguity. That is why we will lay the foundation for a metamorphosed public service, which will no longer proceed from a unitary State, but from the citizens themselves, it's to say, from civil society.

The sovereign debt crisis shows that we need to redefine the relationship between the State and money. We will therefore take a detour through the State budget and the Public Treasury. We will be compelled to fully revisit the ideas we usually have about them.

Thus we shall have explored the main issues at the national level, in terms of money. Equipped with new tools, we will be able to build a *Real Economy International Monetary System (reIMS)*, managed by Civil Society Organisations (CSOs), active in the monetary domain. We shall then have reached the limits of the unthinkable, since it will be about replacing the usual dysfunctional political game at this level, by an organization consisting of a network of institutions that are administered and controlled by Civil Society.

When we will have acquired the foundations for a new *Real Economy International Monetary System* (reIMS), we will be able -in the second Volume- to attend to the three other branches of the Economic Cross, starting with Financial Capital. As a result of the understanding gained about monetary creation for financing purposes, a form of financial capital will arise naturally, which will have nothing more to do with the stock market share capital of public limited companies[14]. Within the perspective of an *Economy of Human Added Value*, this stock market shareholder system is meant to disappear. The damage it has caused in the economy can no longer be doubted. But until now, the possibility of offering a real alternative failed; with State capitalism not being such an alternative, as the experience of the countries of Eastern Europe has shown.

The new type of Financing Money we propose will allow us to solve this critical problem, and to consider

---

14 Translator's note : The original French of "Société Anonyme" (S.A), designates a type of corporation in countries that mostly employ civil law. In common law jurisdictions, it is roughly equivalent to a "Public Limited Company" (plc) in the UK, or a Publicly Traded Company in the USA.

financial capital, not as a means of possession and control, but as a loan to the corporate enterprise, and thus repayable. This will result in a double question: who owns the corporate enterprise, and to whom are the operating profits due?

It will not mean the replacement of stock market shareholding by employee shareholding. It is necessary to think differently with regard to profit and also to taxation. It will be apparent that the surplus generated by a corporate enterprise should be used to fund seven different domains, and that the health, both of the enterprise and of Society, depends on it.

We will then have an essential tool to address the third branch of the Economic Cross: Labour.

Separation of the salary from the work is an idea that is increasingly gaining ground, for instance, the Unconditional Basic Income is mentioned by several thinkers in the field of economy. But the tools to achieve this are still lacking, firstly because the idea remains tied to the same monetary and capitalistic organisation; and secondly because of the essentially idealistic view that is developed regarding this question. If one were to think concretely about this question, one would understand better where the problem is situated. Making an obser-vation which encompasses the entire economic life, whether in the commercial or noncommercial circuits, reveals that there is no lack of work to be done. On the contrary, in the so-called developed countries, there is not enough personnel to meet all needs. The problem lies in the fact that under the current organization of financial capital and money, the money for remuneration does not arrive where it is needed. It is this question we have to consider in the first place. This will lead us to propose, instead of the employment contract, a double contract: one for collaboration and another for remuneration.

We shall then have the foundation to address pensions. We will see that this is an issue that is as defectively formulated as is the issue of unemployment. Disaster capitalism, locked in its own logic, tries to instill the idea in people that pension plans will soon be bankrupt, and therefore the age of retirement must be delayed. The separation of the salary and work, as we propose it, will reveal how inadequate this thinking is, and that an alternative exists.

But there are other reasons why the separation of work and wages is necessary. They are more subtle and appear only when considering the whole of the life of Society, and particularly the notion of human creativity, in the widest possible sense. So we will have to consider the economic consequences of its development.

We will thus have examined three quarters of the Economic Cross. But anyone who attentively considers this new approach, even if they approve of it, will not fail to notice that some of the necessary funding is lacking. Whatever method of allocation one chooses, the amount of money generated by the commercial circuit of the economy will be insufficient to fuel the development of the noncommercial circuit. Unless you make indispensable changes in the domain of land and real estate.

Here we touch upon a vital issue for the health of an *Economy of Human Added Value*. But it will probably meet with the strongest of resistance, since it affects not just the rich, the so-called well-to-do, but anyone who owns land or housing. Indeed, we need to observe what happens in the economy, when property that has already been paid for in full, but which the owner rents out at a rate that is far in excess of its maintenance costs.

In answering this question, we will bring out the concept that renting should be replaced by a right of use, which then will be less than the amount of current rentals. Thus, the share of wages used to pay the rent may decrease proportionately. Over the whole of a country, such a measure will significantly reduce the so-called payroll without diminishing the standard of living of each one, except for those who derive their income from house rental. The money thereby released will provide the necessary complement to the financing of the noncommercial circuit of the economy.

In exploring the fourth branch of the Economic Cross, we will see how far the *Economy of Human Added Value* is from that of disaster capitalism. Today, the gap between them has become an abyss in which any civilization may be swallowed. Unless we as citizens, are going to decide to stop what is digging this abyss, which is called speculation ; the generator of the *unreal economy*. The truth is that an economy will have human values when it will be real and only real.

It is therefore necessary that society acquires tools to prevent speculation from occurring the instant it tries to do so. We cannot expect the current political system to take the necessary measures. It is up to citizens to impose it. But, with the exception of Switzerland, no country has the full complement of instruments allowing citizens to intervene directly and totally in democracy, by changing the laws. Generally, [in France] we do not have the vital minimum of a genuine democracy that would allow the citizen to make it evolve directly, at the measure and speed demanded by social evolution. Yet these instruments are simple. These are the right to Popular Legislative Initiative and the right to Popular Legislative Referendum, two quite distinct notions that the new provisions of the French Constitution mix together.

Thus we see that the transformation of the economy, as I propose it, requires a change in the form of our democracies. We should enter into a new era, that of *Evolutive Democracy.*

4

The debt crisis:
a deficit of economic thinking?

The multiple dysfunctions of the economy are now crystallized in different parts of the life of Society. Among them, there is, of course, the debt of States. This crisis has many causes, and each one helped make it take on abyssal proportions. The causes include in particular the prohibition on central banks in EU countries, especially the European Central Bank (ECB), to create money that could be made available to States at low or zero rates of interest. For example, in late 2012, the French debt was 1,830 billion Euros. If, since 1973, the State had been able to borrow at zero interest, the debt would be close to 400 billion. The difference is enormous and one can imagine the impact on the economy. France would not devote 49 billion (82% of income tax or 109% of corporate tax) to pay the annual interest on its national debt.

But these facts, in themselves, are secondary causes or even tertiary. Behind them is the concept of economy that we have. From this concept, everything else follows.

If we look more closely, it turns out that our usual economic thinking is not precise enough to be able to identify root causes. We are going to illustrate this by a specific example.

In the milieu of *"alternative"* economics, there are frequent references to a kind of monetary fable, that of *"the Lady of Condé"*[15]. It portrays a woman who takes a hotel room in the town of Condé, and pays in advance with a banknote of 200 €. With this money, the hotel owner pays his debt to a supplier, who, in turn, pays an invoice for the same amount to another business. The banknote passes from business to business until it reaches someone who owes 200 € to the hotel owner, and who then goes to settle his debt immediately. At this moment, the woman traveller, who instead of going directly to her room had been out walking, comes back and decides to leave town. The landlord refunds her the original banknote, which meanwhile, was used to settle trade debts between seven businesses.

To push the logic of this story even further, some add an unexpected ending: the Lady tears up the banknote in front of the amazed hotel owner, and hands him the pieces, saying that it was a forgery.

This money has therefore played the same role as a catalyst in chemistry. It enabled a chain reaction. It entered into a circuit and came out as it was at the beginning. Some economists see this as an illustration of what they believe to be the primary monetary problem: a lack of money in circulation. They conclude that an

---

15 Translator's note: the Anglo-Saxon version of the same fable being *"A slow day in Texas"* (See Additional Bibliography: Henderson, 2012).

injection of money into the circuit would be the remedy. It would suffice to create the necessary money, and in the right place, so that the economy works. But as money creation is in the hands of private banks, supported by the Central Bank, they advocate the creation of local currencies; or even that the State introduce such money into the noncommercial circuit of the economy; or that the central bank could be nationalized and could lend without interest to the State.

One way or another, behind these proposals, there is always a reasoning similar to that which underlies the fable of the Lady of Condé. One could even say that it was this reasoning that led to the invention of the story.

We may note that this way of thinking is not new nor alternative. It is the one that prevails in all central banks, whose primary role is to regulate the amount of money in circulation in order to optimize the economy. At least that is what supports conventional economic theory and it is what central bankers are trying to do, who have been fed these theories during their studies. Given the disastrous functioning of the economy, it might be useful to revisit these notions. The famous banknote of the Lady of Condé can help us to take the first step.

When I discovered this story, I found it luminous and I was seduced. Then one day, I decided to really think about it. I then realized that my eyes followed the path of this banknote, and did not look at the economic facts underlying the situation of the businesses. For in fact, what is their problem? They all have a difficulty of cash flow. Before declaring that it is a monetary issue, it would be wise to consider what causes this lack of cash flow.

Then we would find that they do not make enough sales; or that they have too much inventory; or else they suffer from mismanagement; or that some of their debtors keep their money invested, instead of paying them in due time, thereby blocking liquidity within the entire supply chain ...

This story shows that the cause of the problem lies in the *real economy* and not in the quantity of money in circulation. Our eyes should become habituated to monitor economic phenomena in a much more precise way and not to be fooled by what, basically, is a smokescreen. For this is what happens if we are obsessed with this banknote of 200 € which passed from hand to hand.

This fable could also teach us other things. Firstly: if the business people gathered around a table, they would discover that the sum of debts and credits they have towards each other is zero. In other words, from the viewpoint of accounting, the accounts payable and accounts receivable clear each other.

If one pursued this idea further, one would arrive at a very different concept, that of money-as-accounting, in which we already are, to a large extent, with what is called scriptural or ledger money[TG] (commercial bank demand deposits). When we make bank transfers or credit card payments, everything happens in the accounts of banks, companies and individuals. Money is dematerialized. It is a set of accounting entries. It is a pure unit of account.

The notion of the quantity of money in circulation or, as it is said, the money supply, thus becomes totally irrelevant. The problem is that we are still attached to this concept. This *"anachronistic"* attitude has a huge impact on the present economy. If we would look in the right place, we would see it and find efficient remedies.

Besides, the punch line of the story of Condé invites us to take a different look at money. It is as if the Lady, by tearing up the counterfeit banknote, told us: *"Look, you do not need physical cash. In any case, they were fake. My banknote has enabled a clearing of trade debts. You could have done this directly."* In other words, it is by looking through an accounting lens that one will be able to examine the causes of the problems.

This fable shows us an ailing economy. The hotel owner, whose business seems already not to be flourishing, uses the money of a sale paid in advance, for a service that was not consumed, to clear his existing debt. What would have happened if, instead of the *"happy ending"*, his debtor, the last business, had other trade debts and had chosen instead to privilege their reimbursement, rather than going to settle his debt with the hotel owner? This would have been an embarrassing situation vis-à-vis the Lady. The whole story would then appear as if he had borrowed from the Lady and was unable to repay it. He would therefore have paid his trade debts by taking out a new loan.

What the author of this story intended to show, was that it is enough to inject money, and therefore to create some, in order to run the economy. There is great confusion here, which we find is pushed to the extreme in the present crisis, in regard to the debt of States. The routine functioning of the State is financed with loans.

These loans serve to mask past economic shortcomings, instead of fuelling the creation of new money for future-oriented projects.

Here we are confronted with one of the major causes of the present difficulties: the conflation between what I call Purchasing Money and Financing Money.

The fact that today there is the desire to separate, within the banking system, deposit activities from those related to financial transactions[AB16], is a manifestation of an early awareness of the problem. But we are still far from having grasped the key issues.

In reality, the story of the Lady of Condé shows the opposite of what it is supposed to prove. The injection of money into the local circuit, by the arrival of the Lady, resolved nothing. The sum of the trade debts was already systemically stable (i.e. the sum of accounts payable and accounts receivable was zero). The fact that they were mutually cleared brings nothing to the economic reality of these actors. They are left with the same problems. From the perspective of the *real economy*, their situations have not evolved. It is interesting to note that this banknote of € 200 does not enter into the *real economy*. It did not contribute to creating value, namely goods and services.

Working on this observation might lead us to reverse our understanding of Purchasing Money. In this domain, money appears after a creation of value and its exchange. Money is nothing but accounting. Wanting it to preexist, that is to say, injected from the Central Bank

---

16 Leftly, (2011).

or a commercial bank, into the economy, is like *"barking up the wrong tree"*. Because money creation can only happen as a result of credit issued for financing new production activities, and not for resolving problems of current purchasing, nor for the operation of enterprises and institutions.

This fable may seem minor, especially considering the scale of problems needing to be solved. Yet it reveals many of them, and gives us the opportunity to train ourselves to think about the phenomena, with much more precision than is done usually. We were thereby able to delve into the facts. By doing the same for other situations, we will sharpen our ability to look with rigorous attention, at their evolution and their consequences on the overall economy and life of Society.

This story has allowed us to illustrate the primary cause of the crises we are facing: a deficit of economic thinking, which renders us helpless in front of the steamroller of finance.

5

Money for the *real economy*

There is no lack of proposals from thinkers and actors of an alternative economy, which is meant to be more respectful of the human. Their proposals aim to improve the income of workers, to share wealth, to eliminate poverty and hunger, to establish a participatory management of enterprises, to put an end to the excesses of unbridled capitalism, to move toward a respect for the environment, and so on.

We could extend the list. Each proposal is supported by good intentions and a sincere concern for humanity. The problem is that these proposals do not touch the fundamentals of the system. Rather, they seek to adjust it, without going so far as to rethink the framework itself. We can even ask ourselves if this lack of analysing root causes, is not reflected by a lack of confidence, on the part of these people, in their capacity to make such projections to really change things. Thus it happens that the ills that they would like combat do not cease to multiply and worthen the gangrene of the social body. Around the world, poverty is increasing, income inequality is growing, and every day, hunger grips the equivalent of the world population during the middle of the last century.

The current economic crisis only reinforces this trend, and highlights the disease that the economy suffers from. We are now at a turning point. Will we be able to take it, or will we continue to go where we are obviously heading for: into the wall? If we fail to resolve the issues that have challenged us for decades, and which erupted with reinforced vigor since 2007, we risk experiencing shocks stronger than those we are living at the moment. We cannot then exclude the possibility that our civilisations will be shaken by new forms of barbarity, which would signal their decline.

However, since the late 1980s, there have been movements that seemed capable of implementing ideals with strong popular support; especially Solidarnosc in Poland and the ANC in South Africa. These movements found themselves in control of their respective countries. They had everything in hand to achieve a transformation of capitalism, by implementing measures in favour of the participatory management of enterprises. Both had included this in their programs. Why did they not do it?

In her book *"The Shock Doctrine"* (Klein, 2008), Naomi Klein traces the sequence of events that led to an identical turnaround by both these movements. She shows the strong pressures exerted on the part of the advisers sent by international financial institutions (International Monetary Fund and World Bank).

In both cases, those who were in a position to decide gave in to the threatening spectres brandished by these advisers. Fear made them back off and turn their backs on their ideals for which they had fought for years, sometimes at the risk of their lives. This fear was that of seeing the flight of capital needed by the economy. The IMF and World Bank advisers had no difficulty in depicting the serial disasters that would occur if investors renounced the investment of their financial capital in these countries: recession, closure of enterprises, unemployment, currency devaluation, and so on. This mechanism is well known.

One may be surprised to find that any changes that meet human ideals in the field of the economy, can be blocked by such a simple mechanism. The threat of a few large investors is enough to defeat the movements advocating such high hopes which are supported by millions of people. We risk repeating this scenario in the case of the recent Occupy movements, in Tunisia, in Egypt, and so on.

But, at the risk of disappointing those who aspire to greater social justice, it must be noted that, in the logic of the current economy, the IMF and World Bank advisers are right. Their arguments are irrefutable.

The heads of Solidarnosc and the ANC well understood it. They did not betray their ideals. Faced with the reality, they found that their ideals were inapplicable, as all such proposals will be, which could lead to a reduction in the remuneration of investments.

For example, a political party can always include measures in its program to immediately raise the minimum wage from 1,000 to 1,500 € net per month. If this party came to power, it could never put this measure into practice, because it would have to face the threat of capital flight and the start of a recession scenario. To circumvent this problem, the party could move toward the nationalisation of banks and enterprises. But after the experience of the countries of the East, we know that this path is doomed.

So, are we discovering the impossibility of social progress, as well as an *Economy of Human Added Value* ? Are we in contradiction with the purpose of this book?

Yes, as long as we do not think the unthinkable.

Most currents of thought go in the direction of a greater humanisation of the economy, and have in common, the inclusion of a framework in their proposals that is not questioned. This framework is that of money. As long as we limit ourselves to the same concept of money, as are all the existing currencies in the world, no transformation can be achieved. For the simple reason that those who control the existing monetary framework, have the capacity to withhold the money from those who would show tendencies to act differently.

Thinking the unthinkable is therefore, in the first place, to imagine a form of money that makes unnecessary the recourse to money held by those who want to prevent the realisation of an *Economy of Human Added Value*. The money which could thus emerge should be of such a nature that we can say to investors: *"You can run away with your money and invest it in another country. We do not need it any more. We have the ability to create the financing money that is necessary for our economy to function, and to do so in the most stable way."*

We will therefore rethink money, and clarify what it would need to meet the criteria for a healthy economy, that is to say an *Economy of Human Added Value*.

We will not be the first ones to imagine other means of payment. In recent years, a growing number of books are addressing this issue. Experiments are also made, sometimes on an already large scale. We will talk about these experiments, without devoting too much space to them.[17] We will see how often they are based on some confusion, as we have already mentioned in the previous chapter.

In volume 2, we will discuss the other three branches of what I call the Economic Cross[18]. Obviously, it is not possible to address them simultaneously. Inevitably, in reading what is said about money in this volume 1, the reader will ask questions that will relate to the other domains of the Economic Cross, and which will be discussed in the relevant chapters of volume 2. He will therefore have to take this into consideration. It is only at the end of the second volume that the reader will be able to get the whole picture.

We cannot move towards an *Economy of Human Added Value* without developing a global vision of the economy. Reforms that would only represent a

---

17 See the chapter 29, Let us not fight the wrong battle
18 See Diagram 1: The Economic Cross, (ch.3)

mechanical adjustment, and which would not proceed from this holistic perspective, could not have a lasting effect.

We are not saying that the whole of the economy should be reformed in one go. That would be unrealistic and contrary to the concept of *Evolutive Democracy*. Progressive steps on different levels will be needed. Partial measures can be introduced. They will represent opportunities to make a real improvement insofar as they are inspired by a global vision of an *Economy of Human Added Values*.

6

A new Bretton Woods?

With the crisis of the banking system, and that of the debt of States, there has been much talk of Bretton Woods. Some political leaders would like, as happened in July 1944, a new international conference to identify the financial rules, which may prevent disasters, such as those we are living through since 2007.

Before imagining such a renewed basis, it would be useful to examine the real causes for the failure of Bretton Woods. It has often been said that it resulted from the huge advantage that the Americans reserved for themselves, by the fixed parity of the dollar relative to gold, while the other currencies have to adjust and therefore provide the necessary efforts.

In my opinion, this is not the main problem, although it had a devastating effect by accelerating and amplifying the manifestations of an economic malaise that was already there since a long time.

Even without the possibility of a *"deficit without tears"*, as Jacques Rueff[19] called it, and even if the plan of Keynes would have been adopted (which included highly innovative elements), the international monetary system established at Bretton Woods would still have experienced severe crises, which would inevitably have led to its implosion.

Before considering what new measures to take, it is appropriate to look at what were the objectives of the Bretton Woods agreement, and why it bore within itself the seeds of its own destruction.

Apart from the bickering for supremacy between the pound sterling and the dollar, the immediate objective of Bretton Woods, the one that was displayed, was to establish a relationship between currencies that allows both for the expansion of the money supply in each country, according to economic growth and, simultaneously, the stability of currencies, relative to each other. The ultimate objective was, on the one hand, that the development of world trade should not be impeded by a lack of money, nor, on the other hand, by the instability of exchange rates[TG] between currencies[TG].

We will come back to the immediate objective. Firstly, let us examine the ultimate one, by asking ourselves: what is it that enables a currency to be stable?

Over the years, central banks and governments have used several mechanisms to adjust the exchange rate of their national currency relative to others. Currently, the most common measure is to adjust the base rate of

---

19 Jacques Rueff (1896-1978) was a French economist and adviser to the French Government.

the Central Bank, that is to say, the interest rate that commercial banks will have to pay to get money from the Central Bank. We will discuss the question of interest later. Let us already note that this method consists of acting on money through an external means, and not through something that is intrinsic to it.

The utility of money is that it enables a disconnection in economic exchange, between sale and purchase, on three levels: (i) on the level of time (I can sell something today and buy something else tomorrow or in six months); (ii) on the level of place (I sell here, I buy elsewhere); (iii) between buyers (I sell to Paul, I buy from Nicole). These three elements make monetised exchange asynchronous and multilateral[20], and thereby economically superior to synchronous bilateral barter, because they overcome the limits of time, place and people.

If we consider money in this way, we can see that it is only a right to purchase a certain amount of goods. With 100 €, I can buy a pair of shoes or a certain amount of cheese, or petrol. The 100 € banknote was initially used to account for the sale of one commodity, and then it accounts for the purchase of another commodity.

Considered in this way, money functions as a unit of account. If it is confined to this role, then it can only be stable. It cannot vary of itself. Only the price of commodities can change. Money is first and foremost a measuring instrument. The meter remains the meter, the

---

20 Asynchronous means that the exchange is outside the constraints of time and place among a network of people, in contradiction to synchronous exchange, which occurs only in the same place and time. Multilateral means that the exchange involves more than two parties, and is therefore not *"barter"*, which is exchange limited to two parties only (i.e. bilateral exchange).

same for the kilo or the litre. Units of measure are fixed. Why is money not fixed? The answer to this question is key to understanding one of the most important issues of the modern economy. To achieve this, we must go back to the time when money first appeared.

When human beings decoupled the purchase from the sale, they used a means of payment that could be accepted by all. This was mainly gold. Other metals were used. But for our considerations, there are no fundamental differences. Gold was a commodity. The transition from any form of barter[21] to money was to favor a particular commodity, to make it a universal means of payment. Gold made possible the accounting of the sale and purchase. It could also be stored like any commodity, and even better than any other because it is indestructible. Owning gold was to possess *"The Commodity"* par excellence, the commodity that enabled acquisition of all other commodities.

Let us try, in a compressed timeframe, to embrace the evolution of money. We see gold progressively withdrawing from monetary circulation. Firstly, coins contain less and less precious metal. Then banknotes appear, which are convertible into gold until approximately the beginning of World War I. After that and until now, monetary gold only circulates between central banks.

A little later, the Bretton Woods monetary system raises the prominence of gold, since the value of each currency is determined according to the reserves of gold

---

21 Today, there is a controversy concerning the original means of payments. Was it barter or accounting? We will not discuss that in this book for both have probably coexisted and one can consider that there were intermediary forms.

and foreign currencies held in each nation's central bank. But the Bretton Woods agreements are made in such a way that all currencies have to position themselves against the dollar, whose parity with gold is fixed.

In other words, central bank reserves are always calibrated, ultimately, by gold. At least we thought so, in 1944.

Here, we are faced with a strange phenomenon of human consciousness. We see it unable to change paradigm and to be in tune with the evolution of the economy. As happens in other areas, particularly in that of democracy, human beings cling to archaic forms, not realizing that they no longer meet the needs of the moment, and even hinder healthy developments.

With hindsight, we can wonder that in 1944 we persisted with a monetary system based on the gold standard. It should have been obvious that the world production of gold would not be sufficient to cope with the growth of the economy. In other words, the amount of money required for trade would become such that it would be backed by an increasingly smaller proportion of gold.

At Bretton Woods, the backing of currencies by gold should have been seen as impossible, as something belonging to a bygone era. Events have since confirmed it. Today, monetary gold has only a figurative role in the functioning of the International Monetary System (IMS).

Yet there are still people who believe that one of the causes of disruptions of the economy lies in the abandonment of the gold standard in 1973, by the President of the United States.

To defend such a position, one has to be somewhat ignorant of the evolution of the IMS during the 1960s and, especially the tragicomic episode of the London Gold Pool. A somewhat careful study shows that the defense of the gold standard had become untenable, and that if Richard Nixon made this decision it is because he could not do otherwise.

Some will think that the United States was in that position because of their lax monetary policy, which led to the creation of the Eurodollar bubble. Certainly, this bubble accelerated the awareness of the gap between the mass of dollars and the stock of gold held by the Federal Reserve Bank. But even without the Eurodollars, this gap already existed and it could only grow. For proof, in 1973 the Fed's stock of gold amounted to 8,600 tons for a GDP of 1,400 billion dollars. In 2012, the GDP is 15'600 billion, and the stock of gold is just over 8,100 tons. In other words, the share of gold coverage against the GDP represents 8.5% of what it was in 1973.

Obviously, a turning point was not taken at Bretton Woods. The model was not questioned and is still not. A closer observation of the evolution of money should have led to the conclusion that money was moving away from its assumed native state of being a financial commodity. It had to free itself from its supposed origin, and get out of the tension illustrated by the following diagram:

Diag. 2 - Tension on money

Money lives in a permanent tension between these two paradigms. Economists accommodate them both by saying that money embraces them both. From the perspective of an *Economy of Human Added Value*, we ask the question otherwise: how can we ensure that this tension is resolved; so that money ceases to be a commodity, and becomes a pure unit of account, an instrument to measure the exchange of economic values?

Because of conservatism in economic thinking, this issue did not emerge during the twentieth century. Economists did not go so far as to arrive at a systemic observation, which could have led them to question the validity of such a paradoxical idea, that money is condemned to be both a financial commodity and a unit of account. It is even likely that many will, on reading this, say immediately that it is unthinkable to want to resolve this duality of money.

It is precisely this unthinkable that we must think about, if we want a new Bretton Woods, which is truly new, and not one of those international agreements that makes the new out of the old.

7

The *real economy* versus the *unreal economy*

The famous financier George Soros, who built his fortune speculating on currencies, proves the old axiom that *"money begets money"*[22]. However, we might ask, as did macroeconomist Jeffrey Frankel: *"When Soros the speculator helps force a currency into crisis, what does Soros the philanthropist think about the social or moral implications for the country under attack?"* (Frankel, 1999). Soros already gave us an answer when he stated: *"As an anonymous participant in financial markets, I never had to weigh the social consequences of my actions. I felt justified in ignoring them on the grounds that I was playing by the rules."* (Soros, 1998a). According to Soros, *"Markets reduce everything, including human beings (labor) and nature (land), to commodities."* (Soros, 1998b). This observation is interesting from

---

22 Translator's note : *"Begets"* is an old English word meaning *"reproduces as offspring"*. The old English axiom *"money begets money"* is contrary to Aristotle's more ancient theory of the sterility of money.

someone who has a lifetime experience in the buying and selling of foreign currencies on a large scale, and who, throughout his career, necessarily considered money as a financial commodity.

I sell the Dollar, I buy the Euro, I play the Yen against the Pound ... Money is treated as if it were a raw material or a consumer good. And yet, it is evident that it is not. Copper, for example, is used in the manufacture of electrical wires. As a raw material extracted from the ground, it enters as a commodity into the *real economy*.

Money does not correspond to any such process in the *real economy*. It is not within the nature of money to be a commodity in the *real economy*. According to its true nature, money is a right to purchase. Money therefore exists within the domain of law, of agreement, not of the *real economy*.

From the moment we sell money itself, as a commodity, we enter into an economy that is unreal[TG]. We create a parallel virtual world vis-à-vis the everyday *real economy*.

How does this parallel world affect the everyday *real economy*? A very simple example will show it. A financier sells a stake of ten million euros for dollars, in order to play the money markets, and in turn sells and buys Yen, pounds sterling, Swiss francs, and so on. After some time, he repatriates the money, which in the meantime has become 11 million euros. He has therefore gained 10% of his initial investment, thanks to these operations. If he is a *"repentant"* financier, like George Soros, we might rejoice at such a gain, by imagining that it will contribute to the philanthropic actions of his foundations. But let us follow more precisely what occurs at the moment when this financial capital is repatriated.

Ten million euros were extracted from the Eurozone. At the moment when the money is repatriated in euros, the conversion has to provide 11 million euros. Therefore the money supply in the eurozone will increase by one million euros. Whatever path is taken to convert these funds into euros, everything will ultimately come back to the creation of one million euros by the European Central Bank.

This increase in the money supply[23] does not come from an increase in the volume of trade in the *real economy*. A discrepancy has occurred. This is tantamount to a devaluation of the monetary unit of account, which will lead to price inflation. If other factors do not interfere, prices will increase until equilibrium is restored between the money supply and the volume of trade in goods and services.

In other words, it is the *real economy* that finances the million gained by the financier who played in the foreign exchange markets. This capital gain is paid for by the consumers.

Some might say that such a small amount will not suffice by itself to cause a destabilisation of prices. But if we follow the path of that million, if, for example, it is invested in real estate, one will find that the effect on the prices, however small, will be real. From there it spreads to the rest of the economy.

---

23   We use the term *"money supply"* in the usual sense, since it is money creation as it is currently done. So there is no contradiction with what is said in chapter 18 *"The illusion of the money supply"*.

As yet we have only considered the effect on the eurozone. There is another effect, and even several, in each currency area through which the original ten million euros passed for speculative purposes only. The disorder thus generated is multiple.

If one understands the process highlighted by this simple example, and can see that it concerns billions every day, then one will face the fact that there is there a real disease of the economy, and that it should be treated as such by looking for the remedies. This is what we want to concentrate on in what follows.

Already, we can formulate a kind of economic law:

A necessary condition for the economy to be healthy is that the amount of purchasing rights are determined solely by the needs of the *real economy*, that is to say, by the exchange of goods and services.

Note that this condition is a prerequisite. As we shall see, it is not sufficient to the life of a real *Economy with Human Added Values.*

To be precise, we are talking about purchasing rights and not about money supply. Put simply, a sum of 100 € may, within a few days, go via the customer's bank card to the account of the restaurant where he eats, then to that of a wholesaler of fruit and vegetables, who will pay a farmer, who will buy clothes, and so on. As a result of these transactions, GDP increases without any money creation. In classical economics, it is said that a given money supply enables a trade volume of more or less the same scale. We will see later that this is a kind of optical illusion. In reality, only commodities are circulated. Money's function is to enable the circulation of commodities, through an exchange process based on a disconnection between the sale and the purchase; in space, in time, and between people.[24]

The law that we just formulated only says, that factors external to the *real economy* must not interfere in determining the amount of purchasing rights.

Thus, in stating this principle, we exclude all money creation, and therefore any kind of loan, which does not result from a direct need of the *real economy*. We will see what this implies, when we talk about financial capital and real estate. In fact the subprime crisis originated in loans granted to the domain of real estate, in a way that permitted factors external to the *real economy* to intervene. This crisis spread to the banking system as well, because the banks provided loans to capital investment funds, for operations that were unrelated to the *real economy*. These elements will have to be taken into account if we are to avoid the repetition of this kind of crises.

Based on what we have just observed, we can deduce that the *unreal economy* has an adverse effect on the *real economy*, and that it is necessary for citizens to take measures that would prevent its occurrence[25]. Now, the

24   See chapter 18: The illusion of the money supply

25   Those who have an orthodox conception of the economy will object, because from the orthodox perspective, money earned in the *unreal economy* allows for the formation or increase of financial capital, which is necessary for the existence and development of *real economy* enterprises. Money generated from speculation is therefore said to be useful, or at least a necessary evil, for the functioning of the *real economy*. This reasoning holds true only under the current concept of money. With the concept that we will elaborate, this reasoning becomes obsolete, especially when we will discuss Financing Money.

cause behind the development of the *unreal economy* lies in speculation, that is to say, in the buying of something and selling of it at a higher price, without having added any value to it through one's own activity. To illustrate what we mean by that, we are going to discuss the creation of values.

8

The creation of value

The concept of added value seems simple. It is well known to all those who have a basic knowledge of economics, especially since the introduction of value added tax (VAT). However, there is a way of looking at added value, which opens up very interesting perspectives, and allows one to get a more dynamic picture of what constitutes the foundation of the whole economy. The Austrian philosopher, Rudolf Steiner, first developed this perspective at the beginning of a course he gave, at the request of economists. We will discuss the principle of Steiner's perspective (Steiner, 2013), and consider whether a link can be found with the unreal financial economy. In Volume 2, we will get onto the theme of labour and the third type of money, called Contribution Money[26]. These concepts will again be useful.

First let us make it clear that it is necessary to distinguish between value and price. Two identical objects on sale in two shops located a few hundred meters from

---

26 See chapter 22: A third form of money: Contribution Money

each other, one in France, one in Switzerland, probably represent the same value from the point of view of the economic process. But the price, for reasons related to many factors, will likely be different.

The simplest formation of economic values occurs when something is extracted from nature to be traded. A fish caught in a river and eaten directly by the fisherman does not become an economic value. If the fisherman puts the fish in a small bucket of water and brings it to a nearby farm to exchange it for something else, he creates a value that enters into the economy. If he puts the fish in a cooler and transports it to the nearest village, to sell it on the market, he has added a new value. From the economic point of view, the fish that is on the market does not have the same value as when it is exchanged at the farm. If a restaurateur buys the fish and prepares it for a customer, he adds a new value to those that the fisherman had already introduced into the economy.

We could take other elements from the soil or from underground, from the air or the water, and follow their passage through the economy, according to the values that are added to them through human activity. We would then have before us all the occupations that are directly linked with nature: farmer, forester, beekeeper, fish-farmer, fisherman, woodcutter, and so on. If we add all activity associated with the extraction of raw materials and food production from the land, including underground, we get what is called the primary sector.

We have thus described the basic principle of the economy. We can see how human activity is applied to nature. We do not contemplate nature as, for example, a painter or a scientist would. We examine it with the eye of the economist. Nature is thereby observed through human labour. It implies that an apricot on a tree or sold at roadside or in a supermarket is not the same apricot. From the economic point of view, we are dealing with three different apricots.

Let's see how labour itself evolves and what effect this has on the formation of economic values. A simple example will enable us to understand what this is about.

Let us go back to the time when the use of chainsaws began. A woodcutter buys one of these devices and uses it to cut wood in a forest. From a visual point of view, the trunks he saws up are about the same as those he previously obtained when using traditional tools.

From an economic point of view, the formation of value, is very different in both these cases. With the chainsaw, labour has been transformed. It is not anymore the same labour that is applied to nature. In fact, what caused this change comes from the creative abilities of the human being. The human mind, through its inventions, creates tools and machines that change, sometimes radically, human labor, and thereby transforms the process leading to the formation of economic values.

If, on the basis of this concept, we consider the evolution of the economy over time, we can see how the secondary sector was formed, from pre-industrial artisanal production, to mass production on an industrial scale. Simultaneously, we notice the phenomenon of the division of labour. By pushing this concept a little further, we would see how other economic values are formed, through the fact that more and more inputs of nature fade away and human creative abilities come to the fore. Think of a lawyer, a doctor or a computer scientist who invented a new software. This is the tertiary sector, which then appears to our eyes of an economist.

We have thus demonstrated a polarity in the formation of values. On one hand, nature transformed by labour; on the other hand, labour is modified by the human mind.

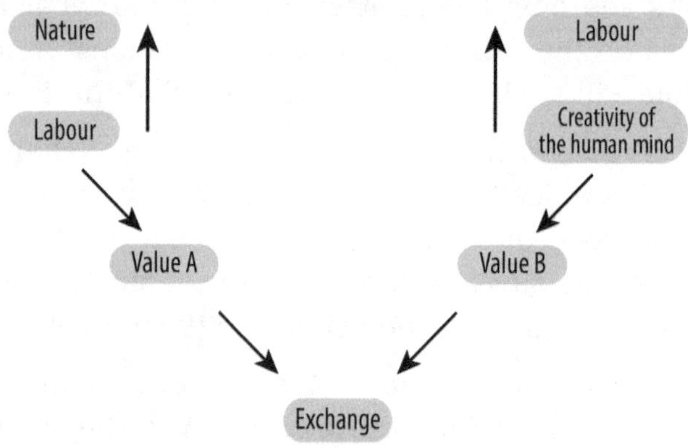

Diag. 3 - Polarity in the formation of value

We will see later how this diagram is also useful for understanding the formation of prices.

This polarity in the formation of values enabled us to capture the dynamics of the three production sectors of the economy. We can now illustrate this in a schematic form:

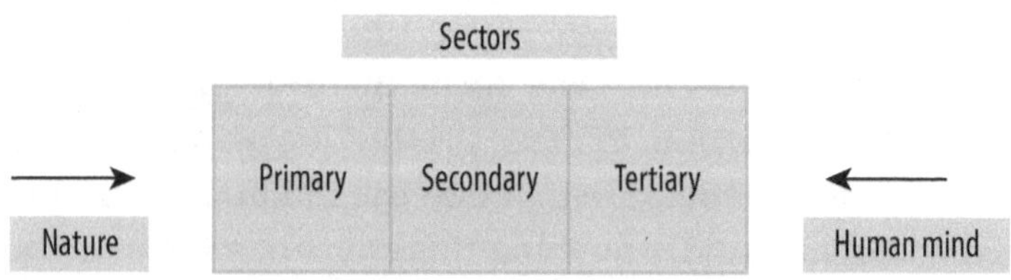

Diag. 4 - Polarity in the formation of values and the three economic sectors

This diagram contains within it the whole of *real economy*. All professions both, those of the commercial and noncommercial circuits of the economy, have a place in it.

We will go into detail regarding this point in the chapter on Contribution Money[27]. However, for now, we have to ask ourselves whether the *unreal economy* has anything to do with the creation of value. In other words, can earning money with money, or making money work, be considered as an economic activity? That is to say: is being speculator a profession?

If this were the case, it would obviously not be a profession of primary or secondary sector. The intelligence necessary for the exercise of this activity, is preponderant compared to the input required from nature, which recedes into the background. We would therefore place speculation in the tertiary sector.

There are other situations that also involve inventiveness and intelligence; for example, burglary and fraud. No one would think that being a burglar can be considered to be a profession. In the act of theft, there is no confrontation of values, as the thief does not bring any value for the purpose of making an exchange.

One could argue that the speculator brings money in when buying foreign currency. In our example above, the one who sells 10 million dollars on the foreign exchange market, would therefore bring a value. Reasoning in this way means mistaking the economic value for the price of the exchange.

---

27   Chapter 22. A third form of money: Contribution Money

Suppose our speculator received these 10 million through the sale of products he created. The economic value generated by his activity consisted of these products that are now held by his clients. The money he received is a purchasing right, but it is not a value within the meaning of the economy. Similarly the dollars he receives against his Euros are not a value. There is only a transfer of a purchasing right, from the euro zone to the dollar zone. The lack of attributes of an economic act, as they are highlighted in the diagram, does not allow speculative activity to be classified within the tertiary sector. This activity is therefore outside of the *real economy.*

We have gone to great length in the details of this question, because of the great confusion that arises from it. The orthodox concepts are too imprecise, allowing a vagueness to be maintained on activities related to speculation. These activities are amalgamated into the economy as if they were naturally part of it. A more accurate science of economics should take these facts into consideration.

With the current economic crisis, the problems caused by the *unreal economy* have become so acute, that many voices are being raised to curb this type of economy. But a sufficiently thorough study has not yet been done, to realize that this economy is not only harmful, but that it is totally useless. It is by no means a necessary evil.

The first advisable measure to take will consist in preventing the harmful effects of speculative investment from being transmitted to the *real economy.* We will discuss the modalities of achieving this with regard to money.

9

Ethics and Economics

Before continuing, I would like to make a sort of intermediate point.

The reader may have noticed that so far there is no reference to any moral concept. We have not considered speculation from an ethical point of view. We constantly remained within the economy to study this issue of speculation. I will continue to maintain such an approach, because, by taking this phenomenological perspective of *real economy*, I have noticed that ethics are intrisically imbeded within economy. It is not necessary to provide, from outside the economy, moral principles of justice, equality, sharing, generosity, love of neighbour, and so on. These qualities belong to the fundamental virtues that humans may wish to develop on their own life path. It is important that philosophers, psychologists and sociologists focus all their attention on these moral principles. If I wrote a book on virtue, in the sense of Plato, I would not hesitate to study the desire for financial gain, from this point of view.

Throughout this book, my purpose is different. My observation of the economy showed me that if we deviate from what is inherent to the *real economy*, then the economy becomes unbalanced, dysfunctional and diseased. Through its crises, it shows us what we have to rectify. One has just to be attentive and to learn to read within the social and economic phenomena what needs to be corrected.

I would even say that the economy carries its health within itself. Its normal state is to be balanced. If it is not, it means that some foreign elements have been introduced into it, which always prove to be speculative.

But the disease caused by speculation, which itself becomes included as part of the economy is, with the passage of time, getting more and more costly. The economy always ends up presenting us with the bill. When it is high enough, we decide to take action.

The example that well illustrates what has been said above is that of the environment. In the late sixties, the *"green"* activists brought this issue out into the open. They were not taken very seriously. Yet over time, their concerns proved to be justified. Gradually journalists took up this issue. They were listened to.

But the effect was very limited, regarding the taking into account of the environment. When scientists became concerned about the issue, awareness increased. This led to politicians sprinkling some green on their programs. But nothing fundamental was undertaken. It is only when the issue was addressed from the economic point of view, that things started to move.

In October 2006 a report on climate change was produced by a commission chaired by Nicholas Stern, a

British former Vice President of the World Bank. For the first time, a team of economists attempted to quantify the annual cost of global warming for the world economy.

Their conclusion was: *"Using the results from formal economic models, the Review estimates that if we don't act, the overall costs and risks of climate change will be equivalent to losing at least 5% of global GDP each year, now and forever. If a wider range of risks and impacts is taken into account, the estimates of damage could rise to 20% of GDP or more.*

In contrast, the costs of action – reducing greenhouse gas emissions to avoid the worst impacts of climate change – can be limited to around 1% of global GDP each year. " (Stern, 2006).

In 2020, the annual cost of climate change could range between 5,000 and 20,000 billion dollars. This evaluation was made in 2006. Since then, Nicholas Stern has revised it upwards.

In citing these figures, I do not want to defend the ideas presented in this report, especially those related to the market for carbon emissions, in which one sees speculation being introduced under the guise of environmental protection.

My purpose is to show that an extremely serious societal issue has only been taken into account from the time that an economic reasoning has been applied to it, and when it was seen that inaction would cost between 5 and 20 times more than taking action.

The Stern report had the effect of a bomb, which began to shift opinions. In the economic sphere, investors moved towards new technologies in the fields of energy and sustainable development.

Certainly, the response to climate change is still very inadequate, and the political game has started to unravel the advances that were concluded upon. But that does not detract from what I want to highlight.

On the contrary, if we do not progress sufficiently on environmental issues, if we do not take the concrete steps that are necessary, the invoice presented by the economy will be even higher.

What has just been said will shed a different light on the term I use: *Economy of Human Added Value*. It is definitely about added value, and therefore an economic process, and not about a moral notion to be superimposed.

Let us take the example of a person who is responsible for operating a machine that produces erasers. It is probable that the quantity of erasers produced in one minute largely exceeds his personal needs over his lifetime. The tens of thousands of erasers produced by the machine are not destined to him. He produces for thousands of other people who need what he himself does not need. On the other hand, it is other people in the world who produce what he needs.

This is one of the main virtues of the division of labour. It creates an interdependence between human beings. If we look at this phenomenon in detail, we see that because the economy is based on the division of labour, it establishes a de facto solidarity between all actors. If this does not translate into humane living conditions for billions of people, we must look for the cause in external factors, which are hampering this basic process that is inherent to the economy.

If the values that enter into the economy are derived from human activities which transform nature and the organisation of work, then the economy is inclusive and fraternal. Such is its nature. If the price of a good or service is determined by a careful examination of the creation of value, and if all the factors of production are taken into consideration (remuneration, working conditions, social welfare, environment), then the economy is in balance, and is thereby healthy.

A foreign element intervenes in the economy whenever price is determined by factors other than those belonging to the chain of human activity that creates added value. For example, when scarcity is included in the formation of prices. We then exit the *real economy* and introduce the seeds of economic disease.

When we will speak about the fourth branch of the Economic Cross, land and real estate, we will see how scarcity interferes in the price, and how it spreads to the whole economy, creating serious imbalances.

By this example, we see that the determination of price is complex, and requires an ability to observe and think through the *real economy*, down to the smallest detail.

However it is upon this condition that the price, which two partners will determine during an exchange, will be such that both are winners in a reciprocal manner; that one will not have imposed their dominant position on the other. Then the economy will be in equilibrium.

It is not by saying *"less economy and more social actions"* that we will make progress in a practical and efficient manner. We must instead dive deeper into the very essence of the economy, which in reality is based on a conditionality of win-win. Let us go further into an economic way of thinking that grasps reality, and we will avoid creating social problems.

By talking in terms of fair trade or a solidarity economy, is this not an illustration of the fact that we have left the ground of the *real economy*? It will be a sign that we are back in it, when we will no longer need to resort to words that are, basically, only tautology.

If we better understand this, we will cease to use moralising but ineffective exhortations, as a substitute for our need of a clear approach to economic phenomena. Because, in practice, this so-called ethical vision distracts us from the real issues.

Wanting to create ethical circuits in parallel to what exists, does not address the real causes. It would be more useful, and more directly effective, to recognize how the economy carries, within itself, fraternity and solidarity. Today it seems to me urgent that we do not fight the wrong battle.

10

Purchasing Money

Following Bretton Woods and the creation of the International Monetary Fund, financial experts have used the balance of payments as the main tool for measuring the situation of currencies (monetary units) [TG]. IMF publications on this subject were taken as references. With the implosion of the fixed exchange rate system, and the explosion of the development of money markets, this instrument is not anymore sufficient by itself. Nevertheless, the structure of the balance of payments is in itself instructive. They record both the trade operations of firms in a country with the rest of the world, as well as operations of a financial nature.

In other words, a significant movement of hot money[TG] for purely speculative reasons, can destabilize a country's balance of payments, even though the trade balance is in equilibrium or even in surplus.

If, for example, the central bank interest rate of the Fed increases significantly, and the prospects of the dollar are rising, hot money will leave a foreign country to be invested in the United States. As a result, the balance of payments of the foreign country will go into deficit.

In a direct way, by the decrease in the foreign-exchange reserves of the Central Bank, or indirectly, by its sudden abundance in the foreign exchange markets, the value of the currency (monetary unit) of that country will be pushed downward by the decision of the Fed. Imports then become more expensive. It will be the reverse for exports. But if exports do not compensate the variation that will occur in imports, the trade balance will go into deficit, aggravating the overall balance of payments deficit, and resulting in a devaluation of the currency (monetary unit).

Scenarios of this kind are quite frequent. They expose the problem that results from mixing trade and financial operations. The balance of payments is an unsuitable tool. But it is only a symptom of the underlying problem: that we have only one instrument for measuring both the flows of investment and of trade. The same money is used in both cases. It is therefore desirable to create two instruments well separated one from the other. The *real economy* needs a money that flows in a circuit that would have minimal linkage with another circuit, the circuit of the money used to finance enterprises and loans in general.

Note that we do not include hot money in the money circuit for the *real economy*, because, as we will have understood, our purpose is to build an economy without speculation.

The organisation of the Financing Money circuit will be the subject of another chapter. Let's first look at the organisation of the first money circuit. We call it Purchasing Money[28]. It will only record the exchanges in the *real economy*, that is to say the sale and purchase of goods and services between enterprises and institutions, or between individuals and enterprises/institutions, or between individuals themselves.

Purchasing Money is recorded[29] in bank accounts that we call Current Purchasing Accounts (CP Accounts). Their operation is broadly similar to that of current accounts, which individuals and businesses presently use. They will provide the same payment system operations through transfers, bank cards and cheque payments, or cash withdrawals. Transfer operations will only be between Current Purchasing Accounts. For example, it will not be allowed to make a transfer from a Current Purchasing Account, to the account of a company that wants to launch a bond issue. Anyone who wants to undertake such an operation will have to do so in a different way, as we shall see later.

A second account will be linked to the Current Purchasing Account (CP Account). It will receive savings we make in anticipation of future purchases. We call it the Deferred Purchasing Account (DP Account).

On December 31 of each year, CP Accounts are reset. Any positive balance is transferred, by the bank, to the DP Account. Thus, the purchasing rights, to meet the current expenditures, remains always within limits.

---

28 Firstly, we will consider this money as circulating within a defined monetary zone. Later, we will look at what happens in the case of imports and exports. See the Chapter 25: A New International Monetary System.

29 Instead of "recorded" the conventional term would be "deposited" in bank accounts. We use the term "recorded" as it is more accurate regarding the accounting nature of Purchasing Money.

Individuals receive their monthly remuneration on their CP Account and use it day-to-day, for purchases and for paying their bills. If they want to put such money aside for a trip or to purchase a vehicle, they can do so at any time, by a transfer from their CP Account to their DP Account. At year end, if there is a positive balance on the CP Account, the bank will transfer it automatically to the DP Account. Note that the CP Account will not be completely reset to zero. In effect, consideration must be taken of the remuneration of December that will be used for expenditures in January, and which are usually paid by the company a few days before the end of the month. A well designed software will be able to take this item into account.

We are therefore talking in terms of principle about a reset of the accounts. In practice, the *"cash flow"* needed for current purchasing will always be available.

The same will apply to businesses. The money that they will retain, at the end of the year, on their CP Account shall not exceed the expenses of the following month of January. Again, a software can be programmed to check that it happens in this way.

For businesses that need cash flow in excess of their normal expenditures in January, another measure will be necessary. It would be assumed that they are in need of a bridging loan. This modality will be discussed in chapter 20, Financing Institutes.

The diagram below shows the basic operations between two accounts A and B, which can belong to companies or individuals.

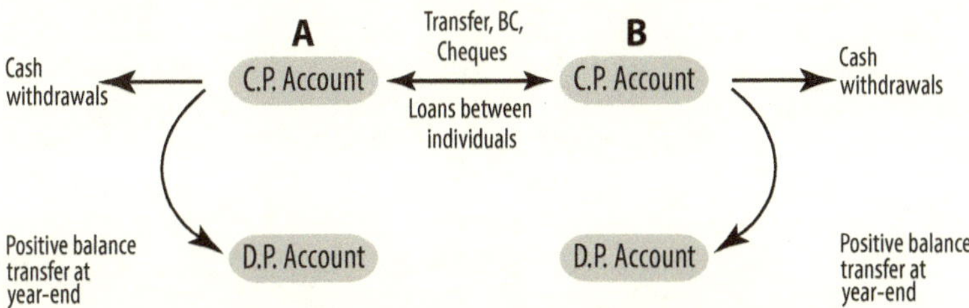

Diag. 5 - Basic opérations between two Purchasing Money Accounts

Let us consider now the reason for a Deferred Purchasing Account (DP Account), which raises the issue of monetary demurrage[TG].

11

Monetary Demurrage

We have seen that money allows deferral of the act of purchase.[30] In this sense, money is useful. It provides a valuable service, provided it is not allowed to develop secondary effects, which are harmful to the economy. These dysfunctional effects emerge when money, instead of circulating rapidly, accumulates in various places as a stored commodity, and thus loses its character of being a unit of account.

In this bi-polar tension between money acting as a stored commodity, or money acting as a unit of account, we are trying to place the cursor as close as possible to the unit of account side of the spectrum. But it is not possible to do so completely, precisely because we defer the act of purchase. The reasons we do so are either because we do not yet have the necessary financial means to make the projected expenditure, or that the time has not yet come for it, or that we need to put some money aside, that is to say to save.

---

30 See chapter 6, para 9: A new Bretton Woods?

Traditionally, economists see savings as a kind of buffer element which enables adjustment of the economy. When savings are too high, purchasing is insufficient. So we will lower interest rates in order to make savings less attractive. The consumer will then tend to spend his money immediately. But it can then happen that there is not enough money left for investment. Again, the interest rate will play an incentive role, but in the other direction. In each of these situations, savings will be considered as a regulatory element. But in reality, it is a mechanical device that moreover masks two unresolved problems.

The first problem consists in the way we consider Financing Money. We will soon look at this. The second problem is related to excessive savings, which can indicate many things: the level of remuneration of some people is too high in relation to their immediate needs; or the need for consumer goods is momentarily satisfied; or, the fear of future crises urges caution. In these three cases, it is necessary to deal with these problems for themselves, as we will. Playing with interest rates to regulate savings solves nothing. In contrast, accumulated money tends to become treated as a commodity, and thus fuels speculation.

The aim is to restrict savings so as to delay the actual purchase, without the money stagnating and thereby being unable to fulfil its measurement function as a unit of account for reciprocal exchange. In other words, money, when it tends to accumulate, must always be recycled to active areas of the economy, where it is needed: such as the financing of enterprises on the one hand; as well as to meet the needs of the noncommercial circuit of the economy on the other. We will consider these two areas.

For now, let us look at a measure that will discourage an individual or an enterprise from accumulating their money on the Deferred Purchasing Account (DP Account). It will suffice to apply a rate of demurrage[TG] of the funds which is high enough, for example, 10% a year. This demurrage will occur on 31 December of each year, and will be applied to the balance of the DP Account at that date. If the account holder wants to use some of their money during the year for a major purchase or for meeting cash flow requirements, the amount they transfer back to their Current Purchasing Account (CP Account) will be decreased by 10%.

Table 1 on the following page shows an example of how the Deferred Purchasing Account evolves.

Here, we assume that Mr. Durand saves annually an amount of 2,000 € on his Deferred Purchasing Account (DP Account), and that in year 6, he transfers 6,000 € of these savings to his Current Purchasing Account (CP Account). In year 6, he therefore saves nothing on his DP Account. At the time of transfer the 6,000 € is depreciated by 10%, so in reality only 5,400 € is transferred back to his CP Account. The 600 € demurrage charge is included in the total amount of 737.12 that is deducted from the balance of his DP Account at the end of year 6 (600 + 10% of 1,371.18).

In total, over 6 years, Mr. Durand transferred 10,000 € from his CP Account to his DP Account, and paid a 3,365.94 € demurrage charge to a holding account of the Bank of Purchasing Money, which we could call the Demurrage Account.

Year	Opening balance at 01 Jan.	Transfer from C.P.Account	Transfer to C.P.Account	Transfer to a Financing Institute	Transfer from the Financing Institute	Sub-total at 31 dec.	Deduction of Demurrage	Final balance at 31dec.
1	-	2'000.00				2'000.00	200.00	1'800.00
2	1'800.00	2'000.00				3'800.00	380.00	3'420.00
3	3'420.00	2'000.00				5'420.00	542.00	4'878.00
4	4'878.00	2'000.00				6'878.00	687.80	6'190.20
5	6'190.20	2'000.00				8'190.20	819.02	7'371.18
6	7'371.18	-	5'400.00			1'371.18	737.12	1'234.06
		10'000.00	5'400.00				3'365.94	

Table 1 - Demurrage of savings on a Deferred Purchasing Account _without_ transfer to a Financing Institute

Everything would be different if Mr. Durand did not let his saved money stagnate on his DP Account, but instead transferred it to an account at the Financing Institute, so that it is available for lending to the economy. When we address Financing Money, we will see that, although the other data of this scenario remains unchanged, the demurrage charge would only be 600, at the end of year 6 (that is to say 10% of 6,000), and that 4,000 would remain on his account at the Financing Institute, after having transferred 5,400 € to his CP Account. Table 2 on the following page shows the recording of these transactions.[31]

What happens to the 3,365.94 € that corresponds to the demurrage illustrated on Table 1, or to the 600 €, illustrated on Table 2 ? They are not destroyed. They are placed at the disposal of the noncommercial circuit of the economy, which will be presented later. This mechanism of monetary demurrage will therefore help to generate the third type of money, the one that appears in the economy as a form of giving.

At this point, we begin to see how all the economic concepts are interrelated, and that it is difficult to treat them separately. Yet it cannot be otherwise. It is only gradually that an overall vision will emerge and that we will understand how each element is articulated with others and fits into the whole. The reader will therefore have to exercise patience and perseverance in the study of an *Economy of Human Added Value.*

---

31 By transferring his savings to a Financing Institute, Mr. Durand avoided a demurrage charge of 2,765.94 (i.e. 3,365.94 - 600). Regarding the total sum of 10,000 saved, this non-demurrage represents 27.65% in 5 years. From the perspective of the concept of Monetary Demurrage, we could consider that this participation in financing the economy will have been accounted for at a reasonable level.

Year	Opening balance at 01 Jan.	Transfer from C.P.Account	Transfer to C.P.Account	Transfer to a Financing Institute	Transfer from the Financing Institute	Sub-total at 31 dec.	Deduction of Demurrage	Final balance at 31dec.
1	-	2'000.00		2'000.00		-	-	-
2	-	2'000.00		2'000.00		-	-	-
3	-	2'000.00		2'000.00		-	-	-
4	-	2'000.00		2'000.00		-	-	-
5	-	2'000.00		2'000.00		-	-	-
6	-	-	5'400.00	-	6'000.00	-	600.00	-
		10'000.00	5'400.00				600.00	

Table 2 - Demurrage of savings on a Deferred Purchasing Account with transfer to a Financing Institute

Perhaps some might be revolted by the idea of a demurrage charge on accumulated money. Maybe they have a nest egg in savings accounts that pays them interest every year. Anyone looking exclusively from their own self interest can only react with antipathy to such proposals. That is understandable. But if they look at the economy as a whole, their judgment may change.

The concept of monetary demurrage that we have just illustrated represents an *"aging of money"*. Many economic thinkers have advocated that money adheres, as far as possible, to the exchange of goods and services. That is to say, money should serve the present, and thus lose its power as it moves away from this present (Gesell, 1916).

We even experienced monetary demurrage in different places, often successfully. A description of these studies can be found in the book by Marie-Louise Duboin (Duboin, 2007), and that of Philippe Derudder (Derudder, 2005).

The aging of money corresponds to a vision of the economy centered in reality. And this foundation is in line with a very holistic approach to life. Precisely because, in nature, all life is accompanied by death. Nothing on earth is in a process of unlimited growth and infinite duration. Only commodified money is claimed to be wrested from the natural cycle that passes through death. Whether through the capitalisation of interest, or the stock market and real estate speculation, we try to bestow money with an infinite capacity for growth and longevity. We thus act contrary to nature. The actual state of nature, of the life of Society and of the economy, demonstrate this more and more clearly.

It is therefore justified to seek methods for making money age, to prevent it prolonging its life into speculative spheres. The aging of the money helps to fight against the tendency of its commodification.

Some people consider monetary demurrage as a form of disappearance. For example, the figure 90 will be stamped, in indelible ink, on a banknote of 100. This banknote will thus have lost 10% of its value. But what happens to the 10 € ? They are purely and simply canceled.

A nuisance value has been taken away from the money, by weakening its tendency to accumulate. But at the same time, a virtue has been taken away from it: its capacity to postpone the right to purchase. By removing money from the speculative sphere in this way, one also removes it from the *real economy*. In other words, a certain amount of purchasing power has been pulled out of the *real economy*. Rather than cancel this purchasing rights, why not transfer them to someone who can use them fruitfully for the economy?

Money could thus acquire a second life that would benefit the entire economy. We start to see a third type of money, that which can serve a role that is equally useful to that of Purchasing Money and Financing Money.

To my knowledge, the Austrian philosopher Rudolf Steiner is the one who discovered this form of aging money, which makes money a dynamic process. His discovery of the three lifecycle stages of money seems to be an essential contribution to the science of economics[AB32].

---

32 Preparata, (2003).

In discussing Purchasing Money, we looked at the Current Purchasing Account and the Deferred Purchasing Account, without going into detail about the organisation that manages them. We will therefore now discuss the Bank of Purchasing Money.

12

The Bank of Purchasing Money

Today, even more than yesterday, the image of banking is associated with big financial capital, equity investments and juicy profits; in short with the world of speculative finance. Admittedly, the image of opulence was temporarily tarnished by bankruptcies or emergency bailouts of some institutions in 2007 and 2008. But already in 2009, the largest banks had put things in order - to their advantage: profits made on the stock markets and the foreign exchange markets, accompanied by enormous bonuses distributed to traders. The leopard cannot change its spots and everything was handled in the usual way and faster than expected, despite the injunctions of the G20. Rather than take offense loudly, commentators might be delighted, because we gained time. It has been proved that the financial system contains within itself this kind of self-serving excess. This excess cannot be restrained by legislation. It is necessary therefore to establish an entirely different design of banking, one that arises from a new approach to money.

To avoid any confusion between the traditional model and the one that we are going to propose, it would have seemed preferable to adopt another name. I have retained the term of banking, because it corresponds to the primary function of these institutions: to receive deposits. Historically, it is only later that other attributes of banking emerged, such as the transfer of funds and the provision of loans.

Banks of Purchasing Money are banks for the deposit and transfer of funds. The granting of loans is not part of their mission. Other organisations, namely Financing Institutes, will be responsible for this, as we shall see later. This separation will allow us to better differentiate between the two types of money: that of Purchasing Money and that of Financing Money.

The Bank of Purchasing Money therefore offers a double service, the management of user's accounts and the transfer of money between accounts, or directly to the users. In the latter case, it is a withdrawal in cash.

But what does the bank do with the money that is recorded in its Users accounts? According to the traditional concept, this money is simultaneously accounted for as an asset to the bank, so that the banker has the impression of having this money in stock as a commodity, which he can sell. He will therefore use the money deposited with him for engaging in the sale and purchase of money or securities, which boils down to the same thing.[33]

33 Translator's note: Although few depositors realize it, legally the bank owns the depositor's funds as soon as they are put in the bank. Our money becomes the bank's, and we become unsecured creditors holding IOUs or promises to pay. But until now the bank has been obligated to pay the money

According to our conception, Purchasing Money only represents purchasing rights. It is only an accounting entry, not a commodity. In the accountancy of the Bank of Purchasing Money, it will be recorded on the asset side of the accounts and is dedicated to this single function. We call it the Movement of Users[34] Funds. It is therefore an asset account which functions like the Petty Cash account, or the Cash in bank account of a firm. But with an important difference. The Cash in bank account enables the recording of very different type of operations: payment by a customer, payment of a service provider, of salaries, the purchase of supplies, etc. This Movement of Users Funds account will have only one function: to record the accounting counterpart of inputs and outputs of money taking place on the accounts of the users, as it is shown in the example on the next page.

The Bank of Purchasing Money cannot consider the balance of the Movement of Users Funds account as money which it can use for investments, loans or even to settle its own bills.

To pay its operating expenses, the bank will need, like any firm, a Current Purchasing Account. To avoid any confusion between User Accounts and the bank's own Operating Account, the bank will be required to open its operating account in another independent Bank of Purchasing Money. Thus, it will act like any other firm or individual regarding its internal management, and it will act as a bank only for the management of its Users accounts.

---

back on demand in the form of cash. Under the 2012 joint plan of the US Federal Deposit Insurance Corporation and the Bank of England, our IOUs will be converted into "bank equity." The bank will get the money and we will get stock in the bank. Brown, (2013).

34 See Depositors VS users in TG

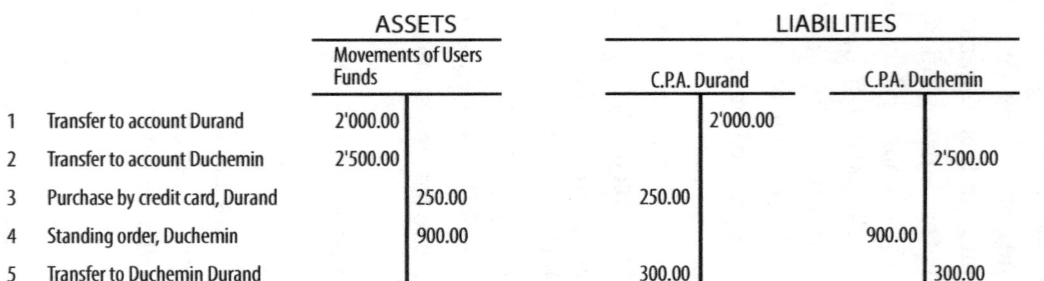

| | | ASSETS | LIABILITIES | |
		Movements of Users Funds	C.P.A. Durand	C.P.A. Duchemin
1	Transfer to account Durand	2'000.00	2'000.00	
2	Transfer to account Duchemin	2'500.00		2'500.00
3	Purchase by credit card, Durand	250.00	250.00	
4	Standing order, Duchemin	900.00		900.00
5	Transfer to Duchemin Durand		300.00	300.00

Table 3 - Accounting of operations on the Current Purchasing Accounts

This mode of operation implies an important element relating to the question of reserves for a Bank of Purchasing Money. Here we are only dealing with one aspect; others will be addressed later, when we study the subject of Financing Money.

How much funding would be needed to create such a bank? Nothing more and nothing less than the amount necessary for a service company to meet its operational costs in the first year.

Since the bank is not committing the money of its users, it does not need reserves to guarantee payment of user funds. Monetary *"deposits"* are accounting entries that represent the purchasing rights of users, and are therefore inviolable, and only a user can order them transferred to another account.

Of course, we need to consider the risk of fraud by a group of ill-intentioned people, or embezzlement by a dishonest employee, as already happens in the actual banking system. This will be the task of a supervisory body, the Monetary Auditing Institute[35], which will establish mechanisms to avoid these problems. We will look again at this issue later.

So far we have talked mainly about Ledger Money. To see what happens regarding physical coins and banknotes, we will now address Cash Money. We will thereby complete the subject of how the Banks of Purchasing Money function.

------

35   See diagram 11, chapter 23: Money as a public service

13

The Institute of Cash Money

Originally, Fiduciary Money designated coins and banknotes that were convertible into gold, at the commercial banks or at the central bank. Since convertibility no longer exists, coins and banknotes are equivalent, in terms of representing purchasing rights, to the Ledger Money recorded as accounting entries by the banks (i.e. *"deposits"*). Basically all money became fiduciary, that is to say based on trust (Latin fiduciarius, from fiducia, trust).

To avoid confusion, we will use the term Cash Money[TG] to refer to banknotes and coins. It is therefore not another money, but one of the forms of Purchasing Money, the other form being the Ledger Money[TG] that circulates between the bank accounts, as we have seen previously.

Nowadays, the use of Cash Money in trade is diminishing. Everyday purchases are increasingly paid by bank card. In the eurozone, cash constitutes only 15% of the M1 money supply, that is to say the one that is closest to what we call the Purchasing Money. The percentage of Cash Money relative to the M1 money supply is likely to diminish further over the coming decades. But even if the use of the digital wallet were to be generalized, physical coins and banknotes will still be used for a long time yet, because many people see it as something more real than Ledger Money. Cash Money gives people the impression of having a more concrete means of payment, to which they can turn to in the event of a banking crisis. Some economists who are nostalgic of the gold standard consider Cash Money to be the new standard, which will guarantee the value of the money. This is particularly the case of the German economist Helmut Creutz. (Creutz, 2010)[36].

Behind this vision of money, we can see the persistence of the concept of commodity money, which reassures by seeming to give an intrinsic value to the money. But there is an illusion and a lack of confidence in this concept. The illusion comes from the notion of legal tender. Since the State has legalised payment by means of coins and banknotes, it is theoretically impossible for a trader to refuse the settlement of a purchase by this means. Therefore a 100 € banknote seems to have a value of 100 €. But we forget that what one can buy with this banknote varies with time. The housewife notices this change in purchasing power when comparing the contents of her basket with that of twenty years ago. The value of the 100 € banknote is therefore exactly the value of what one can buy with it! The value of money is derived from the *real*

---

36 Since the publication in 2014 of the original French version of this book, the situation has changed very rapidly. Several countries have since established smartphone payment systems, with the declared aim of eliminating cash. This endeavour which is now called "De-Cashing" by the IMF, has proved to be more rapid than I originally envisaged, but of course that was always a possibility. See: Alexei Kireyev, (2017) .

economy, unless some factors alien to the *real economy* cause some disequilibrium.

The lack of trust that we spoke of earlier, is a lack of trust in the accountancy. Over time, monetary instruments became dematerialised into book-keeping, which records every commercial exchange. If money is limited to this function, as we want to do with Purchasing Money, then this money becomes accountancy, which, if maintained with rigor, is as reliable as the bookkeeping of a firm[37].

Of course, one might object that if a bank fails, the clients lose everything on their accounts, while the money in their pockets remains their property. We could check whether, in the present system, this argument is still valid.

But in the system that we propose, the loss of recorded deposits becomes obsolete, because a Bank of Purchasing Money has no reason to go bankrupt. It does not make any speculative investment with the monetary rights of its users. It does not use their deposits (registered purchasing rights). It only registers them. If, over time, this bank did not have enough users to cover its overhead costs, and therefore decided to stop its activity, it would simply have to transfer the accounting of its Users[38] accounts, to another bank. This other bank would then open corresponding accounts for each user of the former bank. For the users, this operation would just be a transfer from their account from one bank to another. Their purchasing rights were registered in bank A. Now they are in bank B. These account users have lost nothing by the termination of the bank A's activity.

---

37 See TG : Depositors vs. Users.
38 Known as *"depositors"* in conventional banking.

To be more precise, the separation between the Accounts of the Movement of Users Funds, and the Current Purchasing Account of the bank or its operating expenses, allows total security for the users. The bank cannot use the deposits of its users. For its own operating expenses, the bank uses an account that is in another bank. The wall between the bank's operating funds and those of the Users offers a full guarantee. Therefore, there is no reason to give more value to the Cash Money than to the Ledger Money. They are equivalent and the transition from one to the other must be done in the simplest way.

For the individual who needs cash, there is no difference between the system we offer and the current one. He uses his bank card at an ATM or withdraws the cash at the counter of the bank. But how does the bank get its supplies of Cash Money?

The answer to this question is actually simple when you consider money as a purchasing right. That this right is expressed as figures in accounting, or figures on paper rectangles, is a secondary consideration. So, there is only the need for an institution to manage the manufacture of coins and banknotes, and to provide the Bank of Purchasing Money with it on request. We can call this institution an Institute of Cash Money. Regarding the accounting, this operation would take place as it is shown in Table 4 on the next page.

Accountancy of the Bank of Purchasing Money A

		ASSETS			LIABILITIES
		Movements of Ledger Money	Movements of Cash Money	Institute of Cash Money	C.P. account of Durand
1	Request of Cash Money	100'000.00		100'000.00	
2	Transfer of Cash Money		100'000.00	100'000.00	
3	Cash withdrawal by Durand		400.00		400.00

Accountancy of the Institute of Cash Money

		ASSETS		LIABILITIES
		Movements of Ledger Money	Movements of Cash Money	Bank A
1	Request of Cash Money by Bank of Purchasing Money A	100'000.00		100'000.00
2	Transfer of Cash Money		100'000.00	100'000.00

NB : The movements of Users Funds account, as seen on Table 3, here is divided into two sub-accounts: the movements of Ledger Money account and the Movements of Cash Money account

Table 4 - Accounting of transaction between a Bank of Purchasing Money and the Institute of Cash Money

We use the term Institute to designate the organisation providing the Cash Money. It cannot be seen as a bank with deposit accounts. The Institute only converts, in Cash Money, purchasing rights that were previously expressed as Ledger Money.

Of course, if the Bank of Purchasing Money "A" has too much Cash Money, it will do a reverse conversion operation with the Institute of Cash Money.

The Institute of Cash Money must pay the costs of manufacturing coins and banknotes. Moreover, like any organisation, it has its own expenses to pay and it therefore would charge a fee for the conversions it handles. For all these operations, it has a Current Purchasing Account (CP account) in a separate Bank of Purchasing Money. Again, a wall must exist between the money that the Institute uses for its functioning, and the money that it converts to allow banks to have Cash Money, or the reverse.

In this proposal, we will see a big difference with that of the central banking system, as it currently exists. The Institute of Cash Money does not ask the Bank of Purchasing Money to deposit securities or other assets in exchange for Cash Money. Nor does it engage in the kind of tricks called *"Swaps"*. It does not care to control the amount of money in circulation, by playing on interest rates. The Institute of Cash Money does not need to do so, because there is no monetary creation or destruction within the Institute of Cash Money. Clearly, it is not an issuing institute in the usual sense.

An important point should also be mentioned. The regulations of the Banks of Purchasing Money will stipulate that they get their supplies of Cash Money only through the Institute of Cash Money. In particular they cannot borrow or lend to another bank. If we clearly understand the function of the Institute, it will be evident that such transactions between banks would be meaningless.

Thus we see emerge a new form of money that derives its organization from what it is at its foundation: a purchasing right. It is by not losing sight of this basic notion that we can solve the most difficult monetary issue, that of the rate of exchange between monetary units. In treating it in this way, we will see completely new perspectives for an International Monetary System that serves the *real economy*, and which enables an *Economy of Human Added Value*.

14

The convertibility of Purchasing Money

In the economic jargon of the French media, the years that followed the post-war reconstruction are called "*the 30 glorious years*". From the perspective of the most developed countries (economically), this denomination may have sense. But from the perspective of the poorest countries, this period could also be called "*the 30 shameful years*". Because this is the period during which the institutions emanating from Bretton Woods behaved unspeakably towards many countries of the Global South. Under the pretext of bringing these countries into the concert of the market economy, supposedly for giving them the possibility of good economic development, the World Bank and the International Monetary Fund, in reality, orchestrated the economic, social and cultural dismantling of most of these countries.

In many cases, Global South countries were left with a huge debt vis-a-vis the World Bank and the club of investors that followed in its wake. By following the advice and plans of the experts of the IMF and the World Bank, these countries found themselves in a spiral such that they had to borrow to pay for what we call, most seriously, *"debt service"*. Generally, after a few years these Global South countries had paid in interest more than the amounts they borrowed, without even having begun to repay the principal. This is not the place to describe all that happened and the catastrophic consequences of *"structural adjustment programmes* (SAPs)" imposed by the experts. Many observers documented it and books on the subject abound[39].

But the disaster caused by the Bretton Woods institutions should encourage us to go back to the real cause of the problem, and to seek ways to ensure that their actions are no longer effective in such a way.

It will always be possible to say that all evil comes from the incompetence of experts serving the voracious appetite of unscrupulous financiers. Unfortunately, such remarks only show that we are mired in second-tier phenomena. We need to go back a notch and see that the problem is first of all monetary, and that it concerns all countries. We will describe this monetary problem in broad outline, and then see how it would be resolved in the *Economy of Human Added Value.*

To understand what we are talking about, we simply need to imagine, as an extreme situation, a country which has no gold, few raw materials, and which would essentially be an importer; and therefore has virtually no export and few tourists to visit it.

At this point, we are facing something unthinkable. However, we will dare to cross this limit.

---

39 See, in particular (Toussaint, 2005).

In his book on the work of Robert A. Mundell: "A Theory of Optimum Currency Areas"[40], Philippe Narassiguin[41] suggests that the issue is not so incongruous. Taking the example of Italy, at the time of the Lira, he shows that, in its exchanges with the North, the southern part of the country is in a chronic deficit situation. In other words, if instead of two regions we had two separate countries, each with its own monetary unit, we would have Italy-South that would be in a constant adverse balance of trade with Italy-North. The Lira-South would tend to permanently devalue, relative to the Lira-North. The fact that these two countries have had the same currency (the Lira) masks the problem. According to Narassiguin, the problem is transferred because compensation will take place elsewhere, for example by State subsidies as transfer payments from the Northern region of the country to the Southern one, or by workers moving from the South to the North, where the wages are more attractive.

This economist takes as an example, in-country economic disparities that are so characteristic, in order to highlight the same situation that occurs between many countries and, more generally, within each monetary zone, in that case the countries of the eurozone.

According to traditional monetary concepts, a country with low exports and little income from tourists would experience insurmountable difficulties. Its trade balance

---

40 Translator's note : In the 1960s, Robert A. Mundell pioneered a currency theory based on geographical area, which adopts a fixed exchange rate regime or a single currency within its boundaries. Mundell is known as the "father" of the Euro, as he laid the groundwork for its introduction through this work and helped to start the movement known as supply-side economics.

41 (Narassiguin, 1993)

would permanently be in deficit. Its money would leave the country to pay for the products it imports. To prevent devaluation of its money, the country would have to buy it back ... with other currencies.

We are therefore before a very curious situation : Importing companies of this country pay for the goods they buy. Then, the central bank of that country must repurchase in foreign exchange markets or from other central banks, the money that was used to settle imports. Everything happens as if the country has to pay twice. As we can see, regarding money as a commodity leads to the bizarre.

In doing so, we do not look at what is happening in the *real economy*. We implement a monetary superstructure that works above this reality. In fact, it would be necessary to take into consideration what is happening in production and trade.

In the country that serves as our example, let's call it country A, we can imagine that there is a diversified agriculture able to satisfy a large part of the population's needs. The country also has the crafts and industry to build houses, produce clothing, furniture, books, etc. Part of the population is dedicated to the tertiary sector. Normally, all these activities generate an economic surplus. The companies are therefore generally profitable. One might imagine that the people of this country seek to acquire goods and services which they have not had up till now. They could seek to produce them locally. But they can also get them from abroad. Import companies will be created and will offer products purchased, for example, from country B. The customers of the importers of country A will settle their purchases with what comes from the surplus of their economy. The importers will be profit-making through their sales. They will also give more work to the suppliers located in country B. The latter will be paid for their services. So far so good and everyone wins. But here is where the problem begins, because the money of the importer is not the same as that of the exporter.

The money that originally was used to facilitate the exchange becomes then an obstacle. This is contrary to the *real economy*, and comes from the fact that we have lost sight of what money is; it is not a commodity, but a purchasing right. If we consider it as it should be, we would see that the chain of trade does not stop with the suppliers that are located in country B. They have received in return for their services, the purchasing right expressed in the money MA of country A. They can use this right to buy products from country A. Or they can use this purchasing potential, expressed in terms of their money MB, to buy products in their own country B. In the latter case, the country B suppliers would give work to the companies of their country. If we observe well the process from start to finish, we can say that the people of country A increased the economic activity of the enterprises of the country B. Why should they, in addition, buy back the purchasing right that they themselves have provided?

This example, although theoretical, exposes a vital problem for the world economy and which climaxed in poor or developing countries. To resolve it, we have to start with the fact that if a country imports, it means that its economic activity generated the necessary resources to do so. This should be enough. Why should the country, on top, have to export in order to have the means to buy its money back? Or to pay its imports in an easily convertible currency like the dollar? This is tantamount to a double penalty, which particularly penalises countries with few products to export. This is the case of the poor and developing countries. During the *"30 shameful years"* they were forced to artificially direct their economy towards exports. This was especially so in agriculture, which has had disastrous consequences on local populations. The problem is different for countries that have an easily convertible currency, like the dollar, the British pound, the Euro, the Yen, etc.

In the first instance, this type of easily convertible money is not bought back by the central bank of the issuing country. It continues to circulate on the foreign exchange market. It is only when a currency becomes too abundant that the issuing central bank intervenes to buy it back. This fact is not without consequences on the global equilibrium of the economy.

To understand this, let us again take the example of the countries A and B, in a transfer of goods from country B to country A, paid for with money MA of country A. The quantity of MA money passes into the hands of the supplier located in country B. The supplier will then convert this quantity of MA money into a certain amount of MB money. Let's suppose the supplier does so directly in the foreign exchange market. In consequent, in the monetary area of country B, there exists simultaneously, two equivalent quantities of money: MA money and MB money. If MA money is an easily convertible currency, then whoever owns it has the possibility to lend it (at interest), even several times over. The quantity of easily convertible MA money will therefore multiply, leading an autonomous existence as such, unless the central banks of countries A and B intervene.

This scenario occurred on a large scale after the second world war, with the dollar. It led to the creation of a great mass of money known as Eurodollars. But at a smaller scale, this scenario is repeated with every foreign exchange transaction, and leads to the fact that, for a while, the amount of money that had been used to settle an export is doubled. This amount then exerts, even in a light way, an influence on the value of the money and, ultimately, on prices. With such an operation taking place thousands of times each day, the generated inflationary pressure on prices becomes more noticeable.

As a result, there is a continuous tendency towards systemic disequilibrium in the economies of countries with easily convertible money. This comes from the fact that the money supply is permanently higher than what is required to mediate all trade. Such excess of the money supply will then feed the speculative economy, unless the central bank intervenes by buying the easily convertible MA money with its own MB money, which it has to create for this purpose. In this case, instead of having a quantity of MA money, plus an equivalent quantity of MB money; we will end up with twice the quantity of MB money circulating in the economy of country B. This phenomenon is well known to economists. It is called imported inflation. But this phenomenon is not looked at from the right perspective, that is to say, from the perspective that money is a purchasing right. Because otherwise the remedy for the resulting imbalance would have appeared long ago.

Let us look at this phenomenon through the lens of Purchasing Money. The purchasing right represented by a quantity of MA money, which results from the export of products from country B to country A, has doubled due to the foreign exchange transaction. Overall, in country B, it became 2MB. Therefore there is 1MB too much. In reality, the foreign exchange transaction should result in the cancellation of the quantity of MA money. The banker would therefore record the quantity of MA money on the Current Purchasing Account of the exporter. But he would record its equivalent quantity in terms of MB money. The purchasing right by the exporter, which is measured by a quantity of MA money, is then recorded as a quantity of MB money. The bank therefore only indicates the purchasing right that the exporter will exercise in his country B.

In reality the process is similar to that we saw in the case of the conversion of Ledger Money into cash, by the Institute of Cash Money. We could envisage to create a money conversion Institute, which would work by the same model as that of Cash Money.

But in the case of conversion, the task is only about recording accounting entries. A Bank of Purchasing Money may as well do it, which simplifies the administration.

From a technical point of view, the software would have three more columns on the account: Movements of Ledger Money. The first column would indicate the denomination of the foreign money received (in our example as MA); the second column, would record the amount of MA received (eg 100,000), and the third column would show the conversion[TG] rate (e.g. 1.5). The accounts would be as shown as per Table 5 on the next page.

MA money is only indicated. It is not part of the accounting itself. It no longer exists as a purchasing right in country A, since the exporter Lambda has decided to exercise this right in its own country B. The exporter Lambda will exercise his purchasing right using MB money.

Conceived in this way, the conversion transaction sticks to the reality of the *real economy*. It does not introduce a distortion in the supply of MB money. It does not oblige the central bank from country A to purchase an amount of MA money which corresponds to nothing in country A, since the purchasing right indicated by the quantity of MA money is not exercised in country A.

By doing so, Purchasing Money completely loses its commodity character.

So a question arises which will quite naturally come to the mind of any economist: how to determine the conversion rate between the monetary units of different countries? Since the collapse of the Bretton Woods system, the parity of currencies is determined by supply and demand. If a currency is in excess, its rate decreases; and vice versa. Many factors affect the amount of money supplied or demanded. Some factors are linked to trade, but the most determining ones come from the speculative financial sphere.

Accounting of the Bank of Purchasing Money Y (in Country B)

	Monetary unit	Amount	Conversion rate	ASSETS	LIABILITIES
				Mov. of Ledger Money	C.P.A. Enterprise Lambda
Transfer from the Bank T (Country A)	MA	100'000.00	1.5	150'000.00	150'000.00

Table 5 - Accounting for foreign currency transactions

Within the framework of Purchasing Money, the parity between different monetary areas is determined by the purchasing potential of each monetary unit of account. Thus, if MA money can buy 1.5 times more goods in country A than in country B, we will have 1MA = 1.5MB. So the real price of goods, would by itself, determine the parity between currencies.

It would then be necessary for the countries to agree on the products used in the composition of the *"basket of goods"*, so that an identical baseline is established[42].

In this matter, it would not be possible to achieve mathematical precision, since a product can be more expensive in one country whilst another product is cheaper. We therefore will need a kind of average that reflects a general trend in the purchasing power of each monetary unit of account (currency) in its own country. But, in this way, we will be closer to economic reality than if we rely only on currency speculation and on the manipulation of interest rates by central banks.

We have shown that there is an answer to the question posed at the beginning of this chapter. Within the framework of Purchasing Money, a country can participate in the global economy whilst being essentially an importer. The requirement of an equilibrium of the trade balance falls by the wayside. And this is alright, since that country, through its imports contributes to the welfare of other countries, by purchasing their goods and services.

The world economy would benefit tremendously by turning to the proposed approach to Purchasing Money.

---

42 See the Basket of Purchasing Power Parity; chapter 25: A new International Monetary System.

For exporting countries, it would eliminate the problem of imported inflation that is present, even at tiny doses, each time a foreign money enters a country. For the poor and developing countries, the gain would be enormous. They could return to an economy that fits their climate, traditions and lifestyles.

Many voices are calling for the cancellation of third world debt. It would only be fair to achieve this. But this measure should be accompanied by an even more important decision: to adopt a monetary system that removes the cause of such indebtedness.[43]

The perception of money as a purchasing right leads to an entirely different approach to the economy than that which prevailed, and which still claims to rule today. For all theories that presided over the destiny of the post-war world, whether they came from John Maynard Keynes or from Milton Friedman, be they from left or right, all have in common the consideration of money as a commodity. Certainly those who have fed these theories, and those who have feathered their own nest with the consequences of these theories, will not grant any credence to a money that would only be a purchasing right. And they will shout even louder when they discover what is coming in the following chapters, where we discuss the Financing Money.

The reaction of such people is, of course, predictable. One can understand that they have a strong attachment to ideas, or an attachment even stronger to personal benefits they get from the incumbent money system. But

---

43 Other aspects of this issue are discussed in chapter 25: A new International Monetary System.

they should be reminded that the system they defend is not working; it produces more and more poverty and damage to society.

Theorists of this type of money system and the financiers who benefit from it, are probably the least qualified to make an objective judgment on the benefits of Purchasing Money. They have too many vested interests to defend, and therefore their judgment cannot be objective. Unless they open their eyes to the reality of the world, and develop a radically different approach, by abandoning that which they depended on, and were animated by in their lives until now. Given the magnitude of the current economic crisis, it is not impossible that such reversals could occur, even on an individual basis.

So we have established the foundations for a Purchasing Money adapted to the needs of the *real economy*, and at its service. We can now turn to the second form of money, that which is needed to finance the *real economy* activities. By discovering its nature, we will find an initial response to questions that emerged from reading the above. In particular, we will see the classic image of the bank completely dissolve, and we will do away with the concept of the balance of payments.

15

The interest-free loan

Traditionally, the financing of economic production is largely based on the notion of loans, whereby accumulated savings are invested. If one understands the nature of the Purchasing Money, it is no surprise that the question of the loan becomes even more important, with regard to financing production in the *real economy*. This is because the accumulation of money as savings is discouraged in Purchasing Money, through a liquidity tax (demurrage) [TG], which transfers 10% of the accumulated value to the regenerative circuit of Contribution Money. Therefore, to finance new production, it will be necessary to resort to the allocation of new credit.

Usually, when there is a loan there is interest. We are conditioned to think that one does not exist without the other. Before discussing the new Financing Money, it is therefore necessary to clarify the concept of interest.

When it comes to the budget of an individual, the impact of the interest on the credit for purchasing is already significant. For a lease on a car whose value is 20,000€ to be paid over 4 years, at the rate of 5.5% interest, the amount of interst payable each month amounts to about € 50. In total, the borrower will repay 112% of the borrowed amount. The car will have therefore cost 12% more than the original purchase price. Although this overhead is spread over four years, it corresponds, in gross terms, to an increase in the purchase price for the customer. But for the seller, the price has not moved. The difference between the selling price and the real purchase price is collected by the credit institution.

In the case of financing real estate, say over 20 years, this difference between the selling price and real purchase price climbs to 45% for a mortgage rate of 4% and to 72% if the rate is 6%. As the amounts involved are so much more important than in the case of car leasing, it becomes obvious that the cost of mortgage credit far exceeds the costs to the credit institution, for its management of the mortgage file. For example, in the case of a mortgage of 300,000€, the borrower will pay, in the form of interest, 136,000€ (at a 4% rate) or 215,000€ (at a 6% rate). If the loan is spread over 30 years, the figures are even more telling: the cost of interest being 62% of the principle for an interest rate of 3.5%, 82% for a 4% rate, and 216% for a 6% rate.

Some may argue that these amounts make up for the inflation of prices (or conversely, the devaluation in purchasing power of money). Indeed, inflation of 2% over 20 years multiplies prices by a factor of 1.486. A rate of 3% over the same period increases the total price by 80.6%[44]. In other words, the property, if purchased twenty years later would cost more because of inflation.

---

44 The calculation is as follows: $1.02^{20} = 1.486$ and $1.03^{20} = 1.806$

That is to say, the lender, applying an interest rate, seeks at least to preserve the purchasing power of his money[45].

Advocates of this view seem to neglect an important aspect: that interest is itself one of the main generators of increasing prices. The price of every good, and of every service, includes the amount of direct interest that an enterprise pays for its loans, plus the amount of indirect interest that the enterprise must pay as a share of wages to employees, to enable its employees to pay the interest on their personal loans due each month, especially their mortgage payments. Eliminating both direct and indirect interest payments, would cause prices to fall.

Helmut Creutz studied in detail this issue, and came to the conclusion that in 1997 "households, directly or indirectly, bear a load of 40 Pfennig interest burden for every Deutschmark spent." In other words, interest payments multiplied prices by 1.67[46]

Note that the application of interest also tends to exert an inflationary pressure in another way. When someone borrows money at a fixed interest rate, they are rather interested in prices rising and that wages follow this increase. In the presence of a true inflation, the proportion of their salary spent to repay their borrowings will tend to decrease. Thus, an increasing spiral in prices and wages benefits both the enterprise and the employee, when they are both borrowers.

On the side of the lender, it is necessary to distinguish whether the money comes from an accumulation of past economic activity, or whether it is new money created at

---

45 In addition, it is necessary to consider the fact that, the lender continuously reinvests the regular loan repayments, as soon as they are reimbursed to him.

46 (Creutz, 2010), Chapter 18: The scale of interest in the corporate sector.

the conclusion of a loan. This distinction will be important when we will be proposing a new form of loan money.

This does not differ greatly from the present situation of banks. The volume of new loans that a bank can make is proportional to the amount of reserve funds it has. These reserve funds are meant to precisely represent accumulated past money. In other words, under the current system, interest can only be justified if one wants to maintain the purchasing power of money that comes from a past accumulation. In the case of Purchasing Money, this claim is redundant because accumulation is out of question. On the contrary, whenever Purchasing Money accumulates, the quantity of purchasing rights, but not the value of money, diminishes because it is automatically transferred to the Contribution Money circuit, to finance goods and services in the regenerative noncommercial circuit of the economy. Therefore, the quantity of monetary purchasing rights matches, as close as possible, the activity of the *real economy*.

If some still doubt that interest has a disorganizing effect in the economy, they just need to look at its action, not only at the level of enterprises and individuals, but also at the level of States. And here we have to consider first of all developing countries. But the situation in other States, especially those of the West, is showing us that the monetary loan with interest leads to an impasse.

The debt problem of developing countries is well known to all who have followed the evolution of the economy during the second half of the twentieth century.

We will not treat this in detail. The works on this subject abound[47]. Let us mention just a few figures that speak for themselves.

In 1981, the U.S. Prime Rate, which determined the floating interest rate at which developing countries borrowed, peaked at 18.9%. As a reference point, a country like Switzerland considers an interest rate above 18% as usurious. The Swiss Federal Constitution prohibits lending above 18%. Therefore, according to Swiss law, the interest rates on loans to developing countries in 1981 were usurious.

For a 30-year loan at 18.9% interest rate, the total cost is considerable. For 1 million borrowed, the total interest payable amounts to 5.6 million, i.e. 560% of the amount borrowed. In reality, the repayments that developing countries had to face were even higher. In 1950, the 165 developing countries together had a debt to the rest of the world (external debt) of $ 541 billion. In late 2004, they had paid 5,300 billion. But they were not released from their debt, as they still had an outstanding balance of $ 2,400 billion.

In the words of Eric Toussaint: *"For every $ 1 owed in 1980, the developing countries have already paid almost $ 10 but still owe today almost $ 5"*. After a quarter of a century, and despite a colossal repayment, the borrower still owes five times the amount borrowed. We are well above the 560% mentioned above. How is this possible?

The explanation lies in four words: the spiral of indebtedness. It is triggered when one who has not the

---

47   See: Toussaint and Millet, (2010)

means to meet repayments is forced to borrow to pay interest alone. Many developing countries have entered this infernal cycle, which fundamentally is a nonsense, both economically and in human terms. But nevertheless it is human institutions that are behind this, particularly the International Monetary Fund and the World Bank.

We are facing one of the major problems of our time. It was characterized in the clearest terms by the young president of Burkina Faso, Thomas Sankara, three months before his assassination, in a speech at the 25th conference of the Organization of African Unity, July 29, 1987: *"Debt is neo-colonialism, in which colonizers transformed themselves into "technical assistants". We should better say "technical assassins".*

They present us with financing, with financial backers. As if someone's back could create development. We have been advised to go to these lenders. We have been proposed with nice financial set-ups. We have been indebted for fifty, sixty years and even more. That means we have been led to compromise our people for fifty years and more.

Under its current form, that is imperialism controlled, debt is a cleverly managed reconquest of Africa, aiming at subjugating its growth and development through foreign rules. Thus, each one of us becomes the financial slave, which is to say a true slave, of those who had been treacherous enough to put money in our countries with obligations for us to repay." (Sankara, 1987).

The term *"technical assassins"* might appear strong to some. But a careful examination of the situation of most developing countries shows that it is not. In an *Economy of Human Added Value*, we must get used to following every economic event, in all its consequences, both direct and indirect.

Thus, the increase in mortality from malnutrition, in poor countries, can be linked to the problem of the external debt of these countries. We could multiply the examples that show the destructive effect on peoples and civilisations, of a certain conception of debt and interest.

We note that among these effects, are some of a *"boomerang"* type, whereby the deteriorating social and economic conditions in developing countries, lead to population migration towards the so-called developed countries. The transfer of financial capital from developing countries to rich countries, is accompanied by a form of transfer of people who have no alternative, but to try to find refuge in the rich countries.

In economics, the disruption caused in a particular location, always comes back to us. In one form or another, we must pay the price.

The end of the last century has been particularly marked by the indebtedness of developing countries and poor countries. Added to this ongoing problem, is the indebtedness of countries which have a developed economy. This added indebtedness is following the same upward curve.

In France, for example, public debt was 21.1% of GDP in 1978. In 2013, it reached 93.4%. Some countries have already exceeded 100%. It follows that the burden of debt has reached alarming proportions. In 2013, this debt cost the French State 47 billion euros, or 14.2% of its budgetary revenues. France spends more in this area than for education.

Such figures are often abstract. They become concrete when they are translated into certain realities. What France pays in interest, i.e. 47 billion, represents 2 million *"guaranteed minimum wages"*, including Social Security contributions, over a year, or the annual income of 1,300,000 persons paid the median net salary of 1,675 € / month + charges. In times of economic crisis, we can imagine what could cause an injection of 47 billion in the form of purchasing power. This huge sum might support the *real economy*, instead of feeding the unreal financial one.

For we must not delude ourselves: the interest on debt goes to the accounts of the big lenders, who reinvest them in speculative finance. We can see how speculative finance pumps increasingly large sums, from the *real economy*, thereby threatening the entire world economy.

In the coming years, this problem may become insoluble if we do not address directly the very notion of interest. The bankruptcy of States, local authorities and cities is not excluded. We have the specific case of Greece, and a US payment default is likely to happen, as for example already happened in August 2011 and October 2013.

Again, we are not going to address this issue from the angle of moral or religious considerations. The economic facts are sufficiently revealing. Over time, the economy never lies. It always ends up revealing the problems that have been introduced into it.

The term *"Debt service"* is actually instructive. When a Developing Country comes to pay, in the form of interest, 10 times the amount borrowed, or when France pays 47 billion in annual debt service, one is entitled to wonder what link this debt service has with the service provided.

The sovereign debt crisis that is shaking the euro also invites us to look at things from another angle. Indeed, we may wonder if the excesses of the interest mechanism do not themselves lead to its annihilation. Already the ECB, to avoid a bankruptcy of the European commercial banks, implements colossal loan provisions at the rate of 1%, which is significantly lower than what they can get on the market. But during the subprime crisis in 2008, the Federal Reserve Bank went much further. It secretly loaned US banks, 1,200 billion dollars at the rate of 0.01%. In other words, to avoid an implosion of the system, the base rate is reduced to virtually zero[48; 49].

As shown by former French Prime Minister, Michel Rocard, and economist Pierre Larrouturou, the ECB could do the same, but for the benefit of the States (Rocard and Larrouturou, 2012)[50]. In reality, we should go further and ask the fundamental question: what is the justification for interest?

---

48 At the height of the depression of the 90s, Japan's central bank did the same, by setting the base rate at zero. In August 2012, the French State borrowed at a slightly negative rate. That is to say that the situation had become so serious, that owners of financial capital did not know where to invest their money and they paid for lending it!

49 Remember that this book was published in French in 2014. Since that time, several central banks and even junior banks have practised, or are still practising, negative deposit rates. So we live in a time when the very notion of interest is self-destructive. The future will show whether the Fed's desire to raise its key interest rate will last. A future financial crisis could very well destroy this intention.

50 For an English language version of this argument, see: Give our States some room to breathe, (2012)

In an *Economy of Human Added Value* there would be no more talk about interest. Such an economy would evaluate the credit allocation service provided by the lender just like it would for any other service, such as that of an accountant, a lawyer or a computer specialist. Only the value added by the lending organisation should be involved in the so-called debt service.

Of course, we should consider the cost of this service in terms of a public service of money, as we shall see in the chapter dealing with this issue.

Thus we are again led to think the unthinkable. In front of the chaos of the present economy, we cannot anymore avoid questioning the notion of interest as it is practiced today. But to achieve the design of an economy without interest, we must thoroughly review another notion: that of Financing Money.

16

Interest rate policy and central banks

In the economy that was put in place since the Bretton Woods agreements, the issue of interest rates has taken an important place, which was further increased after the collapse of fixed exchange rate system, and even more so in recent years, when the role of gold in the currency reserves of central banks disappeared into the background. Today, the base rate of central banks has become the main tool of monetary policy. Economic actors, political decision-makers and the media are attentive to the decisions of the Fed or of the ECB. Will they raise or lower their interest rates, or will they leave them as they are?

The determination of central bank base rates affects all other interest rates on the planet, and thus the cost of borrowing money for businesses and individuals. But this is not the only impact. For example, a base rate increase in the United States may, under certain conditions, have the effect of attracting financial capital, and thereby raise the value of the dollar.

For a central bank, the control of inflation requires a subtle balance of variations in their base rates. Thus the value of a currency is largely conditioned by changes made on these rates. We can see how the question of interest rates plays a central role in the overall economy. They have become its pivot.

But this situation is due to the fact that the money itself is seen as a commodity whose price may vary.

Let us examine this problem. Normally, a standard of measurement does not vary according to circumstances. The meter always measures the same length. The litre always offers the same capacity. In economics, what should vary is price, not the instrument for measuring economic value, that is to say, the money. A price may vary due to circumstances related to production. For example, it may fall because a new method of production has been invented, or because of improved management efficiencies by the enterprise. The factors of price variation can be many. But to properly measure them, a standardized reference is indispensable. If you change this reference, you no longer have a firm ground to stand on.

When the Euro goes up relative to the US dollar, a commodity produced in Holland is suddenly more expensive in the US market. But the reasons that cause the Euro to increase, are almost always financial, resulting from speculative finance. In most cases, changes in value of a currency are not related to factors within the *real economy*. We have to remember that the proportion of global financial flows, represented by the *real economy,* is less than 8%.

We saw that in the case of Purchasing Money, the determination of conversion parity between two monetary units was based on actual economic conditions, that is to say in comparing price indices. On this basis, changes in parity should be slow and infrequent.

In our disoriented economy, conversion rates vary from one day to another, even from one minute to the next. In this way, the economy can only go out of control. It is arrhythmic. It is like a heart that suffers permanently from palpitation crises. To regulate such a heart, we will use the pacemaker. But this apparatus acts external to the body, like a sort of electronic crutch. Its regulatory function does not proceed from the very vitality of the heart. If the heart has reached the end of its life, one can understand the need to implant such device. But no doctor will claim that a heart equipped with a pacemaker represents the normal functioning of this organ, and that its use should be generalized to all human beings.

The variation in base rates by central banks acts as a pacemaker. It sends impulses to the monetary system from outside, as if the economy was considered to be something that could only live in a pathological state, without any internal forces capable of providing an endogenous means of autoregulation.

But it may be worth looking at this differently. Our economy, based on the commodification of money, is sick. Our monetary system itself is in an end-of-life situation. It is suffering from chronic arrhythmia, which can no longer be controlled by natural means. Various means have been tried in the 20th century. One of them has, over time, imposed itself by its effectiveness. Indeed, the impulses given by central bank base rates produce an effect. But the effect of the best pacemakers is time bounded, and the heart dysfunction will eventually overcome the pacemaker, or the problem causing the arrhythmia will move to another organ.

In the huge deflation experienced by Japan during the last decade, we see the limits of a therapy by manipulating the base rate. To revive the economy, this country has applied a zero and sometimes negative base rate. Yet the economy struggled to revive. The financial crisis that began in 2007 also shows the redundancy of this therapy. With interest rates at 0.25%, not only does the *real economy* not appear to restart, but a new financial bubble has been created, and its implosion could cause further devastation.

The method of regulating money, through the manipulation of interest rates, is therefore tantamount to considering the economy as a diseased body.

Ultimately, the economy never lies. It reveals what has been introduced into it. If acting on interest rates has become the pacemaker of commodity money, it means that commodity money has reached its final stage.

Many books have been written in praise of the interest rate tool. They are full of intelligence and demonstrate great science, just like the development of the pacemaker. But let us not deceive ourselves. Use of this tool implies a pathological state of the monetary system, and hence of the economy.

Just as the human being is not born to be implanted with a pacemaker, neither is it inherent for the economy to be driven externally by changes in base rates. If we take this fact seriously, we will direct our research towards understanding the factors of economic health. We will learn to discern what makes the economy sick, and what makes it healthy.

Just as an organ carries within its own nature the conditions of its health, likewise the economy innately carries the potential of its healthy state, as long as foreign bodies are not introduced, which it cannot support long-term. The commodification of money is one of those foreign elements. Interest is one means to remunerate this commodification.

Making changes in interest rates to cure imbalances born of commodity money, is equivalent to introducing the pathogen of a disease into a body already affected by that disease. The condition of the patient will only get worse. This is precisely what we are witnessing in the repeated crises of the economy, especially in the crisis that began in 2007, which now prolongs itself as a sovereign debt crisis.

So we still had to deepen this issue of interest, by showing how it manifests itself today at the heart of institutions responsible for regulating the monetary system.

Now we are going to see why these institutions are not a necessity for the economy, and how they could be replaced.

17

The central bank, an anachronism

With the subprime crisis and consequent indebtedness of States, central banks are again on the front stage. The role generally attributed to them, that of lender of last resort, is strengthened. To deal with the defaults of banks, insurance and reinsurance companies, to address the risks of default of European countries, starting with Greece, only the central banks were left. If we wanted to avoid a general freeze-up of the monetary system, which would have led to a global crash, we had, as the Banque de France wrote, *"to make unlimited amounts of liquidity available."* (Matherat and Mongars, 2010, p. 42)[51].

To this end, these institutions have not hesitated to resort to practices that, not a long time ago and particularly during the creation of the ECB, were deemed to be contrary to their own constitution, and also considered heretic, relative to prevailing economic doctrine.

---

51 According to a Banque de France publication: *"Central banks, and the European Central Bank in particular, took several measures to support short-term liquidity, (...) to make unlimited amounts of liquidity available."* (Matherat and Mongars, 2010, p. 42)

When the Greek debt crisis broke out, the weapon of interest rates that was meant to address the functioning of the money, was used to its maximum capacity: The Fed went from 5.25% in 2001 to 0.25% in 2010, the ECB from 4.25% in 2008 to 0.25% in 2010. The rates of the Bank of England and of the Swiss National Bank have reached the same lower thresholds; while Japan had exceeded them since 2000, with up to zero and even negative rates. The classic tool of interest rate reveals itself to be insufficient, therefore central banks have resorted to what they call unconventional measures[TG52].

The first measure is Quantitative Easing, which the Banque de France presents in the following way:

"The central bank attempts to "saturate" economic agents' demand for money in the hope that they will spend their excess holdings directly. This is why the money is very often channelled to the only agent that is sure to spend it, meaning the government, which will spend it through its fiscal deficit. Central banks' purchases of government debt securities represent one of the most commonly used forms of quantitative easing." (Matherat and Mongars, 2010, p. 46)

The second unconventional measure is Credit Easing, which is presented in the same publication, two paragraphs later:

"Ultimately, if the credit channel is blocked, the central bank can take the place of commercial banks and markets to make loans directly to the economy. In practical terms,

---

52 Smaghi, (2009), for a keynote lecture at the International Center for Monetary and Banking Studies (ICMB). Published by the European Central Bank (ECB).

the central bank starts by broadening the range of loans that it refinances.[53] *It can then make outright purchases of securities representing lending to the economy, such as commercial paper, corporate bonds and mortgage bonds. These operations have two effects: they stimulate the market for debt securities and they provide financing directly to the economy. In exchange, however, the central bank is exposed to credit risk and interest rate risk, which are not ordinarily part of its function."*

By both these measures (quantitative easing and credit easing), the conditions of monetary creation are relaxed. That is to say that money is no longer backed by the usual values. It is created on arbitrary grounds. The money creation framework is no longer efficient enough, so it is expanded[54].

The system must be on its last legs to reach such contradictions! But when all the expedients have been exhausted, what will we do? Will we have the courage to ask the hard questions about the nature of money and the reality of central banks?

Past crises provided several opportunities to address these issues. But we did not take them up, because we continue to see money as a commodity. Although we are now equipped with very sophisticated economic tools,

---

53 Quoted from the Banque de France publication: *"Banks must provide colla-teral for their refinancing with the central bank. This collateral is usually government securities or loans to very highly rated borrowers. By relaxing its requirements, the central bank encourages banks to extend the loans that have just become eligible as collateral."* (Matherat and Mongars, 2010, p. 46).

54 This expansion has reached astronomical heights. Between 2009 and 2015, the Fed flooded the US economy with \$4 trillion. At the beginning of 2015, the ECB took over, at a rate of EUR 60 billion per month, soon to be increased to EUR 80 billion. In total, the ECB has already created more than 2,000 billion euros in quantitative and credit leasing.

our monetary conceptions remain within the paradigm of barter. We exchange a stock of goods against a stock of money.

It is understandable that we had this impression during the epoch of precious metal currencies, like gold coins. But when gold was withdrawn from the monetary circulation, we should have questioned the fundamental change that fiat issued coins and banknotes were bringing. Then, with the universal spread of Ledger Money (bank money), this issue should have become obvious to economists.

It is interesting to notice that the removal of convertibility of fiduciary money into gold, on the eve of the First World War, happened at the same time as the emergence of central banks, (including the Fed, which was founded in 1913). The objective of these institutions was to regulate the issuance of money according to the stock of gold, held by them.

It is interesting also that at the end of the First World War we had not realized that the world production of gold would never match the scale of economic exchange required under modern economic production; this was still understandable. But it is surprising that we continued with this approach, at Bretton Woods, when the parity of the dollar was defined in relation to gold. Even despite the problems raised in the interwar period, through the maintenance of a gold standard for the pound sterling, which were well known.

Of course, powerful interests were at stake. The Americans wanted to impose the dollar as the reserve currency instead of the pound sterling. But this does not explain everything. For all other countries continued to maintain gold reserves in their central banks, and the shares that each country paid to the International Monetary Fund were made partly in gold.

We were indeed in a kind of Gold Exchange Standard. And if it had not been fixed on the dollar, it could have been fixed on a Currency Basket, or on an international Central Bank-money, like the Bancor, which was proposed by John Maynard Keynes.

In all cases, we have continued to teach in the universities, the same vision of money as a storable commodity. It is this misrepresentation that should first be transformed, if we want to realise a new form of international monetary system. There is no commodity in the world that can exist in sufficient quantity, to cover the exchange requirement of the modern economic production, unless we use gravel or sand, which would make little sense.

If money cannot be backed by a particular commodity, that is because it is backed by all commodities. Money represents all tradable goods and services available within a given economic area, either immediately, or in the very near future. This is what gives money its reality. By itself, money does not have a reality, at least in material terms. Like any unit of measurement, money is a social agreement. It therefore falls within the conceptual domain.

Study of the evolution of money shows this well. With the emergence of bank transfer, the immaterial nature of money has become evident. It is often described as playing with the virtual. But this is not a game. When a salary of 1,500 € is transferred from the account of a company into that of one of its employees, it is a very real recording of accounting entries, although it is not accompanied by a transfer through material monetary instruments (such as physical cash or cheques).

The emergence of bank transfer, has revealed money to be an accounting of purchasing rights and production obligations. Whether as a written order on paper, or made by Internet, whether as a payment by credit card or digital wallet, in all cases it is a transfer from one account to another account, which boils down to the recording of accounting transactions. No physical cash is used.

This use of Ledger Money, also known as *"bank money"* has become more pronounced during the twentieth century, and will continue to do so in the twenty-first. This trend of dematerialisation is inevitable, because it is inherent to the nature of money itself, especially when it is regarded as a measuring instrument, or more specifically, as a unit of account. But if we continue to regard money as a commodity that can be accumulated, even though it no longer has any material substance, we are faced with a contradiction. To resolve this contradiction, or rather to give ourselves the impression that we will resolve it, we invent processes and mechanisms to back money against something that would seem more tangible.

Under the Bretton Woods system, the foreign-exchange reserves of central banks consisted of gold and currencies. In 1967, during the full crisis of the convertibility of the dollar into gold, the countries which were members of the International Monetary Fund, created from scratch the Special Drawing Rights (SDRs), as a kind of money that circulated only between central banks, for the purpose of settling balance of payments deficits. Subsequently, the use of SDRs was extended. After having become obsolete, their use has been reactivated and updated, following the 2010 European sovereign debt crisis

The value of the SDR is determined by a basket of currencies. With the collapse of the Bretton Woods system, currencies began to float against each other. The exchange rate of some currencies[TG] can vary significantly. For example, the dollar can lose 40% of its value within a few months or, on the contrary, be increased in value by as much, relative to other currencies.

The main currencies that make up the foreign-exchange reserves of central banks, undergo at regular intervals, fluctuations in value of major magnitude. Therefore, how can foreign currency reserves and SDRs represent a stock of guarantees, regarding the stability of central bank base money? We are hereby faced with something very relative.

In reality these foreign-exchange reserves are one of the pillars on which money creation is based. The other pillar, also appearing in the balance sheet of central banks, is what is called the refinancing of commercial banks.

To supply commercial banks with central bank base money, central banks either buy government bonds and other securities from them, or hold them as collateral for loans. Without going into the details of this mechanism, we can note that the central bank buys receivables from the commercial banks, that is to say, promises of payment (IOU's). The Central bank therefore supplies the commercial banking system with central bank base money, in exchange of future payment.

The Central bank records the value of these securities on the assets side of its balance sheet; and on the liabilities side, it records the value of the base money that it has issued to the commercial banks.[55]

But where do these elements that are thereby recorded as assets come from? For the most part, these are Government bonds, that is to say, receivables, which, until recently, were thought safe. But if they are, why transfer them to the central bank? The commercial bank might as well keep them. Anyway, it's not with the money generated by those securities that the commercial bank will repay the advance of Base Money that the central bank granted to it. For these securities will be paid to the commercial bank at maturity, that is to say, maybe in 5 or 10 years. Usually the provision of central bank Base Money is only extended for a few days, or even for 24 hours. Therefore it is another type of money that will return as settlement to the central bank ... to immediately restart the process afresh, in the reverse direction, and in greater quantities if the need for liquidity increases. The commercial bank will then provide other securities. Or it will conduct a swap that will allow each of the parties to include an asset in its balance sheet. And if that is not enough, if the need for liquidity increases, then the central bank did what we quoted earlier in this chapter.

---

55 AB : How central banks create money, (no date).

It undertakes *"unconventional measures"*[56], such as Quantitative Easing or Credit Easing. That is to say, it relaxes its rules and accepts less reliable securities, if not rotten securities, as the Fed has been doing since 2009.

Every day thousands of people are mobilized all over the world, to calculate which securities to buy and sell. Considerable energy with sophisticated tools, is devoted to optimize, on both sides, these exchanges of securities for central bank money. All this looks like a game of fictive accommodation papers. What is it for?

Is it really necessary? Does one need to supply the economy with central bank Base money as if delivering spare parts to a car manufacturer? From the perspective of money as a commodity, the answer seems to be affirmative. But for how much longer can it continue, and at what social cost?

Once we have understood that the accumulation of money is precisely what allows speculation, which is the cause of economic malady, and once we accept to see that feeding the economy with central bank money, is based on the notion of storable money, then we will be ready to change the present model. We will be able to see central banks for what they are: old redundant forms carried over into the present; in a word, they are anachronisms.

But to convince ourselves of this, we still need to understand more precisely the concept of the money supply, in the context of the Purchasing Money. Only then will we have the necessary foundation to address Financing Money.

---

56 AB : Smaghi, (2009)

18

The illusion of the money supply

This chapter debunks complicated technical theories that justify the existence and role of central banks, as institutions which supposedly ensure economic stability, by regulating "the supply of money" that "circulates" within the economy. Three interlocking theories that represent the principle justification for this purported "economic stability" role of central banks are examined: (1) the notion of "the money supply" itself; (2) the notion of "the velocity of money"; and (3) the various classifications of the money supply, such as "M1, M2 and M3".

Readers unfamiliar with these theories might get lost in the detailed argumentation necessary to debunk these convoluted theories. Lay readers thereby have the option to skip the technical argumentation (that begins at 18.1) if they so wish and go to 18.2 (p. 173) where they will find the main conclusions of the debunking argumentation, using words that are more understandable by the layperson.

18.1   The theory of money supply and velocity debunked

We will now show that the concept of the money supply is only valid in the context of the unreal financial economy, where we make money with money. In the *real economy*, the question of the money supply is quite different. To well understand it, let us put ourselves in the situation of the Bank of Purchasing Money. There, the users have Current Purchasing Accounts. Let us suppose that the credit balance of all of these accounts is 100 million Euros (100 M). On the asset side of the balance sheet of the bank, in the Movement of Purchasing Money account, is recorded the counterpart of this 100 M (on the debit side - see Table 6).

ASSETS		LIABILITIES	
Movements of ledger money	100	Current Purchasing Accounts	100

Diag. 6 - Simplified balance sheet in a Bank of Purchasing Money

In the traditional banking concept, the 100 M on the asset side would be considered as a stock of money that would be usable for loans, because the bank knows statistically that its customers will not use all of the 100 M at the same time.

The Bank of Purchasing Money does not consider that it has this 100 M as *"cash on hand"*. It cannot dispose of it for making loans, nor even for its own cash flow, since its own Purchasing Money Account is held in another institution.

This 100 M represents the purchasing rights of the accounts holders, be they individuals or companies.

We have seen that the Bank of Purchasing Money could not go bankrupt because of poor financial operations or risky loans. Finance and loans do not fall within the scope of its activities. Only poor management, which would result in overhead costs being too big, relative to the volume of its activity, could lead it having to shut down. In this case, the users (depositors) will run no risk, since their money is not stored. It cannot disappear. Their purchasing rights would simply be transferred to another institution. What we will have thereby moved is not physical cash (coins and banknotes), but accounting.

In the same way that a company can change accountant, and transfer all of its bookkeeping from the old to the new firm, through a simple mouse click, the detailed situations of each customer's account in the bankrupt bank, would be sent to the new institutions chosen by the holders of those accounts.

So we are dealing with the transferal of accounts and not of funds. We can already understand that the whole of the credit balances of all the Purchasing Money accounts, within a monetary area, does not constitute a hierarchical money supply. However, we will get a more precise understanding if we consider the concept of the velocity of money, as it is seen by conventional economists.

Let us take the example of six enterprises: A, B, C, D, E, F, which are in the following economic relationship: A buys from B goods or services costing 1,000, B buys from C for the same amount and so on to F.

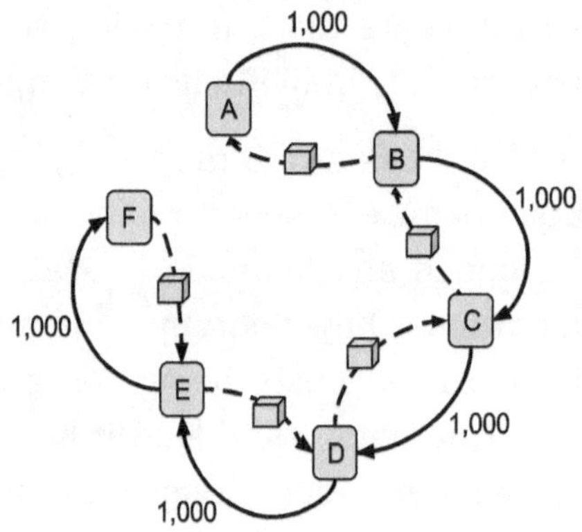

- Total value of 5 sequential transactions
  of supplied goods = 5,000

- Value of total quantity of cash used = 1,000

Diag. 7 - Purchasing chain of 6 enterprises : A-F

The total volume of transactions in goods/services that was generated, amounted to a value of 5,000 monetary units. In other words, the value of sales by enterprises: B, C, D, E and F, increased by 1,000 for each one, and by 5,000 in total.

If every payment was made in cash, that is to say in banknotes, and sequentially over time, then the total transaction value of 5,000 was generated by a quantity of banknotes equal to 1,000. If the five enterprises/ people completed this series of 5 economic transactions within one morning, it would still be possible, in the afternoon, for the same 1,000 in banknotes to generate 5 more transactions, each worth 1,000, which would thereby double the volume of transactions within the economy during that day. Therefore, with the same quantity of banknotes, a total turnover of 10'000 would have been generated.

However, at the other extreme, if the 10 enterprises (A-J) all want to make their purchases simultaneously in cash, at the same time, paying cash with 5 banknotes of 200, it will require a total of 50 of these notes.

If purchases between enterprises A - J are sequentially offset in time, but some are not paid immediately in full, then the quantity of banknotes required will be somewhere between 5 and 50. Ultimately, it would take very few banknotes to generate a high volume of exchange activity. The velocity of circulation of banknotes is therefore directly related to their amount in circulation.

Orthodox economists therefore establish a relation-ship between the velocity of money (V) and the money supply (M). For example, the same overall turnover of the economy (GDP), denominated in euros (E), gives the formula:

$$E = M \bullet V$$

The greater the velocity of cash, the more the mass of banknotes in circulation has to decrease.

Now, this quantity (E) itself depends on the prices (P) and the volume of transactions or production (T):

$$E = P \bullet T$$

If the volume of transactions is constant, the GDP (E) remains the same, assuming that prices do not vary. By bringing the two above equalities together, we obtain the Fisher *"equation of exchange"*[57]:

$$P \bullet T = M \bullet V$$

---

57 Irving Fisher (1867-1947) American economist.

Consequently, some schools of economic thinking, such as the Chicago School, deduce that if the velocity of money (V) remains constant, an increase in the money supply (M) will induce an increase in prices (P), or in the volume of transactions (T), causing an inflationary effect.

In other words, the quantity of money in circulation is crucial to the stability of the economy. This therefore is taken to be the first and foremost concern of the central bank. It must regulate the volume of the money supply, through the base rate and by constraints on the commercial banks (such as reserve requirements).

Here we are faced with a purely mechanistic approach to the economy. It does not take any account of what happens on the side of consumers, who are not necessarily robots. They may, for example, not need to buy something because they are already well equipped. We will come back to this way of assimilating the economy to a mechanism, and shall see that it is certainly not the right way to humanize it.

For now, let us discover that this link between the money supply and the velocity of money is an illusion.

Let's get back in the situation of Purchasing Money, and assume that all transactions are settled through ledger transfers. We will reintroduce paper money a little later.

Let us assume that the six enterprises have account balances as below at time t:

	A	B	C	D	E	F	Total purchasing rights
Current Purchasing Accounts balances	3'000	7'000	2'000	5'000	1'000	9'000	27'000

Table 6 - Account balances of 6 enterprises at time t

Altogether, these six enterprises have combined purchasing rights equal to 27,000.

The five situations resulting from the five sequential transactions (1,000 € each) at times t1, t2 ..., t5 are shown in Table 7 on the next page.

In the first example, we saw that the quantity of banknotes in circulation depended on their velocity of circulation. When transactions are cashless ledger accounting, the notion of velocity of circulation has no influence on the total quantity of purchasing rights.

The five purchasing enterprises could make their payment transactions simultaneously, each one to the amount of 1,000 monetary units. In this case, there would be no need to increase the amount of purchasing rights. While, as we have seen, in terms of non-sequential (simultaneous) payment by physical Cash Money, each enterprise would have to have 1,000 in hand, and the mass of banknotes in circulation would have to increase from 1,000 to 5,000.

Still within the framework of Purchasing Money, if the five companies wish to pay for their purchases with banknotes, their bank will proceed to do a conversion operation with the Institute of Cash Money, as we saw in chapter 13, (see p. 118, parag 3). For each enterprise, their purchasing rights, which was expressed in Ledger Money, will be converted into paper money. Both amounts cannot coexist simultaneously. Therefore, the overall amount of purchasing rights remained invariant, without any new injection of money into the circuit of Purchasing Money.

Current Purchasing Accounts	A	B	C	D	E	F	Total purchasing rights
initial balance	3'000	7'000	2'000	5'000	1'000	9'000	27'000
t1 balance	2'000	8'000	2'000	5'000	1'000	9'000	27'000
t2 balance	2'000	7'000	3'000	5'000	1'000	9'000	27'000
t3 balance	2'000	7'000	2'000	6'000	1'000	9'000	27'000
t4 balance	2'000	7'000	2'000	5'000	2'000	9'000	27'000
t5 balance	2'000	7'000	2'000	5'000	1'000	10'000	27'000

Table 7 - Account balances of 6 enterprises at sequential times t1 - t5

In the concept of Purchasing Money, the velocity of money does not exist. The notion behind the equation $E = M \cdot V$, that is to say, the link between the money supply and the velocity of money, is a theoretical construct that is born from three problems:

1. Observing the velocity of circulation of real economic goods and services

Economists have their eyes fixed on the circulation of physical money instruments (coins and banknotes). In our example, they would track visually the 1,000 transferred from enterprise A, to enterprise B, and then from B to C, and so on. But in terms of velocity of circulation, what counts is not the Cash Money, but the purchases. Our economist eyes should focus on observing the purchasing circuit between enterprises A, B, C, D, E and F. There we can observe a velocity of real circulation, which is a function of the needs of these companies, relative to the offers of available goods and services. It is therefore obvious that our economist eyes should follow the real phenomena of the real economy.

2. The speed of payment

The second problem is that of the speed of payment. Let us go back to our example, in its initial situation, and assume that enterprise B only has 200 in its account.

	A	B	C	D	E	F	Total purchasing rights
Current Purchasing Accounts balances	3'000	200	2'000	5'000	1'000	9'000	20'200

Table 8 - Account balances of 6 enterprises at time t, where B starts with 200 purchasing rights

Let us imagine that B wants to sell to A for 1,000 in cash, but that A does not have the cash in hand to pay it immediately. B will then not be able to make the cash purchase of 1,000 that he planned to do with C. Or he will postpone his payment to C who will then have to bear the consequences of B's cash difficulties. Unless C transfers the problem to D by delaying his payment, and so on.

Here we see a major problem of the present real economy, that of payment period. The speed of settlement of purchases increases all the more, since payments will be made immediately in full.

This problem should be addressed for what it is. To attribute this problem to notions about the quantity and velocity of money in circulation, is to displace it. So when the central bank is asked to intervene to solve this false problem, it only adds another dysfunction to the real one that was not addressed as such.

3. Cash flow problems

When the speed of the sales and that of the settlements are optimized, there may nevertheless remain a payment capacity problem. The enterprise might then have a problem of cash flow or of profitability. In both cases, this is a management issue that should be addressed for what it is. The managers of the enterprise might then conclude that, for example, the enterprise needs to borrow money.

At this point, we raise the issue of Financing Money. We shall soon see how the enterprise can obtain it.

But from the moment that the borrowed money appears on the Purchasing Money Account of the enterprise, it represents additional purchasing rights, which can generate real economic activity. In using these rights, the enterprise will increase the velocity of circulation of goods and services in the economy. And, if it pays immediately in full, it will increase the speed of payments.

So we are back to questions 1 and 2 above. The acquisition of additional purchasing rights, through a loan granted to the enterprise, was not linked to a need to increase the velocity of circulation of money, nor to a need to increase the money supply. It is some needs of the real economy that have generated the creation of money through loans by financial institutions, and not the reverse. However, the reversal of what should drive money creation has been theorized and institutionalised in the classical approach of central banking.

18.2   Principle conclusions of this chapter

Anyone who would address what we have just presented without linking it to concrete facts, that is to say to the *real economy*, could say we *"quibble"* on questions of detail. But that is what is precisely lacking in the actual theories that led to the present state of disaster capitalism. What is required now is this ability to track economic phenomena in their reality, in detail, and to follow them through to their economic, social, environmental and cultural consequences.

The theorist who imagines that he can optimise economic activity by acting on the velocity of monetary circulation, in accordance with central bank measures, looks like someone who would sit in front of a computer that manages the circulation of traffic on a motorway, and who notices that the average speed of the traffic is too slow. And, to remedy this, he would program the computer, so that the signs on the motorway indicate a higher mandatory minimum speed limit. Having done so, he would presume that he has acted on the situation to resolve it, without seeking the actual cause of the slowdown, such as an accident on the motorway.

Let us summarize what we have discovered in this chapter:

a. In the balance sheets of Purchasing Money Banks, the aggregate of credit balances of the Current Purchasing Accounts (as liabilities), do not have as a counterpart (as assets), a stock of money. So we do not have a money supply there. In the traditional view, the aggregate of credit balances of these accounts represent between 50 and 55% of what is called the money supply M1.

b. The 15-20% of M1 that are not recorded as commercial bank Ledger Money, are central bank Cash Money, in the form of physical banknotes and coins. They come into circulation as a result of withdrawals in banks or at ATMs. Within the framework of Purchasing Money, the bank transfers the purchasing rights, from bookkeeping ledger entries, into physical cash, which is then given to its client. Only the monetary instrument has changed. Not the money supply.

c. According to conventional concepts, the velocity of money would vary in inverse proportion to the money supply. If the money supply does not exist, what about its velocity? We have seen that the concept of the velocity of money has no reality anymore. It is not money that circulates. In the real economy it is goods and services that are circulating. With regard to Purchasing Money accounts, the bank simply records a transfer of purchasing rights. Then the velocity of money has no more reality than the money supply[58].

We thus see the level of fallacious abstraction that we have reached in so-called modern economics. Central banks spend their time trying to influence something that has no reality in the *real economy*, where only the exchange of goods and services is what counts.

The total amount (aggregate) of credit balances of deposit accounts is meaningless as an economic variable that can be acted upon. It is an abstraction of the same order as the cumulative amount of traffic jams within a country at a given time.

If one hears on the radio that there is a cumulative traffic jam of 300 km across the whole country, what does it usefully tell us? We have left all effective reality, it is just a babble of numbers that mean nothing.

From the perspective of the *real economy*, the important thing is what enterprise A will do. Will it buy something from enterprise B? Will enterprise D acquire supplies from enterprise E, or prefer to purchase those produced by enterprise L? From the perspective of these

---

58 Translator's note : In short, the orthodox notion of the "money supply" has no reality, because it is real economic production and exchange that endogenously generates money, as an accounting record of the real-world transactions involved, and not the other way round, i.e. of money produced as an exogenous supply of (financial) transactions, which would allegedly "stimulate", as a consequence of their creation, real economic production and exchange.

enterprises, it is useless to know what the French national aggregate of credit balances of demand deposit accounts was, for example, 3,700 billion euros in 2009.

If we are already in a fallacious abstraction with regard to the money supply M1, then where are we with regard to the money supply M2 ? Not to mention the money supply M3 -which the Federal Reserve bank stopped to take into consideration since March 2006 (Discontinuance of M3, 2005).

Here too we should follow the phenomena. For example, M2 includes deposits as savings in small savings accounts. But this money does not stay in the bank. It will, among others (such as M3 time deposits), be made available, for example, to the State via bond purchases for State expenditures.

In one way or another, money in deposit savings accounts, whether categorised as M2 or M3, will be used to settle transactions in the *real economy*. This money will therefore end up on the demand deposits accounts of enterprises, that is to say in what is called the M1 money supply. There is nothing wrong with this provision of recycling accumulated money to serve others.

A systemic incoherence arises when we want to consider the monetary aggregate at the global level. Because in the M2 and M3 levels of aggregate money supply, the same money is counted twice, first as accumulated savings of money in M2 or M3, and then as money loaned to and used in the money supply level of M1.

Here we reach the confusion that is made between Purchasing Money and Financing Money. Amalgamating these two monetary accounting functions together, in the form of M2, is like having our bread and eating it too.[59]

With M3 level monetary aggregates, we enter another dimension, that of the unreal financial economy. As well as M2 monetary aggregates, M3 includes other monetary aggregates used for short-term speculative investments, such as various investment funds. But let us leave this level for those who want to make more bread with the same bread![60]

---

59 Translator's note : The original French played on the idiomatic slang for *"making money"* and keeping it, despite spending it too, which has been transliterated into the English equivalents of *"making bread"* and *"having our cake (bread) and eating it too"*.

60 Translator's note : This is a transliteration of the idiomatic French expression for "making money with money".

19

Future-orientated money

We now turn to the most crucial question to be resolved, if we want to transit from disaster capitalism to an *Economy of Human Added Value*.

Many people do not understand why there is not an emerging political will that would limit the power of speculation. Many believe that this is due to collusion between the political and financial powers. This is probably true in many countries. But there are examples that show that the issue is not so simple, and that even the politician with the right intention, finds himself powerless to implement what he had planned. In particular, there have been two moments in recent history, where the representative of a popular movement became the head of State, and they seemed to be in a very good position to initiate a transformation of capitalism. In both cases, the aim of these movements was to establish a form of enterprise self-management, with the employees becoming stakeholders.

This happened in Poland and South Africa, and it is described with precision in the book: The Shock Doctrine, by Naomi Klein (Klein, 2008). Beyond anecdotal differences, the same scenario played identically in both countries. State ministers and officials responsible for implementing these reforms were subjected to overpowering pressure from economic advisers strongly committed to the promotion of ultra-liberalism; the so-called Chicago boys, who were trained at the Chicago school of economics in accordance with the ideas of Milton Friedman.

Each time the same extremely simple argument was used, which I can sum up in a few sentences: *"if you carry out your planned reforms, capital will flee your country. You will not have enough to meet the investment needs of your enterprises, which will lose their competitiveness. Exports will plummet, the trade balance will deteriorate rapidly, further accelerating capital flight. Your balance of payments will enter a vicious downward spiral. This will be accompanied by a collapse in the value of your currency, and a steep rise of unemployment, and so on ... "*.

This chain of events seems inexorable. In the logic of the present system, it is actually true. In other words, and at the time, the governments of Poland and South Africa had no other choice, but to submit to the dictates of finance, by turning their backs on their ideals, and thus betraying the people who had brought them to power.

Both these governments were given the opportunity to realise how ideals and good intentions are not enough to transform the situation of their countries, particularly in the economic field. We can understand why all progressive government, even if it is honest and uncorrupted, will eventually do the opposite of what they had announced. All left-wing parties and environmentalists will be brought up short by this threat alone, and end up in taking half-measures, which fail to meet the promises on which they came to power.

Are we saying that any economic reform to limit the consequences of disaster capitalism is impossible? The answer is clearly yes, as long as we do not question the present foundations on which the economy is financed; as long as we do not grasp the true nature of Financing Money; as long as we do not view this Money through concepts inherent to its true nature, instead of putting it in the same institutional vault as the Purchasing Money.

We need to make a complete turnaround in our conception of finance. If we do so, we will find remedies to the disaster of capitalism, and we will have the tools that were lacking to the representatives of Solidarnosc in Poland, and to those of the African National Congress in South Africa.

The entire current system relies on the fact that the financing of a building, a new business, or the deficit of a State, comes from financial capital accumulated in a more or less recent past. It is on the basis of pre-existing funds that a financing operation can be launched, either by collecting the total funds necessary, as in the constitution of the share capital of a company; or by supplying a fraction of the funds required, for example 20%, and borrowing the rest, as in the case of mortgage loans. The mortgage down payment of 20% having been saved up over time. The remaining 80%, if it comes from a commercial bank loan, results from money creation. Therefore we will tend not to see the commercial bank loan as resulting from a past accumulation of financial capital. But this is only an appearance. Because the possibility for the commercial bank to create money is essentially based on the reserves at its disposal, which is money amassed progressively. In both cases - whether as an equity contribution of 100%, or only of a fraction of the amount required - that funding is based on money that has been stored over time[61].

In other words, the money used to finance something is past-oriented, meaning that it results from past actions which have been completed.

The question then arises: what is the link between these results of the past, and what is going to get under way, through the new activity that seeks to be funded?

This past accumulated money does not bring, in itself, any guarantee that the one to whom it will be entrusted will make good use of it. This element of risk is also why we talk about venture capital. Even the most colossal fortune does not guarantee the success of a new business. As soon as funds are made available to anyone for the development of an initiative, what will permit the repayment of this money depends entirely on what the borrower will do with it. The guarantor resides in the future.

It is the same for a consumer loan. If an individual borrows 15,000 € over four years to buy a car, it is his activity during the forty-eight months ahead, which represents the counter value of the money created by the banker.

---

61 It may be that the money comes from the sale of a business or property. But in this case, it is the buyer who has accumulated the funds. This question of financing new economic activity with past accumulated money is then moved up a notch, and is just as problematic, although it has a different nature.

The purchasing power (value) of Financing Money is therefore based on the future. We can say that it has no prior existence. In an economy which differentiates between Purchasing Money and Financing Money, it can not be otherwise. Because Purchasing Money corresponds to purchasing rights created by the present economic activity. The sum of these rights tends to be equal to the sum of goods and services provided in the monetary area.

Whoever establishes an enterprise, for example a manufacturer of goods in the secondary sector, does not yet have the purchasing rights that will allow him to purchase machinery, equipment, raw materials and office furniture. Nor does he yet have the money to pay employees. These purchasing rights do not exist at the outset. They can only be created.

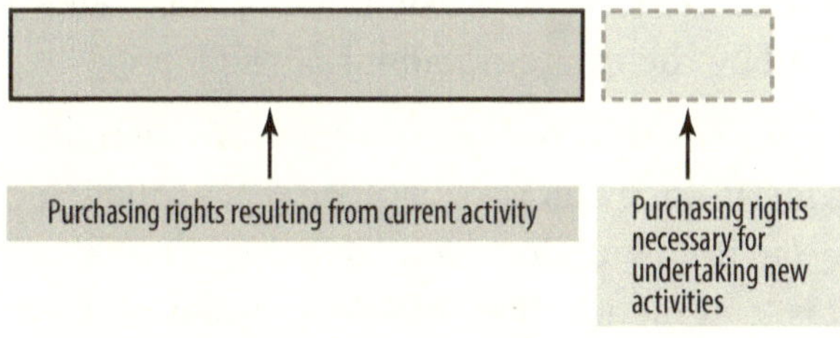

Diag 8 - Purchasing rights : current and new activity

From the moment we put ourselves in the context of money as a purchasing right, saving is minimized, so that money becomes a more accurate reflection of actual economic activity. Therefore, new economic activities necessarily require the creation of new purchasing rights. These new economic activities give rise to the future, they thus need future-orientated money, which comes into being at the same time as the activity which is about to begin.

This money is not created ex nihilo, meaning *"out of nothing"*, as one often reads in the specialised economic literature. Some even believe that it would be possible to stabilize the economic and social disorders by stopping loan-based money creation. In my view, they propose wrong remedies, because they do not grasp how the birth of new money is necessary at the point of undertaking new productive activities, that is to say, when the economy needs financing.

"Future-oriented" money is inherent to the economy, and it takes its place alongside existing Purchasing Money. It is not based on arbitrariness or nothingness, but on an activity that will become a reality. The realisation of the project will generate value that will be represented by the money thus created. The existence of this value will be confirmed by the reimbursement of the loan.

Thus, we see the emergence of a profession that seems to have lost its lustre as a result of the crisis of housing loans. For we have now understood that this *"future-oriented"* money is loan money. If all financing relies on loans, then the role of those who grant them, and thus create money, is essential. They bear responsibility for the value of new purchasing rights that they create and award.

The subprime crisis has exposed what it is about. Originally the problem did not come from the fact that banks did not have enough reserve capital to cover loans. Faced with the mass of payment defaults, the banks would have needed colossal reserves. The failure that led to the present systemic banking crisis is above all human, and lies in the fact that the rules of the profession, in terms of loan allocation, have not been followed.

But rules are not everything. They must be accompanied by know-how and human skills. Financing Money, as we propose it, will require large capacities, both technical and human, to assess the feasibility of a project. Those who will award a loan to an enterprise must know well its field of activity. They will evaluate the soundness of its financial plan. They will also be helped by an Operations Insurance, i.e. an insurance on operating losses due to economic situation, which I mentioned in my previous book (Laloux, 2007. Chapter: Aux ressources de l'humain)[62]. In addition, they will have to evaluate the project team, especially their ability to achieve their intentions. This last point requires great human skill which goes far beyond dealing with figures.

The profession of banking saw its image severely tarnished as a result of the crisis. The implementation of the model of Financing Money here proposed could give the banking profession an opportunity to recover itself, and even acquire a new dimension. However, note right away that the Institutes that will manage the creation of Financing Money will not be banks, in the usual sense. Their nature and their functioning will be presented in the next two chapters, and we will understand that this task falls within the ambit of a new form of public service.

---

62 The question of Operations Insurance will be dealt with in more detail in volume 2 of this book.

The beginning of this chapter enabled us to sketch the foundations of a Financing Money that would be managed independently of Purchasing Money. It is important to see that their natures are different. Purchasing Money has both feet in the present, in that it represents purchasing rights under the current *real economy*. Financing Money is future-oriented, because it allocates purchasing rights to be used for new production, which will add new value in the future to the existing economy.

The specific nature of these two Moneys must be differentiated, to the extent that the institutions which will manage these two Moneys (the Financing Institutes and the Banks of Purchasing Money), will be completely separate, as we shall see .

However, the fields of activity of these two Moneys will be linked by gateways permitting a transition from one Money to another. As for the transition of Financing Money to that of Purchasing Money, it is obvious, and happens almost instantaneously. Indeed, a loan is granted to be used as soon as possible. When the Financing Institute allocates a loan, it is transferred immediately to a Current Purchasing Account in the bank of the beneficiary. Thus Financing Money instantaneously becomes Purchasing Money. It will be used to buy whatever was envisaged in the business plan of the loan.

We will now see how the transition from Purchasing Money to Financing Money happens. At the moment of a loan repayment, the purchasing rights created at the time of the loan allocation will then be cleared from the monetary accounting system. They will have become useless because the enterprise, through its new productive activity, creates new purchasing rights that correspond to the level of the economy at that time. This will allow the system to remain balanced. The transfer between the two monetary circuits, of Financing Money and Purchasing Money, in both directions, poses no problems in terms of accounting principle, nor any technical difficulties.

The situation is less straightforward for accumulated Purchasing Money which might tend to go towards investment. We definitely distinguish between investment and financing. Remember that money is under a permanent tension between its status as a unit of account and as a commodity[63]. Money always tends to accumulate in one place or another. This will never be settled once and for all. It requires constant attention by economic stakeholders.

Why does the accumulation of money happen? The reason is twofold. Firstly there is what might be called voluntary restraint of immediate spending, ie making savings instead. And then there is also the surplus of purchasing rights that are inevitably created by the economy itself. Let us look at these two points:

1. *Money accumulated by individuals saving*

   These are savings, that are accumulated by the tendency to not use all of one's purchasing rights, in anticipation of future needs.

   If these future needs correspond to the purchase of something for a relatively little amount of money, they can be financed by the savings of a few months during the calendar year. In this case, as we have seen, the

---

63 See Diagram 2, The dual nature of money, (ch.6)

money remains on the Current Purchasing Account of the individual user. The user has no interest in putting this money on his Deferred Purchasing Account, since he would lose 10% when transferring it back again to the Current Purchasing Account[64].

If the individual user intends to save money for a period longer than one year, to meet a bigger expense, then he will use his Deferred Purchasing Account, where he will lose 10% of his savings each year. To avoid this, he will have the possibility to transfer his savings to an institute of Financing Money (a Financing Institute). We know that he will not gain interest from doing so, but his savings, accumulated over more than one year, will only be subject to one application of the 10% demurrage, when it is transferred back to his Current Purchasing Account.

We have here a passage between these two types of money. The solution we propose avoids the systemic dysfunctions arising from the commodification of accumulated money. It also offers the opportunity for everyone to contribute to financing an enterprise of their choice[65].

Finally, note that where someone envisages an expenditure that would require a significantly longer period of saving, for example for buying a car, they can ask

---

64   See Chapter 11, Monetary Demurrage

65   In traditional economic thinking, one would expect an investor to participate in the financing of an enterprise by becoming a shareholder or entering into an investment fund. As was said at the beginning of this book, it is not possible to address simultaneously all four branches of the Economic Cross. When we later reach the topic of the branch of Financial Capital, that issue will become clearer.

for a loan. In this case, they would go to a Financing Institute, just as would an enterprise.

2. *Accumulated money that represents an economic surplus*

Now let us examine the question of the surplus generated by the economy, which is usually called profit. Before seeing the link it might have with financing, it might be useful to examine the whole concept of profit.

Among those who aspire to a more humane economy, many have a negative view of profits, as if someone who makes a profit would take advantage of, and thus abuse, others. If an abuse exists, it is in the way profits are distributed, not in the generation of profit itself, because generating profit is inherent to the economy. The example of an enterprise in the manufacturing (secondary) sector will make it understandable.

The entrepreneur establishes a financial plan. He assesses the financing required to be able to buy everything that is needed. He calculates the sale price and formulates a progressive plan of his prospective sales over three years. From this sales plan, he forecasts that the enterprise will reach an equilibrium between its total operating expenditures and its total operating revenue, (i.e. the break-even point), sometime in its third year of operation. The entrepreneur will not base all these predictions on a 100% utilisation rate of the production machinery. If he were to calculate a break-even point solely based on a 100% utilisation of his operational potential, no

Financing Institute would grant him a loan. He will therefore take in account fluctuations in the economy, and will formulate his plan on reaching a break-even point based on perhaps a 60% utilisation rate of his productive capacity.

Prudence requires such an attitude. This means that as soon as the volume of production and corresponding sales exceed the break-even point, an operating surplus (profit) will be generated. The same goes for the artisan or an enterprise of the tertiary sector. Prices should be calculated by taking into account the economic variables. And the generation of profits by the enterprise will be a sign of normal functioning of the economy.

The question that now arises is: what are we going to do with the profits? To whom do they go? We cannot fully answer this question without having addressed the issue of share capital. So we will return to it later. This is not just about having or not having shareholders, but also about the problem of operating reserves that each enterprise is required to set aside out of its revenue.

We shall see that one can look at this problem from another angle, and thus prevent the money from accumulating. With regard to profits, there is also a part that goes towards self-financing. In this case, the money is used to purchase goods and services, so it remains in the Purchasing Money circuit.

Generally speaking, at this stage, we can say that the profits generated by an enterprise are Purchasing

Money, and should stay in this circuit as much as possible.

We will better understand this issue when we shall discuss the third type of money.

A small enterprise might be tempted, just like an individual, to save for a future investment. In this case, the money of the enterprise would follow the same circuit as the example of an individual given at (1.) above. But we must ask ourselves whether it is worthwhile to do so, since the Financing Institutes can provide these small enterprises with the Financing Money they need and without interest.

What we propose in separating Purchasing Money from Financing Money tends to discourage savings or at least limit them to a necessary minimum. In this way we will avoid the accumulation of Money and its consequential tendency to become treated as a commodity. But, even though this separation is a necessary condition, it is however not sufficient. Other measures will need to complement these proposals when, in Volume 2, we will address Financial Capital, Real Estate and Labour, that is to say the other three arms of the Economic Cross.

On the basis of these general principles of Financing Money, let us now look at the Financing Institutes.

20

Financing Institutes

From the moment we put into effect a turnaround solution that anchors the value of Financing Money in future production, and not on the accumulation of funds resulting from past actions, we will see a new form of monetary organisation emerge. Its organisation and operation will be much simpler than the incumbent central banking system. What we propose makes the present model and function of central banking redundant. Neither will we have a single monolithic body that is cumbersome and therefore expensive to operate.

Financing Institutes are institutions with a light organisational structure, but which are capable of exercising a *"profound"* task on behalf of society. Their responsibility is to enable innovation and evolution of the economy, and they devote themselves entirely to this service.

Financing Institutes are not part of the market economy, in that they do not offer a commercial service like a merchant, trader or an accounting firm. The service they provide is of a non-commercial nature. We can then deduce that their legal structure must clearly indicate that they are nonprofit. In a later chapter, we will see how Financing Institutes can be modeled as another form of public service[66].

The fact that Financing Money is created on the basis of demand for future activity within the *real economy*, means that a Financing Institute does not need reserve capital to back the money it creates. At its creation, this institute does not have to raise funds to build its capital as does a business in the actual economy. What the Financing Institute needs to function is relatively small compared to the amounts of Financing Money that it will have to create. Its needs are determined by the nature of its activity, in a manner similar to that of a public accounting service, such as a public accounting firm, or government tax office. It needs office space, of which it is not necessarily the owner, furniture, computers, etc. It must also pay current expenses, including the remuneration of the people who work there.

As the provider of a public service, Financing Institutes will partly cover their operational cost with public money. In a later chapter, we shall examine a new kind of tax mechanism[67], to source and channel public money that will fund part of the operational cost of Financing Institutes.

Public funding of Financing Institutes can be supplemented by revenue generated from the invoicing of services provided by each Financing Institute. Like existing banks or Post Office, as a public service, each

---

66   See chapter 23: Money as a public service
67   See chapter 22: A third form of money; Contribution Money

Financing Institute may request a contribution from its users that is proportional to the service it provides them with.

It should be clear that funding the operational cost of Financing Institutes will not involve the charging of interest, as interest is considered to be a significant factor of economic disruption. Service charges to users by the Financing Institutes must not penalize small initiatives that need to be financed, and therefore must be reasonable. Several approaches are possible regarding this issue. Within a governance regime based on Evolutive Democracy, it is the citizens who will decide about the optimum approach. Some countries might even opt for a total funding of the operating costs of Financing Institutes by the public sector.

Regarding start-up funding requirements of a Financing Institute, it would represent a significant moral hazard if a financing institution were to allocate to itself the money required to fund its own establishment, therefore this issue will be dealt with in the same way as any other firm. The project team for the establishment of a new Financing Institute, will have to go to another Financing Institute, to justify the need and viability of their project, as well as the measures they will take to conform with the regulatory framework established for these Institutes[68].

If a project for establishing a new Financing Institute gets the required start-up funding, it will open a Purchasing Account with a Bank of Purchasing Money. This account will allow the Financing Institute to settle

---

68   See the end of this chapter, and also all of chapter 23

its operating expenses, collect the payments for its services, and receive public funds. From this perspective, the Financing Institute is on the same level as any other business and non-profit organisation. The Financing Institute will also have to reimburse its start-up funding, that is to say the purchasing rights that were allocated to it at the moment of its establishment, in the form of a loan.

In this way, a watertight separation is made between the Purchasing Money for the operation of each Financing Institute, and the Financing Money that each Institute allocates to businesses and individuals. This is a necessary security measure. This measure should extend to the point where, if at the end of the accounting year, a Financing Institute has a positive balance of money on its Deferred Purchasing Account, these funds should only be transferable to another Financing Institute, and not to its own Current Purchasing Money Account.

Another provision will also highlight a clear reform relative to current prevailing banking practice. If we have well understood the nature of Financing Money, then it will be clear that an Institute that allocates and manages Financing Money can only do so within its own monetary zone, whether that zone is equivalent to the national border of the country in which it is domiciled, or whether the monetary zone comprises a union of countries.

In this sense, a Financing Institute cannot provide its services on an international basis. It will not establish foreign subsidiaries. Why should it? In today's economy, a bank uses funding from abroad when it does not have the required reserve funds to back the loans it makes to its clients. But this scenario does not arise in the case of Financing Money, as we propose it, since Financing Money is*"future-oriented"*, and thus does not depend on the existence of past accumulated reserves to *"back it"*.

It will therefore be stressed in the operational rules of Financing Institutes, that their scope of service provision is limited to the country or even the region where they are located. This will remove one of the main causes of financial disorder. As we shall see in a later chapter[69], the international flow of financial capital will lose its purpose, and this will be a key factor in stabilising the global economy.

Following this overview of Financing Institutes, let us now look at their detailed functioning, by taking a concrete example as we did with the Banks of Purchasing Money.

Financing Money only exists as ledger entries. In other words, it is double entry accounting. Let us examine the successive recording of accounting transactions related to the financing needs of the Lambda enterprise. Suppose that these financial needs amount to 500,000 over 5 years. Lambda goes to see the Financing Institute F, which will examine, with an Operations Insurance Institution, Lambda's situation[70].

Both organisations require clarification on some points and changes to others. They then agree that Institute F will process the credit application dossier of Lambda. Institute F could now credit the Purchasing Account

---

69 See chapter 26: Financing Money in the *Real Economy International Monetary System*

70 See more about an Operations Insurance Institution at the end of this chapter, at parag.27

of Lambda by the total amount of 500,000. However, a certain Mr Dujardin has already contacted Institute F, because he has 20,000 on his Deferred Purchasing Account at the bank A. He would like to make this amount available as a loan over 5 years. The case manager at the Institute F, will now present Mr Dujardin with the activity and funding requirements of the Lambda enterprise. Mr. Dujardin subsequently concludes that Lambda's activity is coherent with a healthy and sustainable economy. Mr. Dujardin agrees to loan his 20,000 in the Lambda enterprise. Therefore Institute F will only have to allocate 480,000 to the Account of the Lambda enterprise.

Table 9 illustrates the sequence of operations as they would appear on the accounts of Institute F.[71]

In step 1 of Table 9, we see recorded as Liabilities, the opening of the Lambda Financing Account, and of the Dujardin Loan Account. As in the case of Banks of Purchasing Money, the Institute has recorded under assets, an account of Ledger Money Movements. This account only records accounting operations. It is not a receptacle for storing money that Institute F could use. Remember, the money that the Institute uses for its own functioning is recorded separately in a Bank of Purchasing Money.

Also shown in Table IX, under the assets of Institute F, is another account named Monetary Issuance. The financing loan of 480,000 allocated by Institute F to the Lambda enterprise, will be recorded on the debit side on this account, at step (1.3).

---

71 Table 9 only shows the principle of recording accounting operations. In practice, it will probably prove necessary to use other elements of accounting technique. On this subject see Appendix : Accounting innovation for the separation of Financing and Purchasing Moneys.

Step 1 : The Lambda enterprise needs 500,000 for a period of 5 years. Financing Institute F lends them 480,000 and Dujardin loans them 20,000

	ASSETS				LIABILITIES			
	Ledger Money Movements		**Monetary Issuance**		**Lambda Financing Account**		**Dujardin Loan Account**	
	Dr	Cr	Dr	Cr	Dr	Cr	Dr	Cr
(1.1) Transfer from D.P.A. Dujardin (Bank A)	20'000							20'000
(1.2) Loan of Dujardin to Lambda						20'000	20'000	
(1.3) Credit allocation by Financing Institute F to Lambda			480'000			480'000		
(1.4) Transfer to C.P.A. Lambda (Bank B)		500'000			500'000			

Step 2 : First reimbursement by the Lambda enterprise to Dujardin and to Financing Institute F

	ASSETS				LIABILITIES			
	Ledger Money Movements		**Monetary Issuance**		**Lambda Financing Account**		**Dujardin Loan Account**	
	Dr	Cr	Dr	Cr	Dr	Cr	Dr	Cr
(2.1) Transfer from D.P.A. Lambda (Bank B)	100'000					100'000		
(2.2) Reimbursement by Lambda to Dujardin					4'000			4'000
(2.3) Reimbursement by Lambda to Institute F				96'000	96'000			
(2.4) Transfer to D.P.A. Dujardin (Bank A)		4'000					4'000	

Table 9 - Accounting operations of Financing Institute F

Table 9 also shows how the money of Dujardin arrives from Bank A to Institute F (step 1.1), where it is then transferred to the Lambda Financing Account at step (1.2). In step (1.3) we see the credit allocation by Institute F to Lambda, for an amount of 480,000. Finally, in step (1.4) the total funding of 500,000 required by Lambda is transferred to its Current Purchasing Account in the Purchasing bank (B). This marks the conclusion of step 1.

Note that if the Lambda enterprise did not need the full funding immediately, the funding would be made available by installment, as needed. That is to say whenever Lambda will have the occasion to use its purchasing rights, for the settlement of its purchases, for example to buy machinery and raw materials. The Financing Money, as such, exists only for an instant. As soon as it is created, it becomes Purchasing Money, which is the accounting counterpart that represents real activities in the *real economy.*

In step 2, we see the reverse movements. At step (2.1), Lambda transfers its annual repayment of 100,000 onto its Financing Account. The counterpart of this entry appears at the debit side in the Ledger Money Movement Account. In step (2.2), Lambda repays Dujardin 4,000. In step (2.3), Lambda repays Institute F 96,000. Note that, since there was a creation of credit, in terms of purchasing rights at step (1.3), there is now a resorption of these rights for an amount of 96,000.

The question remains about what Mr Dujardin will do with the 4,000 that were repaid to him. He could loan it again to another enterprise or even to an individual.

In step (2.4), we illustrate what happens if Mr Dujardin requests that his 4,000 be returned to him, by transfer from Institute F to his Deferred Purchasing (DP) Account, from where it can be transferred onto his Current Purchasing Account. At this last transfer to his Current Purchasing Account, he will incur a 10% demurrage deduction of 400, leaving a balance of 3,600 at his disposal on his DP Account[72].

In our hypothetical example, Mr Dujardin makes a loan to the Lambda enterprise. He therefore bears the risk that the enterprise may not be able to repay him. In exchange of this risk taking, Mr Dujardin gets a reduction on the total demurrage charge of 8,190 [ie: $20,000 * (1 - 0.9^5)$], which would have been applied to his 20,000 over five years, if he had kept it on his Deferred Purchasing (DP) Account. By lending his 20,000 over 5 years, with an annual reimbursement of 4,000 per year, Mr Dujardin incurs an annual demurrage charge of 400. Over five years this makes a total deduction of 2,000 [5 * 400], once his money is transferred onto his CP Account. Thus, Mr Dujardin's loan to Lambda allows him to keep 6,190 more by the end of the loan, compared to him keeping it on his DP Account. This operation therefore allows Mr Dujardin *"to gain"* 31% from his original support to Lambda.

Let us consider the case in which the Lambda project fails, and the enterprise goes out of business without being able to repay Institute F. What happens to the 480,000 purchasing rights on goods and services in

---

72 These last accounting operations will appear on the accounts of Bank A, and not on that of the Financing Institute F.

the economy? On the one hand some companies have received these purchasing rights as payment for goods and services they provided to the Lambda enterprise. But it had not yet obtained these purchasing rights by its own activity, and it will no longer be able to do so, since it goes bankrupt. Therefore, an imbalance of 480'000 is installed in the whole of the economy. How can this imbalance be absorbed?

If we make a consolidated balance sheet of all enterprises that are created every year, it is always positive. Some go bankrupt, but others succeed, and take flight on their own wings. Thus, in aggregate, they generate a large surplus.

As noted by Lucien Pfeiffer[73], we are now talking about something that concerns insurance. Catastrophic loss to individual enterprises, can be minimised by spreading the risk (mutualisation of risk) over many enterprises, in return for each one contributing to a pooled insurance fund. In Volume 2 of this book, we will see in a chapter about Financial Capital, how this technique can be applied to an Operations Insurance. This tool would ensure that any annual or monthly repayment that Lambda failed to discharge through the unexpected termination of its activity, would be reimbursed by the Operations insurance fund.

It would seem appropriate that Institute F should contribute to an insurance fund. This contribution would be charged to its operating budget. Thus, all Financing Institutes within a monetary zone, would mutualise

---

73 See (Pfeiffer, 2006). A description of Operations Insurance is also given by (Laloux, 2007), in the chapter: *Aux ressources de l'humain*.

their risk exposure. In the above example, this kind of insurance would discharge the outstanding 480,000 of Lambda. This money would therefore be taken from the purchasing rights that the Financing Institutes had *"set aside"* for the corresponding year, by the payment of their premiums. Note well, that the insurance institution had not put this money into circulation. It was only recorded in its accounts. In this way, through the payment to Institute F, by the insurance institution, the purchasing rights amounting to 480,000 will have been canceled. The whole system will again be in balance.

What is the interest to involve in such a way the Institute F, instead of simply leaving the insurance institution to pay Lambda its operating deficit, the latter then reimbursing its loan to Institute F, in accordance with the installments schedule? By this method, Institute F is more involved, and responsible, in evaluating and processing their credit allocation decisions. If the employees of the Institute make too many assessment mistakes, the insurance institution will have a lot of claims to pay. Initially, the insurance institution might respond by applying a penalty to institute F, which will adversely affect the operating cost of Institute F. If the problem persists, the insurance institution may refuse to continue insuring Institute F. Then Institute F might not find another insurance institution to work with. It will then have to stop its operations, because its license will be withdrawn.

Setting up such an insurance system, we will enable us to improve the quality of financing.

We now have an outline of how to operate the Financing Money and Purchasing Money components of our proposed monetary system. To complete our vision and understanding of money and its role in the functioning of the economy, we will now look at a third circulation[TG], Contribution Money. This will reveal, from a new positive angle, a serious but unsolved chronic problem of our society: unemployment. We will thereby make the link with another branch of the Economic Cross: the branch relating to human work (labour).

But first we are going to look at an example of monetary creation, with an 80 year successful track record, which in some ways is close to the method of financing that we advocate.

21

The experience of the WIR

With monetary institutions that operate without a central bank; with Financing Institutes allocating financing credit solely on the basis of the demand for real future production within the *real economy*, and not on the investment of past accumulations of interest-bearing money for speculative purposes; with Purchasing Money regarded only as a unit of account, which cannot be accumulated; and with the liquidity maintenance function of Monetary Demurrage; with all these proposals we have so far made, we can finally recognise money for what it is: accounting. In summary we have reached the unthinkable that we announced at the beginning of this book.

Some readers might now be tempted to close this book, concluding that it is just another utopia for idealist dreamers, which will be quickly forgotten, thanks to the wisdom of economic reality.

May any skeptical readers wait a little longer before coming to such a definitive conclusion. Because what we are advocating actually exists, partially, since 1934. This experience of 80 years, which brings together a network of 60,000 Swiss SMEs, has the capacity to face regular monetary system crises with a positive counter-cyclical effect on the life of the enterprises involved. This Swiss experience shows us that civil society has the potential to create and manage innovative monetary tools, required for the proper functioning of the *real economy*. So how did this experience originate, and how does it work?

In 1934, the great depression, resulting from the crash of 1929, weighed heavily on the European economy. The lack of confidence prevented normal bank financing. Enterprises therefore did not get the trade credit required to maintain the liquidity of their cash flow. Because of uncertainty in being paid, there was hesitation in concluding a sale. A domino effect spread this phenomenon to the whole supply network of production and trade, which consequently seized up.

Some fifteen Swiss artisans and small entrepreneurs then took the initiative of creating the WIR Economic Circle Cooperative, in German the *"Wirtschaftsring--Genossenschaft"*. The first three letters gave the name to this experience. But WIR also has a symbolic value, because it also means WE. This indicated a willingness by the founders to joint action, to put in place, by their own initiative, responses to the economic crisis.

These entrepreneurs decided to settle their trade relations with their own money, the WIR franc, which was denominated with the same value as the Swiss franc. They did not put banknotes into circulation. Each trade transaction was recorded by the administrators of the WIR Circle, as described in the sidebar, below.

WIR in practice[74]

In a transaction between two members of the WIR circle, enterprise A opts to pay part of its bill in WIR, for instance 1000 WIR out of a total of 5000 Swiss francs (it is the service provider, or enterprise B, that chooses the portion, which is never 100% of the entire bill). Enterprise A pays enterprise B 4000 Swiss francs and opens a credit line of 1000 WIR with the clearing house (with no interest rate if the credit is short-term). Enterprise B receives 4000 francs and 1000 WIR, which have thus been created out of nothing[75]. They exist as a debt that the buyer owes the clearing house. Next, enterprise B buys goods worth 10,000 francs from enterprise C, 2000 of which it opts to pay in WIR. It spends the 1000 WIR in its possession and opens a credit line of 1000 WIR, just as enterprise A did.

Thus, no one makes a decision about whether the loan should be granted or not. The clearing house simply determines the portion each member can pay in WIR and registers the transactions. Monetary creation is determined solely by the companies engaged in transactions. But it occurs in a single place : the clearing house that records the system's transactions. This is one way in which the WIR system differs from credit lines typically offered by banks: monetary creation is centralised, as with the credit lines available through central banks. In reality, Swiss small businesses use WIR credit alongside traditional bank credit lines, particularly in times when bank credit is tight.

Enterprise B accepts partial payment in WIR because it knows that it, in turn, can use WIR for purchases. Moreover, joining an exchange network typically results in a 5% increase in turnover (a consequence of "club" membership loyalty).

---

74 This sidebar is extracted from (Kalinowski, 2011).

75 In chapter 19, we have shown how the expression *"ex nihilo"* is inappropriate. WIR monetary credit is created from the confidence that the WIR Bank has in the future productive activity of enterprise A

In the same set of accounts, the debit of the purchasing enterprise, and the credit of the selling enterprise, were simultaneously recorded. The WIR money did not transit physically, but was expressed as a symmetric accounting record between the two enterprises, to evidence their respective credit rights and production obligations within WIR trade network.

Initially, the entrepreneurs had no WIR francs. In order to obtain some, they did not convert Swiss francs into this new money. What would have been the usefulness of doing so? If they already had Swiss francs, they would have settled their purchases by directly using the official currency.

To initiate the first operations, each enterprise opened a line of credit, denominated in WIR francs, with the WIR Economic Circle Cooperative. The maximum amount of WIR credit allocated as a standing negative balance allowance to each enterprise, was evaluated according to its production and sales potential, as well as its viability. WIR member enterprises then sold their goods or services to others, within the WIR trade network, with settlement being partly made in WIR francs. This WIR credit line enabled the WIR members to substitute for the non-existent overdraft facility on their business bank accounts.

In other words, the WIR francs were used to finance the cash flow of the WIR members. By their own initiative, in 1934, they thus overcame the problem of an insufficiency of bank credit.

Success of the WIR was immediate. In 1936, after only two years of activity, the WIR Economic Circle Cooperative had 3,500 SME's using the WIR money, which generated an annual volume of trade that was worth one million, and approximately five million, if one includes the share of trade transactions that were paid in Swiss Francs. This represented a pretty sum for that time.

In other European countries, similar experiences were successfully established. But the authorities quickly put an end to them. Switzerland has a different history and citizenship tradition. The authorities were of course wary regarding the WIR initiative. But they did not prohibit it; instead, they imposed the regulatory framework of a banking licence on the autonomous WIR initiative. Thus it became the WIR Bank, which continued to offer its services in two currencies: the Swiss franc and the WIR franc. However, the sovereign capacity of the former WIR cooperative to allocate credit to its member enterprises, became subject to Swiss banking regulations.

It is to be noted that the members of the WIR Economic Circle Cooperative did not feel the need for a banking license, because their system was balanced and under control of the general assembly of its cooperative members. Each member had a vested interest in the integrity and health of the WIR system.

They therefore created procedures of control and of systemic re-balancing, especially in the event of the bankruptcy of an enterprise that was indebted in WIR francs.

When the WIR Bank became responsible for granting a credit line in WIR francs, it also had to bear the risk of loss, resulting from a defaulting debtor. To recover its operating expenses, as well as to cover exceptional losses, the WIR Bank applies an interest rate of 1% on overdrafts, and charges a fee of 1% on each transaction in WIR francs (which is charged to the seller).

Transactions in WIR francs are recorded in real time by the WIR Bank. When an enterprise sells something in WIR francs, it is paid fully and immediately. This represents a double advantage: a better cash flow for each enterprise and no loss resulting from default, in the event of the bankruptcy of a debtor. The WIR Bank bears the charge for such default. In other words, defaults of payment are mutualised, through the Bank. Note that, in 2012, the total amount of default did not reach 0.05 per cent of the total WIR francs *"in circulation"*, which is very low compared to conventional banks.

The WIR Bank also had to make a provision in relation to the conversion of WIR francs into Swiss francs. Since 1973, this conversion was no longer possible, neither in one direction nor the other. To understand the reason for this decision, we must know that the WIR Bank is a co-operative of approximately 2,300 member enterprises. However, 60,000 SMEs use WIR francs, mostly on a regular basis. Therefore, 96% of non-member enterprises using WIR Francs are not much involved in the management of the WIR Bank by becoming a member of the cooperative.

Among these enterprises, a small number are occasional users. They resort to using WIR francs when economic growth is low or when interest rates in Swiss Francs are high. The punctual nature of engagement by these enterprises in the WIR network, means that when economic conditions or interest rates in Swiss Francs become more favorable, these enterprises find themselves left with a surplus of WIR francs, which they then want to convert into Swiss Francs. As a result, a black market in the trade of discounted WIR francs developed, which the management of the WIR cooperative decided to stamp out in 1973, by making the WIR franc nonconvertible. Since then attempts of fraud are rare. Those who are caught in this game by an internal commission of control, are excluded from the WIR system, and must pay a penalty of 50,000 Swiss Francs.

Over time, a new need emerged among the users of the WIR Trade B2B Network. Until the beginning of the 1990's, enterprises had to have an account for WIR francs at the WIR Bank, and another account for Swiss francs in a separate institution. This made the management of the WIR payment system cumbersome, because most settlement transactions were made by a simultaneous mix of the two moneys. On top, to finance the acquisition of machines or premises, enterprises had to prepare two separate application dossiers for two different banks. The enterprises therefore asked the WIR Bank to open accounts in Swiss Francs. They also wanted a single bank card, with which to make payments by a simultaneous mix of both WIR francs and Swiss francs.

Step by step, the WIR Bank has adapted to these functional realities, even proposing mixed credits, savings accounts and contingency funds. Then in 2000, the WIR Bank opened its services to businesses and individuals not using WIR francs, which today represents some 40,000 users. The WIR Bank therefore has a dual operation: both as a traditional bank and that of a Financing Institute of the WIR monetary zone.

In the framework of the proposals made in this book, the evolution of the WIR Bank teaches us several things:

1. *With regard to the WIR monetary zone, the WIR Bank functions in a similar way to that of a Financing Institute, such as we have described in the previous chapter. This initiative has gone through every economic crises of the past 80 years. During this time, it played a supportive role to the SME sector, avoiding many bankruptcies, and supporting their trade activity.*

   This Economic Trade Circle comprises 60,000 SMEs, with a total annual turnover of 1.5 billion WIR francs (1.2 billion Euros); it is able to regulate itself and to adapt to economic upheavals. All these facts show that free initiatives, born within civil society, are useful and should be encouraged.

   The WIR experience also shows that a Financing Institute can be managed by civil society.

2. *The WIR Economic Trade Circle created money, without resorting to a Central Bank. It is a real-life example that resort to a Central Bank is unnecessary, and that the Central Bank is irrelevant to the economy. The fact that a bank licence was imposed on the WIR Bank, so that it is subject to regulatory supervision by the Swiss central bank, does not contradict what has*

just been said. On the level of the issuance, transaction accounting and credit clearing management of the WIR franc, the WIR Economic Trade Circle continues to function, within the WIR Bank, in accordance with its founding principle, independently of the Central Bank.

3. *The evolution of the WIR Bank showed that having each one of the dual money accounts in separate institutions, posed management problems for the enterprise users. Because the enterprises traded in the two moneys, the WIR Bank had to progressively integrate, within itself, the official monetary system. The proven counter-cyclical effect of the WIR franc shows that this money exists solely because the official money does not fully play the monetary role that it should. The WIR franc was born for this reason, and its existence continues, because the official monetary system remains within the paradigm of commodity-money, and therefore cannot function as pure accounting-money, like the WIR franc.*

The WIR franc is considered as a complementary currency. But what is it complementary to? If something requires a complement, it means that it does not fully fulfill the function for which it was created. In the same way, we have complementary pension funds and complementary health insurance, whose financial resources, by the way, go through the circuits of speculation.

In the case of complementary currencies, we have the opposite situation: whilst the official currency is mainly circulating in the speculative sphere, the complementary currency is only devoted to the real economy.

Would it not be better to address the real causes of monetary dysfunction? Should we not be encouraged to do so, by the economic chaos in which we find ourselves today?

4. *Complementary currencies are blossoming a little everywhere, and a lot of people see them as a solution to the problems generated by the economic chaos. We will return to deal with this issue in chapter 29: "Let us not fight the wrong battle".*

For the time being, let us note that the WIR franc has two essential attributes: it is an accounting-money, which can be created on the basis of the future activity of an enterprise, that is to say, it corresponds to what we have called Financing Money.

Today, we see the emergence of some complementary currencies which have none of these attributes. They are often issued in the form of notes, without involving any credit based monetary creation.

If it seems that they do, it is in fact the national money which backs the issuance of the complementary currency. It is therefore not a monetary creation analogous to that of the WIR Bank. Yet these complementary currencies refer to the WIR, which they cite as an example to justify the need for parallel currencies. Is there not a confusion here?

22

A third form of money:
Contribution Money

We have explained the functioning of two moneys, one that is used for purchasing in the *real economy* and one that is for new financing. These moneys are not differentiated by the unit of account which denominates them. For example, the term Euro will still be used to count for one as for the other. What makes the specificity of each lies in its circulation. In fact, when we talk about these two moneys, we characterize two different circuits that communicate with each other.

It's the same with the third form of money. It is not a money with a different unit of account, but of another circulation[TG]. In other words, according to the circuit in which it is located, money takes on other qualities.

We could compare this fact with what happens in the human body, with regard to blood circulation. Anatomy specialists talk of the small and large circulation, the first being the one that goes from the lungs to the heart (and vice versa); the second being that which goes from the heart to the rest of the body, before returning again to the heart. These two circulations have specific functions. Yet in each case, we use the word *"blood"* to denote the liquid circulating therein.

Step by step, we will get a picture of Purchasing Money, which will include not one but two circulations, one large and one small.

And we will see that the small one is as necessary to the vitality and health of the economy as the pulmonary circulation is to the human body.

Let us dare to push the comparison a little further. We know that the small circulation is started up at birth, with the first breath of air outside of the womb. Until then, the embryo depended on a single circulation, which was linked to that of the mother.

If the second circulation was constituted insufficiently, or even defectively, what would be the result? Many dysfunctions would establish themselves in the body of the child. In particular, carbon dioxide would not be evacuated sufficiently, and oxygen, the source of regeneration, would be lacking. We can imagine the serious disorders and diseases that would result from this bodily condition.

Let us now take an overall view of society. Are we not dealing with the same constitutive insufficiency? We see, on one side, that money accumulates in certain places, as do the toxins in the body. On the other, we find insufficient regeneration of our economic models and operating modes. From everywhere come calls for new social forms, fit for a post-industrial society. But we are operating in a closed circuit, under the same stereotypes. We feel that our society is asphyxiating, but do we let go of our old patterns, in order to inspire the fresh air of new ideas?

One may be surprised that we mention this situation when addressing the third money. And it will be even more so if we say that this is a Contribution Money, which basically has the nature of a donation, relative to the current functioning of the economy. The term *"donation"* is rarely associated with actual financial practices, which often show the opposite nature, and instead are in a logic of *"always more"*.

Of course, the big financiers also make donations, which generally have a philanthropic character. However, the Contribution Money that we will describe, has nothing to do with an ethical connotation. It is not charity. We are in the economic domain, and it is from this perspective that the need for a second circulation, within Purchasing Money, must be shown.

In fact, this second circulation already exists in society, but truncated and largely inadequate. Much of it is done through taxes and duties, that in France are also referred to by the term *"contribution"*, but which term has fallen somewhat into disuse. Yet when the term contribution was used, it indicated that through our money, we contributed to the functioning of the whole of society. By paying taxes, I contribute to the construction of roads, railways, waterways, and public services, such as the police, the military, the education, etc.

By the fact that we have taxes, direct or indirect, we signify that we consider it normal and necessary, for part of the surplus generated by the economy to be taken out of the commercial circuit, in order to finance the noncommercial circuit. There is indeed a circulation that goes from the commercial to the noncommercial circuit. So we are not adding an element that is foreign to the actual economy. It is about giving to this circulation the full dimension it needs. To be able to do so, we need to clarify what the non-market economy is.

Let us use the diagram we already made to illustrate the three sectors of the economy[76].

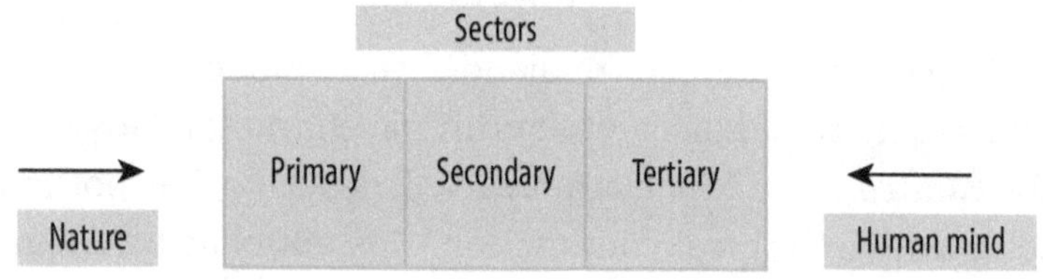

Diag. 9 - Polarity in the formation of values and the three economic sectors

We saw that in the tertiary sector, Nature tended to move to the background of an act of economic production. The services of a lawyer are based, marginally, on Nature. His raw material is the body of law, which is a human creation.

If we look more closely at the tertiary sector, we see a gradual transformation emerging. Let's consider some examples. The aim is not to look in detail at all activities that compose it. In the first place, it is about seeing where the noncommercial circuit of the economy manifests, and to understand how it can be divided into two quite distinct parts.

---

76 See Diagram 4: Dynamic between polarity in the formation of value, and the three economic sectors (ch.8).

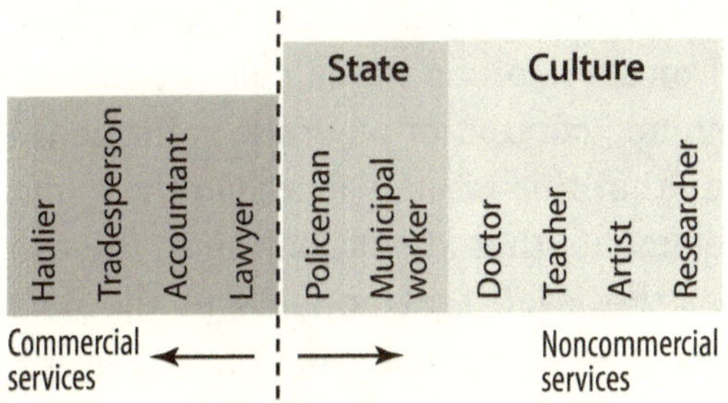

Diag. 10 - The tertiary sector comprising :
commercial and noncommercial services

At first glance, it may seem strange to talk in terms of economic services of a policeman or a teacher, for example. Yet the contribution of the one and the other is essential to the proper functioning of the economy Imagine the chaos that would result from the fact that there would be nobody to enforce the laws. The economic consequences would soon show themselves.

Similarly, a teacher provides the child with the elements that allow the child to develop himself. Without going into the nuances that would be necessary, we can say for example, that the ability of someone to exercise their creativity in their professional life, often originates in the pedagogy that was or was not experienced during their childhood. In this case, the consequence of the service provided by the teacher or the educator, is seen over a duration that can last a very long time.

In both cases, of the policeman and the teacher, we are facing a *"production"* which is not directly measurable. The economic value created cannot be directly translated into a price.

In the commercial circuit of the economy, the production of a good or service can be calculated according to the socio-economic context of where it is formed. We do not wish to say that this issue is easy. On the contrary, when the four elements that should not be in the economy are pulled out, the issue that appears at the center of the economy is that of price formation[77]. It is towards this issue that all the energy of the various actors should converge. We will not enter here into the details of this issue. We have dealt with it in my previous book (Laloux, 2007)[78], and we will look at it again in the forthcoming Volume 2 of this book.

For what concerns us here, we limit ourselves to noting that the service of the policeman as well as the one of the teacher, cannot be measured directly in terms of price. How could one estimate the price of the absence of chaos on the roads, for example? On some occasions during strikes or blockades affecting the road system, economists estimate the economic loss in terms of hundreds of millions. Should we align the salaries of policemen on these statistics? They probably would not be against such a measure, which would be to their advantage. But its economic unreality would cause problems elsewhere.

In the case of the policeman, we cannot quantify his absence, in other words to quantify something that cannot be present at the same time as its opposite. In the case of the teacher, we cannot measure the qualities that, perhaps, appear or not appear in the coming decades. We could take other examples of professions from this

---

77   See Diagram 1: The Economic Cross (ch.3).
78   See chapter: *La formation des prix*.

segment of the tertiary sector, and each time we would make the same observation. The service provided is a real value of the economy, but it cannot be sold directly, as would a consumer product, for example, or the transportation of goods by truck.

So we see emerging a boundary between two distinct circuits of the economy, the commercial and noncommercial. The example we have taken nonetheless reveals an essential difference. One of the professions falls within the sovereign functions of the State. About the police, we can say that we are in the field of law. That means that we are at the very heart of what the State is. Regarding education, this is in the field of culture, as is research and art.

We can therefore conclude that the noncommercial circuit of the economy is subdivided into two areas. The first has to do with all State services as the responsible party for all that is in line with the law. The second sub-area is the cultural domain, which obeys a different dynamic.

We will not go here into the details of what differentiates these two sub-circuits of the noncommercial economy. We have thoroughly done it in three other books, about education, showing the confusion that reigns in people's thinking.

By superimposing public services and the State, we lose opportunities, whose consequences we cannot properly measure yet. But if we agreed to put aside preconceived ideas or dogmas, we might realize that there are public services, which, in our scheme, appear to the right and left of the State[79], that is to say, in

---

79 See. Diagram 10, p. 217.

the commercial circuit of the economy and also in the "cultural" sub-circuit of the noncommercial economic circuit. If, for example, we address the question of the status of La Poste (French postal service) with this notion, we would find formulas that would avoid, on one hand, the status quo of a trading company linked to the State, while it has nothing to do with it; and on the other hand, privatization in the liberal way, which generates multiple problems. The next chapter will provide an opportunity to see how we could create, in the field of money, a public service that would be independant of the unitary State.

From the economic point of view, there is a big difference between the services provided in the field of culture and others. If we consider the products of the primary and secondary sectors, we see that they have a limited lifespan. They are consumed over a more or less long term period. To produce and then sell them takes some time.

And then, the lifetime of the product during its consumption, depends on the nature of the product. A salad is quickly consumed. A garment has a longer lifespan; furniture, still more. A house, if it is built according to the professional rules, and maintained, will have a lifetime that exceeds a century.

But in all cases, there will be a total consumption resulting in a complete disappearance or wearing out of the product. We can represent this with a diagram, showing the variable duration of use of an object, resulting either from a production in the commercial economic circuit, or from the noncommercial State sub-circuit.

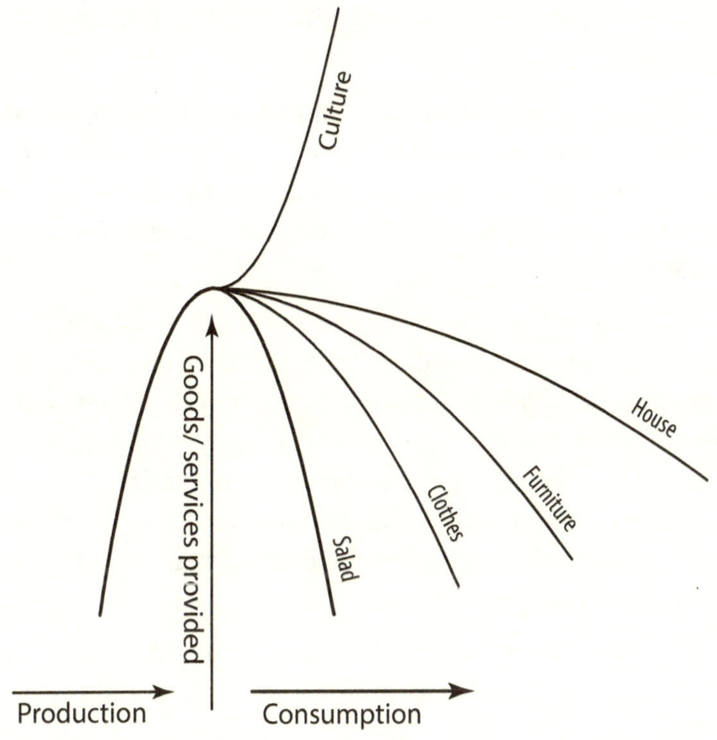

Diag. 11 - The special regenerative role of Cultural services

In the domain of Culture, this does not hold true, or else it is indicative that a service produced in the cultural domain has fallen into the commercial domain.

A teacher or artist can have an effect on a child or adult that is long-term, and which can even grow. Reading a book or a play can inspire ideas, feelings and creative impulses, which will make their way through people and, in the course of time, will manifest their qualities in the professional life.

Within a culture of this nature, we have economic values that continue to grow after their initial production. Their lifespan curves are contrary to those of the productions of the rest of the economy (see diagram 11 above).

Thanks to this concept, we can realise to what extent the economy needs values that continue to grow. They ensure that the economic process is not depleted. What comes from culture should continuously regenerate the rest of the economy. It is therefore essential that this area be considered for what it is, that is to say, something which is located outside of the commercial circuit of the economy, but which is vital to it.

By the way it is interesting to remember that the initiatives of the OECD and the WTO, particularly the MAI[80] and the GATS[81], have triggered strong protests against them in France and Europe. Slogans like "Culture is not a commodity" show an awareness of what is at stake. Those who mobilized were feeling that it touched a vital element of society.

Yet this vital element of culture must have the means of existence. If it does not sell directly its services, it must receive, by other means, that which will allow it to continue. In other words, the entire commercial circuit of the economy is in need of the noncommercial circuit, and therefore must provide it with what it needs to develop in good conditions. For the economy to be healthy and

---

80 See Endnotes: en.1 - The Multilateral Agreement on Investment (MAI)
81 See Endnotes: en.2 - The General Agreement on Trade in Services (GATS)

balanced, the commercial circuit must contribute to the noncommercial circuit.

Since the commercial circuit of the economy inherently produces surpluses of purchasing rights[82], these should be directed to those in need. It is proposed that the surpluses of Purchasing Money, which, in the actual economy, are treated like commodities and penetrate into the economy as speculation, that these Purchasing Money surpluses will therefore move in another direction. Certainly, as we have said, part already does so through taxes and duties. But it is obvious that this is far from sufficient. On the other hand, how this is done, by taxation, is not satisfactory. Let us examine these two questions.

1. *If we characterize the liberal conception, in broad strokes, we will say that only what produces profit is considered to be in the domain of the economy. The rest is regarded as a burden or a hindrance to the development of the economy.*

   Therefore, two attitudes are considered. The first one is to minimize these budgets that the State allocates to the noncommercial economic circuit: cuts in spending on education, health, social protection, etc. This method is applied wherever the neo-liberals can either come to power or influence heads of State. In countries that are disadvantaged or in difficulty, it is these shock treatments that will be applied to maintain the profitability of financial capital. The

---

82 The question of an inherent surplus of purchasing rights, produced by the commercial circuit of the economy, will be dealt with in Volume 2, in relation to share capital.

social services of the State are then reduced to their simplest expression, at the expense of the people. The phenomenon is well known.

The second approach is to privatise whatever can be privatised within the noncommercial economic circuit; that is to say, to bring it into the commercial circuit, which is contrary to its innate purpose.

In each of these situations, we are witnessing a decline in the quality of services and an increase in unemployment, due to a reduction in the number of jobs available. Only those who have comfortable incomes can afford, in institutions that have staff in sufficient quantity, quality services. But these services are subject to pricing policies that are proportional to the maximum ability of clients to pay, irrespective of income inequalities.

This liberal approach to the noncommercial economic circuit contributes to economic maladies. In order to manage the economy in a healthy way, civil society should do the opposite, by directing more money into noncommercial goods and services, especially in the field of culture, health, education (specialized or non-specialized). The money would come from the surplus generated by the commercial economic circuit. It would allow the institutions in the noncommercial circuit to engage co-workers under decent conditions, not like all the kinds of State subsidised employment contracts representing unstable solutions, which do not offer a satisfactory situation, neither to the employing organization, nor to the employee. Much of the unemployment could thereby be reduced[83].

---

83   The other part of the unemployment would be reduced by the fact that agriculture would employ more people. Indeed, policies that respect the

Thus we see that the unemployment problem is an ill-posed problem. It is not jobs to be done that are lacking. There is enough work for everyone. The issue is not located at the level of labour, but at the level of remuneration. To solve it, it is necessary to establish a third circulation of money, which comes from the contribution.

2. *We use the word contribution instead of taxation. By this we mean an action that was chosen and desired by the taxpayers (called "contribuables" in French). A true democracy would allow the citizen to choose where he wants his contribution to go. For example, everyone should be able to choose the field of research they wish to finance. As soon as they know the percentage of their contribution that is to be allocated to research, they can calculate the amount they have to allocate to this domain, relative to their income. Next they should be able to choose the research institute, which will receive the percentage allocated from their total amount of contribution.*

If, for example, someone is in favour of GMO research (assuming that it is permitted by law), they could choose an institute conducting research in this area. But if they do not want their money to be used for this "cause", they could instead direct it to an agricultural research institute that prioritises the existential health of nature and of the human being. In this way, everyone will be able to "vote" for the

---

environment as well as the living conditions of the farmers, need more people working in this area. Currently, there are too few active people in agriculture.

kind of research they wish to fund, according to their individual conscience.

The general principle has therefore been revealed. In passing from anonymous non-democratic taxation, to the contribution decided by himself, the citizen would become more aware of the path travelled by the Contribution Money. He would become a full participant in determining the circulation of that money.

We have identified three types of money. So that they are inserted in a healthy way in society, we still need to consider the aspect of the public services that they should provide to society.

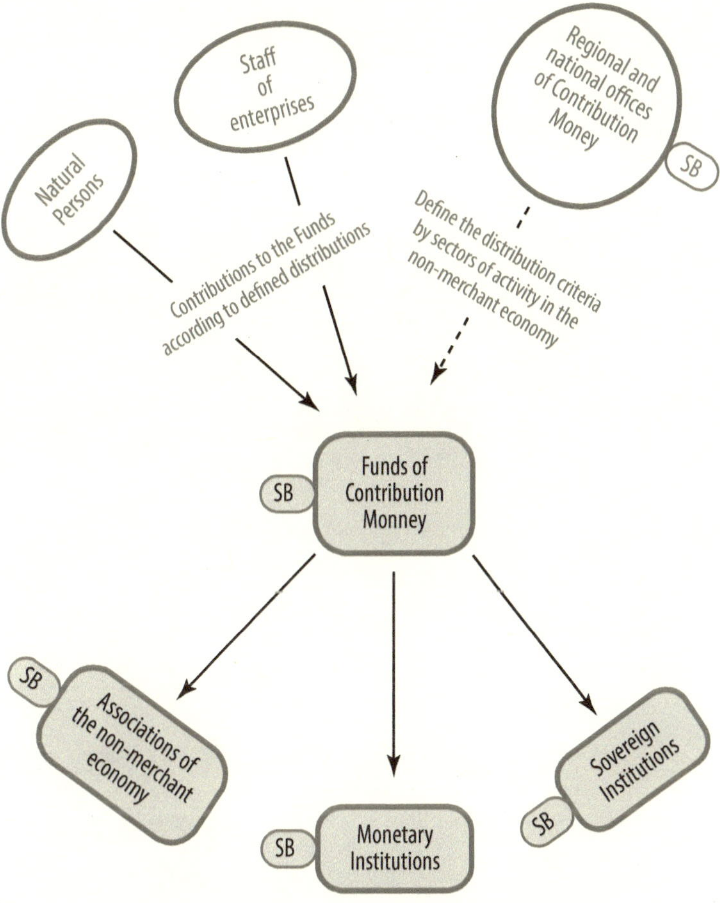

Circulation of Contribution Money

- SB = Supervisory Board, composed of representatives of CSOs and of user or employee associations

- The Monetary Institutions (MI) are : the Banks of Purchasing Money, the Financing Institutes and the Funds of Contribution Money.

- This diagram is to be compared with that of Civil Society Public Services in relation to Monetary Institutions (see diag. 13 at the end of next chapter).

- NB : In the central square of the diagram, it is indeed a plural. The Contribution Money Funds are a multiplicity of organisations created as needed, at the initiative of civil society.

Diag. 12 - The circulation of Contribution Money to public services

23

Money as a public service

The amount of national debt of States has become an open crisis in Ireland, Portugal and Greece. This problem spread to other eurozone countries, and in turn could call into question the existence of the eurozone itself, despite the *"unconventional measures"* (Smaghi, 2009), taken by the European Central Bank (ECB).

Faced with this situation, many wonder what to do about it. Of course, there are the measures taken by official authorities which are short-term answers aiming to plug the gaps. Few observers believe in their effectiveness. In any case, they do not question the fundamentals of the system, and do not act on the underlying causes. Therefore new troubles are expected.

With the series of crises, reality is now showing the limits of one-track thinking, provided we are willing to assess those limits. Several recent developments should give us pause for thought, and the most shrewd economists definitely pointed them out.

Let us look, for example, at the measures taken on 2 May 2010, by countries of the eurozone, to lift Greece out of its sovereign debt crisis. What sense should we give to the words *"to lift"*[84], when we see that the interest rate on the €110 billion loan made available to Greece by those States, amounted to 5.5%, (before moving to 3.5% in the July 2011 plan)?

Why not lighten the already considerable debt service burden of Greece, by lending at a 0% interest rate? This would have had a double effect. In addition to a direct and very practical assistance to this country, it would have send a strong signal to financiers, who always tend to raise interest rates, as soon as a State shows signs of weakness in its ability to repay, thereby aggravating the situation.

The message would be: *"We, the countries of the eurozone, take back a power that we had given up to you, the power of money creation. We will create the money needed to get us out of this crisis. We will do this without you, as you are the ones who are driving us to ruin."*

To be able to speak in this way, several conditions must be met. Let's look at a few:

1. To be willing to break free from the influence of financial powers, which requires courage. But is this not a prerequisite to everything else?

---

84   Translator's note : The French verb *"voler"* means both *"to fly"* and *"to steal"*. When used in the expression *"voler au secours"*, it means *"to rush to save"* someone or something. In the original French, the author played on the word *"voler"*, to bring out the sense that eurozone countries *"rushed to steal"* from Greece, instead of rushing to save it. The English translation attempts to transliterate this word game, by making a connotation regarding the slang use of *"to lift"* as meaning *"to steal"* (e.g. as in *"shoplifting"*).

2. To assert a willingness to question conventional wisdom, those concepts which constitute the actual economic doctrine, and obviously work less and less.

3. To develop an ability to think in a multiple and differentiated way, particularly in the field of money, where three monetary dynamics are constantly manifested, instead of conflating them into only one.

   With Purchasing Money being inherently stable, the Euro would not be subjected to speculative attacks. Thus consumer purchasing power would not fluctuate from day to day.

   The kind of Financing Money described in this book, would make redundant any need to resort to investors, whose actions prove to be destructive.

   Finally, funding the noncommercial economic circuit with Contribution Money, would make austerity policies unnecessary, which policies in any case only exacerbate the actual problem, and force the most disadvantaged sections of the population pay the price of austerity.

4. To call into question one of the fundamentals of the ECB, as set out in Article 104 of the Maastricht Treaty, at paragraph 1:

   "Overdraft facilities or any other type of credit facility with the ECB or with the central banks of the Member States (hereinafter referred to as "national central banks") in favour of Community institutions or bodies, central governments, regional, local or other public authorities, other bodies governed by public law, or public undertakings of Member States shall be prohibited, as shall the purchase directly from

them by the ECB or national central banks of debt instruments."[85]

Faced with the situation in Greece, and the risk of eurozone implosion, the ECB made an infringement to these provisions by buying Greek treasury bonds. But the principle remains, which prohibits the ECB (and the national central banks that depend on it), to create money this way. The ECB cannot therefore issue Euros for public treasury of member States.

When they want to borrow money, member States of the European Union are therefore forced to turn to private financial markets, which require levels of interest rate charge that aggravate public deficits. It is also not uncommon for a member State to have to borrow more money in order to pay what is called debt service. The ECB and the States are deprived of the possibility of creating interest-free money that they need. Instead, States are forced to borrow from commercial banks.

This last point raises the question of money as a public service. Many economists seeking alternative ways to address this question, point out that political parties, on the whole, are silent on this subject. Indeed, the extent to which it is absent from public debate is surprising, except in eloquent calls for an exit from Euroland and the return to a national money. Such calls mean returning to a previous situation, with the same conception of money, forgetting that the previous system did not work either.

---

85 The Treaty of Lisbon (2007), which amends the earlier Treaty of Maastricht on European Union (1993), repeats at Article 123, almost word for word, Article 104 of the Treaty of Maastricht.

Moreover, as several authors pointed out[86] the surrender of monetary creation, by the State, to commercial banks, is prior to Maastricht and the ECB. In France, this mutation was instituted by Valéry Giscard d'Estaing, under the presidency of Georges Pompidou, by the law of January 3, 1973.

Of course, there were reasons for this change. Its aim was to make the Banque de France independent of political power and prevent it from resorting, in a too convenient way, to facilitating budget deficits. Those practices had the effect of operating the printing press. Note that in the current debt crisis of States, this palliative is back in fashion, under the euphemism of quantitative easing (QE), practiced by the Federal Reserve Bank in the US and the ECB. This euphemism gives a serious academic appearance to what has always been considered to be an economic heresy!

According to monetary orthodoxy, any central bank must be independent of the State. Thus there cannot be a public service of money. This concept justified the full privatisation of money, and the total transfer of the money creation power to private banks. One consequence of this orientation is the problem of unsustainable debt, firstly of Third World countries, and now in western countries.

Critical observers of this approach think that countries would not be indebted if they had no interest to pay. Holbecq and Derudder have calculated that the accumulated debt of France in 2006, was equal to the total interest paid on State borrowings between 1979

---

86 (see Duboin, 2007; Holbecq and Derudder, 2008, p. 23)

and 2006. They conclude that if the Banque de France could lend money to the Public Treasury, at zero interest, France would not have had any debt in 2006. In other words, the debt seems to be solely due to debt service, and it looks as if France had borrowed money just for paying interest on its loans !!!

Let us make a digression to look at the reality of these figures. Holbecq and Derudder made their calculations in constant 2006 Euros. Thus the 1979 debt is multiplied by 2.76, that of 1980 by 2.43, and so on. Because their calculation was not done in current Euros, the amount of interest supposedly paid is therefore considerably increased, compared to what was actually paid off. Based on a calculation in current euros, the cumulative interest paid by France amounted to 888.50 billion euros, on a debt of 1,142.20 billion euros. In a zero-interest rate scenario, the 888.50 billion euros would been used to pay off the debt (instead of interest). Therefore the total debt in 2006 would have only been 253.70 billion euros, which is a quarter of what it actually was at the time.[87]

Admittedly, the calculation in constant Euros makes what we want to demonstrate more spectacular. But it does not reflect what actually happened over the years between 1979 and 2006. Reducing the amount of interest in 1979 to what it would have been in 2006 is a purely theoretical extrapolation, which introduces an error. Because the economic conditions at the beginning of the considered period are absolutely not comparable to those of the end.

---

87 See the comparison of two methods of calculation: http://www.democratieevo-lutive.fr/fr/interets-dette-france.html.

For the purpose of their demonstration, Holbecq and Derruder did not need to push up the numbers, which are sufficiently telling in current Euros. To pay nearly 890 billion euros in interest over 30 years is in itself an exorbitant amount.

Extrapolating the correct calculation for the years 2007-2013, we would arrive at a cumulative amount of interest paid by France of 1,200 billion Euros since 1979. The total amount of sovereign debt is 1,950 billion in 2013. Under a zero interest rate, the debt of France would only be 750 billion Euros, about 37% of GDP, instead of the actual figure of 96% of GDP in 2013.

In reality, this figure would certainly have be much lower. For the interest payment of 1,200 billion Euros spread over 34 years, could have represented a productive investment potential by the State, which would have increased State revenue through taxation, thereby enabling the State to reduce its debt still further.

Let us terminate this digression on the method of calculation, and return to the question of money creation power that the State surrendered to private finance.

We are faced with two opposing views. One says that the State cannot have the power to create money, because it would misuse it. The other view contends that we have thus offered an unjustified privilege to banks and investors, and that money creation should return to being a responsibility of the State, thereby making it a public service.

As always with this kind of issue, we have in both cases, a serious problem. We can debate endlessly on how to resolve it, without ever succeeding. Because this problem has no solution, as long as we do not transform our concept of the State and, more specifically, our notion of public service.

Within our minds, we have a picture of the State as having a decision-making center, and a superstructure to manage each area that it is responsible for. In my previous books, I showed that in the case of education, the State's superstructure was not only inefficient, but also harmful to the very cause it claims to serve. And that we could dispense with it, without needing to resort to the private sphere. Instead, we can transcend this non-choice conundrum, of having to jump out of the frying pan into the fire, as soon as we entrust civil society with the responsibility for providing the public service of education. We can also do the same for money.

Let us first consider the notion of public service. Just as there are interconnected networks for the provision of telephone and electricity services, money also needs an infrastructure, to permit its circulation. It is in the public interest that the monetary infrastructure operates under the best conditions, and is accessible to all citizens, regardless of their standard of living.

Just as everyone is entitled to a grid connection or a delivery of mail, even if they live in an isolated place, everyone should be able to make their money circulate wherever it is necessary, and within the legal framework.

We are therefore in the presence of a need for a public service of monetary circulation[TG]. As we highlighted before, this requires a triple circulation.

Banks of Purchasing Money deal with the first circulation; Financing Institutes with the second one, and Contribution Money Funds with the third one. But public service principles apply to all three monetary institutions. They should therefore be subject to the following conditions:

1. Monetary institutions belong to the noncommercial circuit of the economy and are non-profit.

2. Monetary institutions cannot use the services they provide for their own purpose.

   Thus a Bank of Purchasing Money shall not hold its own Purchasing Account within its institution. To settle its own operating expenses, it must hold a Purchasing Account in another bank.

   The Financing Institute cannot grant a loan to itself. If it needs to fund, for example, an office facility, it will make an application to another Financing Institute, which will examine its application for funds with the same criteria that would apply to any enterprise.

   A Contribution Money Fund cannot attribute to itself any of the money it collects. To pay for its operation, it must apply to another Contribution Money Fund, and justify its needs like any other non-profit organisation of the noncommercial economic circuit.

3. A monetary institution can only be active in a single monetary domain.

   Thus a Bank of Purchasing Money cannot undertake any function of a Financing Institute, nor of a Contribution Money Fund, and vice versa.

4. A monetary institution cannot hold shares in another monetary institution, regardless of the domain in which the latter is operating.

5. Monetary institutions are financed predominantly by public funds, that is to say, by Contribution Money.

6. Access to the basic services of monetary institutions is free to all users. Only fees for additional specific services are charged (eg, intervention fees, direct debit fees and insurance premiums for loss or theft of means of payment, and so on.)

   Financing Institutes do not charge interest on loans they grant. They charge a fee for opening an application dossier, at a total rate not exceeding 2% of the loan requested; as well as a fee at the time of credit allocation, at a total rate not exceeding 3% of the loan[88].They also charge an intervention fee in the event of a delay in repayments.

   The Contribution Money Fund charges an intervention fee when, for example, an association does not provide its accounting records on time.

7. The operating budget of a monetary institution is capped in proportion to its volume of service. Any surpluses are returned to a public collection agency. A National Council of Monetary User Organisations will evaluate, region by region, the ratios that determine the capped budget of the monetary institutions.

---

88 The total rate of 5% charged as a fee for the successful allocation of a loan is to be compared with what we discussed at Chapter 15, *"The interest-free loan"*, where the cost of interest as a percentage of the loan, ranged from 45% to 216% of the principle, depending on the interest rate and duration of the loan.

8. The operational management of each monetary institution is subject to the authority of a supervisory
board, acting as a constituent organ of the monetary
institution. The supervisory board is composed, on
the one hand, of representatives of the founders of
the monetary institution; and, on the other hand,
of members of Civil Society Organisations (CSOs),
representing users; as well as members of CSOs that
are active in societal and environmental issues.

   The Supervisory Board appoints and dismisses the
   executive officers of the monetary institution.

9. In each monetary region and for each type of
monetary institution, a Monetary Coordination Board
is established, composed of delegates from each type
of monetary institution, as well as the corresponding
representatives of user organisations, together with
representatives of societal and environmental CSOs.

   The purpose of this Coordination Board is to:

   ▷ Identify the needs of the territorial region, and to
      investigate what type of institution will best meet
      them. The Board is responsible for ensuring that all
      needs are covered.

   ▷ Convene a commission to examine and adjudicate
      disputes and user complaints.

   ▷ Grant or renew the license for each monetary
      institution.

10. Each monetary institution is subject to inspection by
a Monetary Auditing Institute that is independent and
public. It will audit the accounts and functioning of the

monetary institution, to check that they comply with the rules of public service, and with the operational specifications of that monetary institution.

The Auditing Institute prepares an annual audit, as well as interim monthly reports, for the attention of the monetary institution, and also for the Monetary Coordination Board, of which it is a member. The reports may contain warnings and recommendations regarding any identified dysfunctions. The reports also give deadlines for redressing any dysfunction.

In case of non-compliance with these conditions, or serious failure on the part of the monetary institution, the Monetary Coordination Board may revoke its operating license.

11. People who wish to create a monetary institution, must submit their project to the Monetary Coordination Board of the monetary region in which they propose to establish it. If their project addresses an unmet need, or represents a new way of providing a service, which is already provided by an existing monetary institution, the Board will grant them a provisional operating license, for a period that enables the project to prove its usefulness.

12. During the startup phase of a new monetary institution, the Board will also give an exemption that allows the institution to benefit from public money beyond the normal operating budget capping ratios[89].

---

89   Note that the Board does not allocate funds for a start-up initiative. Since the Council is not itself a monetary institution, it is unable to provide any funding. To find the necessary funding for their project, the project owners will apply to a Financing Institute, in accordance with the procedures and conditions described above.

13. Each monetary institution implements a quality management system approved by the Monetary Auditing Institute.

14. All of the foregoing provisions are an integral part of the operational specifications of each monetary institution.

The above provisions lay the foundation for a threefold public service of money, administered by civil society. It is threefold, so as to permit a triple monetary circulation. It is public because it is accessible to all citizens, and at the service of the whole of society. It is administered by civil society, because it is regulated by non-governmental organisations, which ensure that the monetary institutions comply with their public service criteria. Through CSOs, especially those representing monetary system users, citizens have the opportunity to directly control the operation of these institutions, and to propose improvements.

To go through the traditional governmental super-structures is unnecessary, and does not bring anything that CSOs could not do in a more direct way.

It will surely be said that this represents a dismantling of the State, in a manner similar to what supporters of liberalism and privatisation are hoping for. We need to properly consider this point.

What is proposed is not about privatisation. In fact, in the current system, money creation is already privatised. Rather, what is proposed represents a return of the money creation power to the public sphere, from where it should never have left.

In this new organisational framework, the State has not disappeared. On the contrary, it is certainly very present, but not in its usual form. It has taken another form, which is civic and not political. Instead of a superstructure managed by a process of political gaming, we have a civic organisation that is directly engaged in the domain of money and finance as a public service.

But then, where is the State? Whereas the State is usually seen as an executive institution in itself, it now only exists in the rules that govern the functioning of monetary system, and the means to ensure that these rules are respected.

Thus, the State returns to its true role, which it abandons each time it wants to be a player, rather than the referee.

In team sports, these two roles are well differentiated. It is a necessity. When we speak of the State, we create confusion if we give it a double and even a triple role.

For example, we talk about the three branches of the State being: the legislative, the executive and the judiciary. This is a confusion, which is at the source of many disorders facing the world today.

The State cannot have an executive role, unless it has to enforce the rules, that is to say the laws. On a sports field, a referee plays no active role, as long as the game is played according to the rules. When one of the rules is not respected, he intervenes to give a caution, or penalty or to exclude a player. He represents law enforcement on the sports field. If a player goes further than a simple mistake and, for example, violently attacks another player, then his act is considered as an offence that may be taken to court. The referee will simply send off the player. However, a special committee established by the sports federation concerned, will judge the case, or refer it to a civil or criminal court.

In sport, these three roles are not mixed up. The same should apply to societal life. In previous books, I argued this case with regard to the provision of education as a civic public service. And now we can see the same requirement with regard to money.

People who would work on a daily basis in the above described monetary institutions, would be what we might call the *"players"*. The CSOs and associations that sit in the supervisory boards of these institutions, would be the *"referees"*. They are also present in the Monetary Coordination Boards. The arbitration commission within each Monetary Coordination Board corresponds to the *"disciplinary committee"* of a sports federation. In other words, arbitration commissions are a form of domestic court, which make the necessary corrections in the case of light malfunctions. But in the case of an offence, this would have to be referred to the commercial court or criminal court.

The rules of functioning for public monetary institutions, which meet the above described fourteen principles, should be adopted legislatively, in accordance with the terms of the constitution of the country.

If the country has a direct democracy constitution, as it is the case of Switzerland, citizens can propose an enabling law for establishing this new form of monetary organisation. In most other countries, this would have to go through the Parliamentary Chambers, which could delay such reforms for a very long time.

That is why the foremost of all reforms to enable a genuine state and process of democracy is a reform that would emancipate citizens with the dual power of referendum and popular initiative. We will return to this subject at the end of the book.

We have now taken one more step into the realm of the unthinkable. We have described a form of monetary organisation which is a public service of a new type, a public service of civil society, which can then embody the three powers of societal governance - executive, legislative and judiciary - in a form that is more direct and grounded in societal reality and its daily changes.

We started from the innate requirements of money; we concluded that this required three circulations, administered by three types of differentiated institutions, and regulated by specific rules of public service; we showed how the State could be involved, in a civic form that is neither heavily bureaucratic nor governmental, but through the committed engagement of civil society organisations; and the end result of this design process, is a new public monetary structure, which is capable, through its flexible and evolutive nature, of meeting the changing needs of society.

The public service structure that is thus taking shape[90], is inscribed within a new form of democracy, which I call Evolutive Democracy.

But there is still a question we must consider. We started this chapter by referring to those who also advocate for a return to the monetary system being a public service, but envisage it within a centralised and unitary State structure. Their objective is to prevent a worsening of the public deficit, and to enable State spending for social needs, rather than for the profit of financial lenders in the form of interest. In the background of their proposed reforms, is the issue of the State budget and the Public Treasury.

We will now examine how we can take into account both these concerns, within our proposal for money as a public service that is regulated by civil society.

---

90 See Diagram 13 on next page.

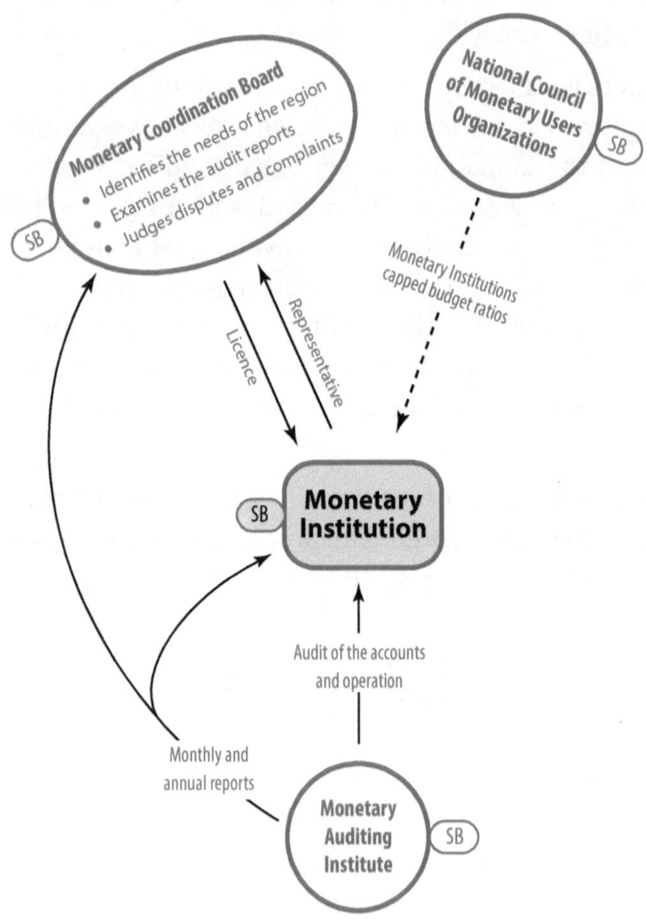

- SB = Supervisory Board, composed of representatives of NGOs, of user associations and employee associations
- Monetary Institution (MI) is a Bank of Purchasing Money or a Financing Institute or a Contribution Money Fund

Diag. 13 - A Civil Society Public Service for Monetary Institutions

24

The State Budget and Public Treasury

At the time of writing (in 2013), the accumulated debt arising from budget deficits of eurozone member States reached on average 91 % of eurozone GDP. Greece was at 160 %, the USA at 103 % and Japan at 245 %. These accumulated debts are growing, despite the rules of good governance that the heads of State would like to impose on themselves.

States devote huge amounts to the payment of interest on their national debt. For example, in 2013, the French State disbursed 47 billion Euros, or 89 % of its revenue from corporate taxation. This debt service represents 2.23 % of France's GDP. In other words, the debt service of France ate up 75% of the 3% deficit margin allowed by the Stability and Growth Pact of the European Union.

Greece still risks being declared insolvent. Other countries in the eurozone may well follow. The American State, itself, has been very close to the suspension of payment for its expenditure. Not for the first nor last time, following a strong fight between Republicans and Democrats in 2013, the American State was able to avoid this humiliation ... by raising its authorised debt ceiling! In other words, the solution is postponed to a later date.

To maintain eurozone stability, the European Union treaties impose strict rules ... that almost nobody is able to enforce. The annual budget deficits are not within the limit of 3 % of GDP, and the accumulated debt of most of the member States has largely punctured the ceiling of 60 % of GDP.

To give himself a virtuous image, a French president wanted the imperative of a balanced budget to be incorporated into the French constitution, as well as within the European Treaty, even though his own government already could not comply with the existing Maastricht rules.

At the same time, other voices argued that these criteria are too strict, and that they should be loosened, so as to revive the economy, and thus reap the tax revenue that would result and, thereby, pay off the national debt. It is easy to point out that these criteria have already been largely splintered, with governments taking on budget deficits that reach 7, 8, or even 10 % of their annual GDP. Their economies have not yet revived, and their accumulated debts are steadily growing, but without the economic growth they desperately hoped for.

Other astute thinkers advocate for an increase in taxation, in particular for the most wealthy people. This idea sounds nice and socially attractive. But these thinkers seem to overlook the fact that the very people that they want to get more tax from, are also the creditors of the States, as well as the investors in the enterprises.

Increasing their taxes carries the risk of making them withdraw their financial capital, to invest it in another country. The economy that one thought of reviving, through increased taxation on the most wealthy, would instead become stagnant through lack of capital funds.

We can turn this question in every direction, and we will still not find a solution, as long as we remain within the same logic. We are facing a systemic problem, which we should address as such. It is no longer sufficient to change this or that detail of the economic mechanism, nor to operate this or that lever. It is about designing new foundations for the system. The impasse in which we are, and which brings even the most powerful State in the world to the edge of suspending payment of its expenses, should encourage us to change paradigm, particularly in the domains of democracy and financial capital. In the framework of this first volume, we will confine ourselves to mentioning the broad outlines of what could be transformed within these domains.

Let us firstly consider the domain of democracy.

To begin with, let us examine public services. In the usual notion of a unitary State, public services are bound to the State apparatus. We have shown how Civil Society could establish money as a public service. Similarly, I also conceived, in the detail, education as a Civil Society public service (Laloux, 2007). This approach could be adapted for the provision of all non-sovereign public services. The result would be public service structures that are lightweight and evolutive, and whose operating costs would be much lower than those furnished through the apparatus of a centralised State.

With regard to sovereign public services, such as the police and the military, we need to reason differently. In these domains, the overall cost burden is not so much linked to the organisation, but results from other factors.

In the case of military expenditure, this should be a choice of society. If we are in a democracy, it is up to the people to decide. The best way would be to ask the people to decide directly, by voting the defense budget. In the case of France, it would be interesting to hear what the people would say about certain foreign interventions by French troops, and what financial means they are ready to devote to such interventions.

The police budget should be looked at differently. It would also be good that it be submitted to a popular vote. Citizens can thus become more conscious about the issues involved, including the consideration that the cost of policing reflects the actual state of society. Therefore investment in other areas, to eliminate the conditions conducive to social disorder, might be voted.

The costs of policing (and to a certain extent, those of health-care and environmental protection) are indicators of the overall state of society. By having to vote directly on this kind of budget, citizens might better question the causes of any budgetary cost increases, and thereby determine the most productive areas on which to focus their fiscal contributions.

I do not claim that this issue is simple, nor that it can be resolved in a few sentences. I just want to draw the attention to the need for a differentiated reflection for each budget heading of a State. By considering the very nature of each public service, we should be able to determine the validity of its budget, relative to the conditions that tend to decrease or increase its overall cost.

Now let us look at the second aspect of the State budget. We have said that it was linked to financial capital. We will get a more precise understanding of financial capital in volume 2 of this book. For now, let us just understand the link between financial capital and the budget deficit.

The fact that the budget deficit is chronic, must encourage us to ask the question: is this an indication that the needs are greater than the possibilities of tax revenue, and therefore a decrease in State expenditure will not be sufficient by itself?

In other words, countries are not directing enough Purchasing Money towards the noncommercial circuit of the economy. Instead, the surpluses of this Money are used for speculative investment, where they create the economic disorders that we are familiar with. Instead of becoming a "potential of oxygenation and revitalisation", these surpluses take on a morbid character. From the point of view of economic health, it is necessary that the operating surpluses of the enterprises of the commercial circuit become Contribution Money.

Unless we realise that this issue is about economic health rather than social justice, we will lack sufficient resolve to rectify it. Only then will we see that the amount of public money devoted to public services can be decreased in some State budget items, but increased in others.

Certainly, it is necessary to act on the expenditures of State public services, as we indicated above. But there is also an urgent need to act on the revenue side, so that society devotes more Contribution Money to the noncommercial circuit of the economy.

To focus only on the budget balance of the State, as is done today, just aggravates the economic problem. This way of thinking leads to decreased public expenditure, where instead, it should be increased. In the economic restructuring plans imposed by the IMF and the European Union, it is the budgets of the noncommercial economic circuit which are reduced. And on the contrary, it is the incomes of the creditors of these countries that are growing, along with the increase in amounts loaned and interest rates. That is exactly the opposite of what should be.

The problem of State deficits will not be solved by increasing taxes and fees in the classical way. Because this approach will not reduce the speculative sphere. Taxing financial capital is not the solution. It is about adopting another conception, as we shall see in Volume 2.

The situation of State budgets reveals real societal issues, related to both the economy and to democracy. Only civil society can address these issues in all their dimensions.

Clearly, civil society acting through Civil Society Organisations (CSOs) and user associations, should establish the budget for each public service, in collaboration with the relevant actors of each field. We are not talking about non-specialised CSOs and associations which are engaged in several fields of activity. The CSOs we are thinking of have to focus on specialised action in a particular field. For each public service, legislation should foresee the modes of voting budgets and the means of arbitration that the CSOs will follow.

For each public service, as in the case of enterprises, distinction will be made between current operating expenditures and the financing of fixed assets. For fixed asset financing, public services will use the Financing Institutes, (whilst their operating expenditures will be funded by Contribution Money Funds). By the way, CSOs are represented in the supervisory board of Financing Institutes. So here again, civil society has a scrutiny right.

Let us reiterate that: civil society already intervenes upstream, in the national and regional Offices of Contribution Money, which determine the budget allocation keys, sector by sector, for the whole of the Contribution Money Funds. Civil society then intervenes in the supervisory board of each institution delivering a public service, as well as in the supervisory board of Financing Institutes that funds their fixed assets. Civil society therefore has three levels of intervention.

If one adds the possibility of popular votes for determining the budget allocation keys of civic public services, as well as for deciding the budgets of sovereign public services, we have the basis for an active participation of the people and of civil society. This intervention can be done in real time and sector by sector. Whereas, in a representative democracy, the mandate is given once for a period of several years, and in broad terms, which leave the governments of unitary States with a latitude that is far too large and ambiguous.

Another transformation which will result from what we have just proposed, is that the Public Treasury, in its current form, will no longer be required. This impersonal entity is a kind of phantom, which suggests an infinite power and which allows all kinds of excesses, especially if the country has a high GDP. We imagined that the Public Treasury could never go bankrupt, and was therefore a reliable borrower. Since 2009, reality is catching up. We now realise that neither the Public Treasury of the USA, nor of Japan, nor of any European Union States, are immune to a temporary payment default nor to bankruptcy.

The Public Treasury issues Treasury bonds. When these bonds have a reputation for being trustworthy, and therefore secure, they are very much sought after by investors. But if their reputation declines, investors will increase the interest rates on these bonds.

The Public Treasury has therefore become, for investors, like a kind of cash cow, which is fed by the citizens, through their taxes.

In the system we propose, each public service will manage its own budget. In the case of a non-sovereign public service, like Civil Society Schools or the Banks of Purchasing Money, the institution should obtain its operating funds by submitting its project plan and operating budget to a Contribution Money Fund. Upon adoption of the project by the Fund, the amounts allocated will be paid into the institution's Current Purchasing Account, in a Bank of Purchasing Money. The

Audit Institutes will verify the requirements regarding the use of the money, and keep the Contribution Money Fund informed.

In the case of sovereign public services, they will obtain their operational funding from dedicated Contribution Money Funds that are managed by civil society. In terms of procedure, there will be no major differences between sovereign and non-sovereign public services.

Thus, we see the great machine of the Public Treasury being replaced by a more flexible organisation, that is more in phase with the reality on the ground, and better controlled by the people.

With such a functioning, it will no longer be possible for the debt of States to go beyond the reasonable. The amount of Contribution Money available will increase substantially. Therefore, the noncommercial economic circuit will have the means necessary for its existence. No public service institution will go into debt in order to fund their operating expenses. Only the funding of fixed assets will be provided by Financing Institutes, according to the same rules as for the enterprises. There will be no more major borrowings by States, nor any issuance of Treasury Bonds.

The three monetary circulations that we propose, enables a balanced financing of public services, with the proper use of public money being guaranteed by the active engagement of civil society.

At a time when we complain about political disaffection of the citizen, should we not move toward forms of democracy that allow citizens to actively exercise their citizenship?

25

A new International Monetary System

Since the global economic crisis that erupted in 2007, we hear political leaders and economists calling for a reform of the International Monetary System (IMS). They would like a new Bretton Woods. All of a sudden, we seem to remember that there is an International Monetary Fund and that, perhaps, it would be useful to give it a role again.

A lot of words, a little bit of posturing, but finally, to leave things as they are. How would it be possible to provide a remedy to the chaos of the world economy if, as Einstein put it, we want to solve these problems *"with the same thinking we used when we created them."*?

We will never solve the present and future crises, if we do not change our conception of the money. Because it is this conception which is at the origin of the disturbances that manifest themselves in the economy. A healthy IMS could arise if it was founded on entirely different bases. That is what we are going to examine in this chapter.

Since 1944, we have had many opportunities to witness the dysfunction of the IMS. In fact, a careful examination shows that what has been put in place at Bretton Woods has never worked. The formation of this cancerous tumor which began in the early 1950s, represented by eurodollar, has been the strongest illustration of IMS dysfunction. Nevertheless, today we are witnessing a sort of replica of this scenario, without having learnt the real lessons of it.

In the 1960s, the German central bank (the Bundesbank) was absorbing a part of the imbalances by accumulating the surplus dollars. Today, the Chinese central bank does the same. Its foreign exchange reserves in dollars amount to, approximately, 3,450 billion, that is to say 21% of the GDP of the USA, or 450% of the US budgetary deficit in 2013.

According to orthodox monetary theories, the Chinese central bank should return these dollars to the Fed, which would certainly have difficulty in redeeming them for Yuan. Or China could sell these dollars in the monetary markets, in exchange for Yuan or the monetary units of other countries. In both cases, existing dollar demand would be substantially satiated, and thereby reduced, whilst demand for Yuan would be proportionately increased.

Contrary to orthodox monetary theory, we are witnessing an artificial maintenance of parity between the two monetary units, as a result of the Chinese central bank lending its accumulated dollars to the American State. China buys interest-bearing US debt obligations with its dollars, in the form of US Treasury bonds.

This artifice has a twofold consequence : first, it allows China to maintain a low value of its monetary unit and, thus, to continue to sell its products at competitive prices to the rest of the world, with very advantageous conditions for itself. The rest of the world pays the price for the use of this artifice, in the form of unemployment induced by the relocation of production to China.

The second consequence is manifested in the USA. Without the surplus of dollars accumulated by China as source of funding for its budget deficits, the U.S. government would have to face the real questions that they have avoided since the country became a superpower. This raises three questions:

The first question would be about whether some budgets should be revised downwards, for example, the defense budget, and everything that maintains American leadership geopolitical leadership. Moreover, it is not impossible that China, when its domestic consumption will be well developed, decides to undermine American hegemony by ceasing to buy US Treasury bonds.

The second question, which is also circumvented, is that of the poverty of more than 40 million Americans, in association with unemployment, a big part of which is induced by the relocation of enterprises to China. The consequent lack of revenue from direct and indirect taxes (resulting from unemployed citizens and relocated enterprises), generates a negative imbalance on the budget of the State.

This leads to the third question raised by this monetary situation. If some budgetary expenditures are reduced and if revenues increase through more consumption and more local production, but if, despite everything, a certain deficit persists, it is appropriate to ask ourselves: what happens to the profits generated by the commercial circuit of the economy?

This fundamental question is excluded from public debate by the fact that the system is still hobbling along. The day when China and Japan withdraw their artificial support to the American budget, this question, and the other two, will become unavoidable. Then the whole problem relating to the structure of share capital and shareholding may be addressed from a new angle.

Thus, three questions with three challenges are present, in a latent state, and cannot be openly addressed because of this abnormal monetary context. Note that each of these challenges concerns one of the components of the threefold monetary circulation that we have highlighted.

The first challenge has to do with the financing needs of the American State. According to what we already discussed, this relates to the question of Financing Money. The second challenge concerns the parity between different units of account of Purchasing Money, as we will see later in this chapter. As to the third challenge, it relates to Contribution Money as we have already described it.

In the final analysis, what hides the abnormal link between the Yuan and the dollar, is an insufficient awareness about the threefold nature of the monetary circulation.

By placing ourselves in the context of these three moneys, we can discover the basis for an IMS that enables the development of an *Economy of Human Added Value*.

Let us examine, from this angle, the problem between the Chinese and US moneys. Let us assume that these two countries have made the separation that we propose, between Purchasing Money and Financing Money. An American company, importing products from China, will settle the invoice in dollars. According to what we have seen in the chapter on the balance of payments[91], the Chinese exporting company will receive purchasing rights expressed in dollars. It will then convert them into Yuan. The bank which will record this operation will cancel the dollars at the time when it credits, in Yuan, the account of the Chinese exporter.

If the same accounting convention were applied to all Chinese enterprises, the Chinese central bank would not accumulate any more reserves in dollars. Thus a mass of autonomous dollars that, by analogy, we could call sino-dollars, would no longer have the opportunity to form.

We have seen that, if we consider the currency as a purchasing right, there is no justification to keep the dollars that have been converted into Yuan. Otherwise, we are creating a duplicate of purchasing rights, which is disruptive in the world economy.

If such accumulation of sino-dollars no longer existed, to artificially maintain parity between the two monetary units, what would happen to this parity?

---

91 See chapter 14: The convertibility of Purchasing Money.

In the concept of Purchasing Money, parity is determined on the basis of the price of goods. We would therefore establish a sort of household shopping basket, containing everything essential to live for a month or a year. Let us call it the Purchasing Basket.

For simplification, suppose that in the current system, 1 Yuan is worth $1[92]. If the price calculation of the Chinese Purchasing Basket shows that it is worth 1,000 Yuan and the American Purchasing Basket is $ 2,000, then the Yuan would see its value doubled against the dollar, i.e. 1 Yuan = $ 2.

Therefore, the export price of Chinese goods would double, becoming less attractive. By doing their accounts, US companies would realise that it would be more interesting for them to relocate their production back onto American soil. China would lose business opportunities. How could China avoid such a drastic decline in its exports?

China would have to address the causes of the problem, examining why its products are cheaper. If it is due to low wages and insufficient expenditure for environmental protection, Chinese companies will benefit from including in their prices, expenditures comparable to the United States, in terms of sufficient wages and the cost of environmental protection.

Such an increase in wages and environmental budgets will result in the Chinese Purchasing Basket becoming more expensive, and thus closer to that of

---

92 In reality, the current market exchange rate at the time of writing is that 1 Yuan equals about 0.16 Dollars. The artifice used here allows us to understand more directly the principle that is being presented.

the USA. In so doing, the conversion rate between the two moneys will revert to what it was originally, before the change of monetary system. But with a crucial difference: the price of the goods in both countries will be comparable.

Will the price of goods in each country become identical ? What factors would make them different?

If both China and the USA had equal wage rates, similar social benefits, equivalent working conditions and identical environmental expenditures, any difference in prices would come from two other factors. The first factor is the capacities developed to improve production and organisation; if both countries provide products of equal quality, creativity will become a key factor in the difference in prices. The second factor is the natural conditions (climate, soil, minerals, oil, etc.).

In the determination of comparative Purchasing Baskets between two countries, it will be necessary to weight prices of included goods and services, in accordance with these two parameters of productivity and the respective available natural resources. Otherwise, the price of these products, which are cheaper because of these parameters, would push upward the value of the domestic monetary unit (relative to foreign ones), and thereby penalize the creators of these products when they export them.

The example of China and the USA shows that the adoption of Purchasing Money in a new IMS would base parity between monetary units on the *real economy*, while encouraging the countries to implement comparable wage, social, tax and environmental policies.

To be more complete on this point, let us consider another example.

Let's imagine a country with an underdeveloped secondary sector, and which has a low standard of living. By comparing identical Purchasing Baskets of this country and America, we may obtain a ratio of 100 to 1. That is to say that one will spend 100 monetary units of this country, whereas 1 US dollar would suffice. Perhaps, in this country, agricultural products will be cheap. But industrial products (TV, computer, car, clothing, etc.) might be very expensive, relative to the external purchasing power of the domestic money. In the Purchasing Money system, the country will export its products at an advantageous price for itself. The money that it will get from such exports will allow it to increase wages and integrate the other factors that we mentioned. By successive steps, the domestic price level will converge with that of the most economically developed countries. Therefore, parity between the domestic and foreign monetary units will also converge. Since wages will become comparable, domestic consumers will gradually gain sufficient purchasing power for them to acquire foreign produced industrial products.

So we can see that the uptake of Purchasing Money at the level of the IMS, would lead to an improvement of the social and environmental conditions of the countries which would adopt it.

The reader will notice that I did not resort to moral discourse about rich countries sharing their wealth with third world countries. I prefer to stay within the economy; and from there, to find the monetary conditions that would avoid an increasing deterioration of the situation of poor countries.

By so doing, we come to a reversal of how the parity between monetary units is usually determined.

So whoever plays with the wages and the social and environmental costs is penalised when exporting. The system of Purchasing Money is such, that it is in a country's interest to produce under conditions that are closer to those prevailing in the countries with which it trades.

Among those calling for a new Bretton Woods, some want to exhume the plan that Keynes proposed at the time. He certainly had a new and interesting idea.

Keynes believed that the economy could only be healthy if there was economic equilibrium between the countries. For Keynes, disequilibrium between their balances of payments is the source of economic malfunction.

The American plan, which was finally adopted, demanded that the countries in current account deficit bear the whole burden of rebalancing. However, Keynes proposed that countries with a current account surplus also contribute to the rebalancing. To achieve this, he wanted to establish a clearing house (clearing union) which would settle the differences between the balances, by means of a dedicated monetary unit of account, which was only circulating between central banks. It was called the Bancor. A set of measures were to be applied to achieve economic equilibrium between the countries in deficit, and to those having a surplus current account balance.

The idea that the economy is healthy when all countries reach a point of equilibrium between them, was revolutionary. It implied that domination of the world by one country was anti-economic.

Unfortunately, Keynes localised this economic equilibrium on the balances of payments, in particular on their commercial part. He thereby applied the concept in the wrong place. Compelling countries to achieve a balance of trade in goods and services does not correspond to real life. Practical reality will always show that it is a mission impossible.

The need for equilibrium is inherent to the international economy. But it is located at the level of price determination, when all the costs of production are included, in particular those costs related to social and environmental conditions.

In other words, parity between monetary units in the *real economy*, should not be determined by the differences in the volumes of trade between countries, but by a price comparison, on the basis of commensurate social and environmental benefits.

The Bancor of Keynes would not have allowed the equilibrium that he dreamed of. This neologism was derived from the French words for *"bank gold"* (*"or"* being the French for gold)[93], which shows that the Bancor was rooted in the concept of commodity money.

However, Purchasing Money will enable a dynamic equilibration of the economy, around a pivot, which will be the price of goods and services.

93　See: Additional Bibliography; Kuttner, (1992) p.34

26

Financing Money in the *Real Economy International Monetary System*

Now let us look at how Financing Money works, in the framework of an International Monetary System (IMS) for the *real economy*.

As we have seen in previous chapters[94], one of the major problems of the current IMS is that no distinction is made between Purchasing Money and Financing Money. This translates into a conflated amalgam known as the balance of payments, in which are recorded both the balance of the current account, and the financial balance.

This accounting confusion reflects what happens in reality, where all kinds of monetary manipulations are permitted. For example, the United States often increased the value of the dollar, by increasing the basic rate of the Fed. This measure attracts financial capital, which translates into a surplus of the financial balance, thereby partially offsetting the US trade balance deficit.

---

94 See Chapter 25 : A new International Monetary System and Chapter 14 : The convertibility of Purchasing Money

With the proposed system of Financing Money, things would be very different. The financial transactions recorded in the balance of payments are mainly of two kinds: those that represent short-term debt claims/liabilities (less than 1 year), and others that represent long-term debt claims/liabilities (more than 1 year). Most of the short-term financial transactions are speculative in nature, and act in a manner detrimental to the economy. All the measures we advocate are intended to make this speculative financial capital inoperative, and therefore to disappear finally from the economic landscape.

A good proportion of long-term international financial transactions are for investments in the *real economy*, either through debt obligations of State, or for the constitution of or increase in the share capital of enterprises.

Regarding debt obligations of State, as we have seen in chapter 24 (The State Budget and Public Treasury), the requirements of the State in terms of financing public investments, could be provided interest-free by the proposed Financing Institutes. The State would have to justify its application for Financing Money just like any enterprise. An application dossier for financing each project would have to be made, so that the Financing Institute could decide whether or not to grant the requested Financing Money, based on an evaluation of the validity and viability of the proposed project.

Thus, any recourse to foreign capital, for the financing of the budget of the State, would no longer be needed.

Of course, this method would require a large degree of rigorous management from the Financing Institutes, and therefore the means to ensure the integrity of this rigor, both at the national and international level. We will return to this matter later.

If the mode of operation of these Financing Institutes is well understood, it is clear that they can provide the Financing Money necessary for the constitution and development of enterprises, without a problem arising from a lack of preexisting financial capital. If a project is judged to be viable and socially useful, by a Financing Institute, the enterprise or the public service which is carrying this project will, without difficulty, be allocated the necessary future-orientated financing[95]. There will be no need to appeal to foreign investment capital, since the Financing Institute will be located in the same country as the enterprise.

An essential characteristic of an IMS for the *real economy* will then emerge: that there is no place in it for international financial transactions. They would be obsolete, since agencies authorized to create Financing Money for enterprises and individuals, would be established in each member country.

In so doing, we would remove the lever which gives so much power to the owners of financial capital, which allows them to enslave mankind to the needs of their capital yield.

International transactions of financial capital would therefore not exist, within an IMS for the *real economy*. They would be banned. This represents one of the compulsory changes that would permit renewed health of the economy.

---

95 See chapter 19 : Future-orientated money

Of course there is the question of subsidiaries of foreign enterprises, in particular those belonging to a transnational corporation (TNC). What would happen if an enterprise located in one country, would like to establish itself in another? How would the parent enterprise of a TNC finance a foreign subsidiary? This raises the question of share capital, and we will look at this in more detail in Volume 2.

However, we can already say that the *"parent company"* would find the necessary funding for its foreign subsidiary from Financing Institutes located in the country of its subsidiary. The parent company would no longer need to transfer financial capital from its headquarters to the subsidiary. As the Financing Money thus made available would be in the form of an interest-free loan, this funding would be just as good as the financial capital that the parent company itself could provide. As for the subsidiary, this form of in-country financing, means that it would be immediately integrated within the local economic fabric.

Finally, in an IMS with Human Added Value, only Purchasing Money would circulate between the countries. And moreover, it would be canceled, immediately at the moment of its conversion into the domestic monetary unit of account[96].

But then, what about Contribution Money?

---

96 See chapter 25, A new International Monetary System, at parag 18

27

Contribution Money in the *Real Economy International Monetary System*

The subprime crisis, by its devastating effects on the global economy, has increased awareness of the problem of speculative finance. The huge sums devoted to financial speculation now appear shocking, compared to the survival needs of populations, both in poor countries, as well as in the so-called developed countries.

Amongst those who amassed large fortunes, especially through financial speculation, there are some who consequently felt that something had to change.

Already, Georges Soros has taken a step in this direction, since some years, by creating and orientating a part of his investment profits towards non-profit foundations, with social and humanitarian goals. He who once said *"As an anonymous participant in financial markets, (...) I felt justified in ignoring (...) the social consequences of my actions (...) on the grounds that I was playing by the rules"*[97]. Other major financiers also

---

97   See chapter 7 : The *real economy* vs. the *unreal economy*, parag 1

woke up because of the shock of the subprime crisis. For example, Warren Buffet and Bill Gates launched an appeal to the most wealthy people in the United States, to donate half of what they have through foundations.

There is now an emerging trend towards the promotion of philanthropic funding, including at the political level. In short, the generalisation of a funding system of philanthropic foundations, at the international level, will become a *"must"* for political correctness.

Despite the possible good intentions that motivate these actions, this is nevertheless a distorted manifestation of a deep societal need, which should be addressed by Contribution Money. This type of philanthropic gift by well endowed foundations, only caricatures the function of Contribution Money. Whilst such philanthropy might serve as a way of salving our consciences, it unfortunately brings no fundamental change to address the dysfunction of the present financial system, and therefore allows its harmful effects to continue unabated. Speculation therefore remains at the core of the economy. The only change is that the orientation of capital gains is partially modified.

Contribution Money, as we have already described it, is of a very different nature. It is not an appendix of the economy but, instead, it is a constituent part or kind of component of it. Just as the liver cannot be described as an ancillary organ to relieve the body, neither can we consider the gift, as an opportune gain to alleviate human misery.

By integrating the gift, in the form of Contribution Money, we have a real monetary organ that is required for the health of the *real economy*, on which the well-being of civil society depends. This monetary circulation permits the accumulated surplus generated by the commercial circuit of the economy, to be redirected back to the *real economy*, through the noncommercial circuit, instead of going into the speculative sphere.

If we are cognizant of the vital necessity of this third form of monetary accounting, then we may conclude that it should be an integral part of an International Monetary System (IMS), for an Economy of Added Human Value. The organ of Contribution Money would be the keystone. It would function in a reverse way to the practice of the World Bank (WB) and the International Monetary Fund (IMF).

For example, what method do these two institutions employ to equilibrate the balance of payments of a country in chronic deficit and on the edge of bankruptcy? They only have one remedy, which entails economic shock treatment. It consists, on the one hand, of exporting natural resources, to the detriment of the local economy and the needs of the population; and on the other, of measures that radically reduce social expenditure, mainly in the areas of health and education. The result is consistently the same: impoverishment of the populations and a dramatic indebtment of the country.

In articulation with the other two forms of monetary accounting, Contribution Money would have a diametrically opposite effect. It would permit the funding of the noncommercial circuit of the economy, which, by the purchasing of surplus goods and services produced by the commercial economic circuit, would boost the economy as a whole. Instead of the harsh austerity measures imposed by the IMF and the World Bank, which subject the most disadvantaged populations to the most crippling economic burdens, we would witness a consolidation of the domestic economy of each country, which would allow them to grow up little by little, in accordance with the method of price convergence in their trade with other countries (as we described earlier)[98].

Today, it has become obvious to the whole world, that the IMS no longer works. It is coming apart at the seams. Governments believe they can seal the cracks. But this can only be a makeshift repair, made on the existing faulty foundations, which does not proceed from a substantially new approach to the situation.

Such is the case regarding tax harmonisation proposals. For some governments, disparity between countries concerning taxation on capital gains and corporate profits (Tax competition), is a source of monetary problems. They therefore advocate a uniformity of tax rules. Several countries of the European Union are calling for it. They even would like to establish tax harmonisation at the global level.

What are the chances of reaching such an agreement? They are practically zero, and in any case, such proposals fail to address the real causes. Fiscal disparity between countries is a consequence, not a cause. It arises from the fact that the financing requirements of enterprises and of States, are met from the pool of global accumulated money. Therefore, each country seeks its own self-interest, and takes measures to attract this financial capital.

---

98 See chapter 25 : A new international monetary system.

With Financing Money based on future production, and not on past accumulation, we can act on the cause of the problem. Countries no longer need to attract foreign accumulated financial capital. Financing Institutes can create the Financing Money required in their respective countries, in accordance with the development potential of their enterprises. It follows that the need for tax harmonisation, in the form it is usually planned, is simply no longer relevant. However, another form of harmonisation becomes necessary.

From the moment the payment of taxes becomes a conscious contribution by citizens, then the question would arise regarding the link between Contribution Money and the formation of prices.

The needs in the noncommercial circuit of the economy should determine the amount of funding it requires, in the form of Contribution Money. There is a direct link between the amount of Contribution Money required and prices, as this amount must correspond to the prices actually paid for goods and services. In other words, when the price of a good or service is determined, it should not just include direct costs, but also the whole of the indirect costs of economic production, such as: roads, transport, education, health, the environment, the maintenance of public order, research and development, and so on. In short, everything relating to the indirect contribution in production and distribution by the noncommercial circuit of the economy, should be included in the formation of prices, through a process of consultation between partners, representing producers, distributors and consumers.

However, in the IMS for the *Real Economy* that we are talking about, the conversion rates between the different monetary units are determined by the price of goods and services, as we have seen. These prices are weighted in order to represent a comparison which takes into account the natural wealth and productivity of each country. The calculation of the conversion rate would include these factors. Thus, if price differences between countries are due to these factors, they could nevertheless lead to a convergence in the rates of conversion between different monetary units.

A third element should also be integrated in this conversion rate calculation, that of the quantity of Contribution Money. If, for particular reasons, a country made considerable effort to develop a domain of the Third Sector, the price of goods would be affected. Suppose that a country is affected by an epidemic, it would be necessary to increase the volume of purchasing rights devoted to healthcare, which, according to what we have just seen, would have an impact on prices.

Such an increase in the level of prices, would lead to a decrease in the purchasing power of the domestic Purchasing Money (relative to the money of other countries). If the country needs to import medicines and health equipment, it would be penalized, because of the efforts that it would provide for the health of its population. The calculation of the conversion rate should therefore integrate this exceptional expenditure within the framework of Contribution Money, so that the country is not penalized.

Conversely, suppose a country seeks to promote its exports, by reducing Contribution Money transfers to the Third-sector (healthcare, education, culture, and so on) in order to reduce its export prices. The determination of the conversion rate of its monetary unit should take this into account. The same goes for any attempts to avoid paying the costs of proper working conditions and wages.

We have here an example which shows how the determination of the parity between monetary units of account, should also include everything that is happening with the Contribution Money. Therefore it is not about enforcing an equality of fiscal levies and VAT tax rates across countries. Because we would act in a biased way on what these taxes in reality are: a Contribution Money, which is not considered as such. What we propose takes into account the real economic life of each region and country.

In this way, what is happening at the economic and social level, will act on the parity between national and regional moneys; instead of the speculation caused by Hot Money exerting an unbearable pressure on human beings.

28

The principle features of a *Real Economy International Monetary System*

Summarised below are the principal features for a *Real Economy International Monetary System (reIMS)*:

A. General Principles

A.1. The reIMS aims to develop an Economy of Human Added Value, i.e. an economy based on the production, distribution and consumption of real goods and services. Therefore the purpose of its establishment is to develop monetary tools that render inoperative speculative operations and the financial economy.

A.2. The monetary tools of the reIMS are to allow a triple monetary circulation, comprising: Purchasing Money, Financing Money, and Contribution Money.

A.3. This threefold monetary circulation is provided as a public service by Civil Society, to promote the *real economy*.

A.4. The member countries of the reIMS organise the threefold monetary circulation in accordance with the principles of a Civil Society public service, and the national and international provisions as set out below.

B. Principles of civil society public services

B.1. Monetary institutions belong to the noncommercial circuit of the economy and are not-for-profit.

B.2. Monetary institutions cannot use the services they provide for their own purpose.

Thus a Bank of Purchasing Money cannot hold its own Purchasing account. Its own account for the settlement of its operating expenditures must be located in another bank.

The Financing Institute cannot grant a loan to itself. If it needs to fund, for example, an office facility, it will make an application to another Financing Institute, which will examine its application for funds, with the same criteria that would apply to any enterprise.

A Contribution Money Fund cannot attribute to itself any of the money it collects. To pay for its operation, it must apply to another Contribution Money Fund, and justify its needs like any other non-profit organisation of the noncommercial economic circuit.

B.3. A monetary institution can only be active in a single monetary circulation.

Thus a Bank of Purchasing Money cannot undertake any function of a Financing Institute, nor of a Contribution Money Fund, and vice versa..

B.4. A monetary institution cannot hold shares in another monetary institution, regardless of the type of monetary circulation operated by the latter.

B.5. The resources of monetary institutions are the public endowments, raised through the Contribution Money system, as well as the fees charged to users, which are proportional to the nature and scale of operations, and in accordance with the rules agreed between the institutions and the users associations.

Access to the basic services of monetary institutions is free to all users.

B.6. The operating budget of a monetary institution is capped in proportion to its volume of service. Any surpluses are returned to a public collection agency (Contribution Money Fund). A National Council of Monetary Users Organisations will evaluate, region by region, the ratios that determine the capped budget of the monetary institutions.

B.7. The operational management of each monetary institution is subject to the authority of a supervisory board, acting as a constituent organ of the monetary institution. The supervisory board is composed, on the one hand, of representatives of the founders of the monetary institution; and, on the other hand, of members of Civil Society Organisations (CSOs), representing users; as well as members of CSOs that are active in societal and environmental issues.

The Supervisory Board appoints and dismisses the executive officers of the monetary institution.

B.8. In each region, a Monetary Coordination Board is established, composed of delegates from each type of monetary institution, as well as representatives of users associations, together with representatives of CSOs.

The function of this Coordination Board is to:

▷ Identify the needs of the region, and what type of institutions will best meet them.The Board is responsible for ensuring that all needs are covered.

> ▷ Convene a commission to examine and adjudicate disputes and users complaints.

> ▷ Grant or renew the license for each monetary institution.

B.9. Each monetary institution is subject to inspection by a Monetary Auditing Institute that is independent and a not-for-profit public service. It will audit the accounts and functioning of the monetary institutions, to check that they comply with the rules of public service, and with the operational specifications defined by the monetary institute.

The Auditing Institute prepares an annual audit, as well as interim monthly reports, for the attention of the monetary institution being audited, as well as for the Monetary Coordination Board, of which it is a member. The report may contain warnings and recommendations regarding any identified dysfunctions. The reports also give deadlines for redressing any dysfunction.

In case of non-compliance with these conditions, or serious failure on the part of the audited monetary institution, the Monetary Coordination Board may revoke its operating license.

B.10. People who wish to create a monetary institution, must submit their project to the Monetary Coordination Board of the monetary unit jurisdiction in which they propose to establish it. If their project addresses an unmet need, or represents a new way of supplying a service, which is already provided by an existing monetary institution, the Board will grant them a provisional operating license, for a period that enables the project to prove its usefulness.

B.11. During the startup phase of a new monetary institution, the Board will also give an exemption that allows the institution to benefit from public money beyond the normal operating budget capping ratios.

B.12. Each monetary institution implements a quality management system approved by the Monetary Auditing Institute.

B.13. All of the foregoing provisions are an integral part of the operational specifications of each monetary institution.

C. National provisions

C.1. Purchasing Money

Purchasing Money is used for the exchange of goods and services between suppliers, producers, distributors and consumers.

Purchasing Money is a unit of account which reflects a purchasing right.

The bodies responsible for monetary surveillance shall take all necessary steps to ensure that Purchasing Money does not tend to accumulate within the monetary circuit.

C.1.1. Purchasing Money circulates predominantly as a form of Ledger Money, by electronic transfers, bank cards, digital wallets, perhaps by cheques, and so on.

C.1.2. Banks of Purchasing Money are non-profit institutions that manage the recording, transfer, and withdrawal of Purchasing Money.

C.1.3. Banks of Purchasing Money manage two types of accounts for users: Current Purchasing Accounts and Deferred Purchasing Accounts.

C.1.4. Transfer of purchasing rights (money) between depositors (account users) can only be done through Current Purchasing Accounts.

C.1.5. Each Current Purchasing Account is closed on December 31 of each year. A credit balance equal to $\frac{1}{12}$ of the total of annual receipts will be kept on the account. The rest is transferred to the Deferred Purchasing Account of each user.

C.1.6. From a Deferred Purchasing Account, a depositor can make a transfer to a Financing Institute or to his own Current Purchasing Account. In the latter case, he undergoes a demurrage of 10% of the amount of the transfer.

C.1.7. The money that remains on a Deferred Purchasing Account, loses 10% of its amount each year, on December 31.

C.1.8. The deductions mentioned in paragraphs C.1.6 and C.1.7 are transferred by the Bank of Purchasing Money to the Contribution Money Funds chosen by the depositor or, in default, by the bank itself.

C.1.9. Money transferred from a Deferred Purchasing Account to a Financing Institute, for the purpose of providing loaned funds to enterprises, will not be subject to any deductions for the duration of the loan. However, when such loaned money (in part or in whole), is transferred back to the Deferred Purchasing Account it came from, it will be subject to the demurrage provision mentioned in paragraphs C.1.6 and C.1.7.

C.2. The Institute of Cash Money

    C.2.1. Each member country of the reIMS has an Institute of Cash Money whose task is to put at the disposal of the banks, the banknotes and coins needed for the circulation of Purchasing Money.

    C.2.2. Each Bank of Purchasing Money has an account with the Institute of Cash Money. The latter supplies coins and banknotes, in exchange for a transfer of an equal amount of Ledger Money. When a Bank of Purchasing Money has too much cash on hand, it makes the reverse operation with the Institute of Cash Money.

    C.2.3. The operation of Institutes of Cash Money are subject to the principles of a Public Service by Civil Society.

C.3. Financing Money

Financing Money corresponds to a monetary circulation which is additional to Purchasing Money, and uses the same unit of account.

Financing Money is a Money of loan, intended for the financing of enterprises, institutions and individuals.

Financing Money can only be issued by the Financing Institutes. This monetary creation can comprise the whole or just a part of the total amount needed, depending on whether a third party will contribute as well.

Destruction of issued Money takes place by the reimbursement of loans.

Loans are granted on the basis of the evaluated feasibility of the project. Loans are not backed by accumulated financial capital, nor by any other type of collateralized guarantee (securities) or mortgages.

Loans are interest-free.

C.3.1. Financing Money only circulates as ledger entries:

▷ By transfer to the Current Purchasing Account of the borrower or in reverse direction upon the reimbursement of loans.

▷ By transfer to the Deferred Purchasing Account of the saver upon the reimbursement of his savings.

C.3.2. Financing Institutes open an account in a Bank of Purchasing Money, in order to register their income and settle their operating expenses.

C.3.3. In agreement with user associations, Financing Institutes can charge fees, which will not exceed: (i) a maximum of 2% of the amount of loan requested, to cover their loan-application costs (as a one-off non-refundable payment), and (ii) a maximum of 3% of the loan granted, to cover their management costs.

C.3.4. A Financing Institute only grants loans for activities located in the country where it is legally domiciled. International transfer of Financing Money is prohibited.

C.4. Contribution Money.

Contribution Money is Purchasing Money that has been transferred towards funding the institutions of the non-commercial circuit of the economy, with the aim of securing their functioning. Thus it is expressed in the same unit of account.

Contribution Money is generated by taxes, profits made by enterprises in the commercial circuit of the economy, donations, and monetary demurrage.

C.4.1. In each country, a National Office of the Contribution Money, together with Regional Offices, define annually, the allocation keys for Contribution Money, according to the sectors of activity in the noncommercial circuit of the economy.

These Offices of Contribution Money do not themselves allocate Contribution Money. Their activity is limited to the determination of the allocation keys.

These offices are subject to the principles of civil society public services, defined above at section B.

C.4.2. The bodies authorised to collect and redistribute Contribution Money are the Contribution Money Funds.

Each Contribution Money Fund is active in only one domain of activity at a time of the noncommercial economic circuit.

Apart from the sovereign activities of the State, each domain of activity in the noncommercial circuit of the economy may involve several Contribution Money Funds, created on the initiative of citizens and civil society.

C.4.3. Each citizen allocates their obligatory share of Contribution Money to the Contribution Money Fund of their choice, in proportion to the allocation keys defined by the Offices of Contribution Money. For each sector of the noncommercial economic circuit, every citizen can decide which institutions and associations will benefit from their contribution.

C.4.4. Transfers to Contribution Money Funds, of fiscal revenues arising from the activities of enterprises in the commercial economic circuit, in terms of tax and taxable profits, will be allocated by the employees, to the Contribution Money Funds of their choice.

The employees will have a choice about the decision-making basis for allocating these fiscal revenues, i.e. whether it is on an individual or collective basis.

This allocation will also be in proportion to the allocation keys defined by the Offices of Contribution Money

C.4.5. To obtain funding for the establishment of their operating infrastructure, Contribution Money Funds will make a funding request to a Financing Institute.

C.4.6. Contribution Money Funds open an account in a Bank of Purchasing Money, in order to register their income and settle their operating expenses.

C.4.7. Institutions and associations of the noncommercial economic circuit, requiring Contribution Money for their establishment and functioning, will seek such funding from a Contribution Money Fund of their choice, by presenting them with their operating plan and budget. Upon acceptance of such a funding request, the Contribution Money Fund, transfers the funding to the Current Purchasing Account of the beneficiary institution of the noncommercial economic circuit.

D. International Provisions

D.1. Transfers of Purchasing Money between member countries of the reIMS can only be made from Current Purchasing Account to Current Purchasing Account.

Contribution Money can only be transferred from Contribution Money Fund to Contribution Money Fund.

Financing Money cannot be transferred between the member countries.

D.2. During an international transfer of Purchasing Money, the Bank of Purchasing Money which receives the purchasing rights, records them in its monetary unit, and cancels the counterpart which was expressed in the monetary unit of the country of origin. This operation is done at the official conversion rate of the reIMS.

D.3. International transfers of Contribution Money happen in a similar way to transfers of Purchasing Money, as defined in the previous paragraph.

D.4. The organisation of the reIMS comprises four International Monetary Institutions (IMIs) :

▷ The International Office of Conversion Rates.

▷ The oversight body called the International Monetary Auditors

▷ The Arbitration Commission.

▷ The International Association of Monetary CSOs.

D.5. Each of the IMIs is overseen and directed by a supervisory board composed of representatives of non-profit civil society CSOs that are active at the international level, and members of the International Association of Monetary CSOs.

D.6. The supervisory board of each IMI appoints the executive officers of each of these institutions. These officers are experts in one of the threefold monetary accounting systems comprising Financing, Purchasing, and Contribution money.

D.7. The IMIs are subject to a quality management system (QMS).

D.8. The IMIs have an office in each member country. Two thirds of the management of these offices is composed of personnel foreign to the country.

D.9. The funding of the IMIs comes from Contribution Money provided by each member country, whose share of contribution is proportional to their GDP.

D.10. The International Office of Conversion Rates

   D.10.1. The mission of the International Office of Conversion Rates is to define, each month, the conversion rates between the monetary units.

   D.10.2. The objective of the reIMS is to facilitate a convergence, between the member countries, with regard to wages levels, social benefits, working conditions, and environmental protection. The calculation of conversion rates between monetary units of account, will be done in such a way that convergence between countries regarding the above four factors will be achieved.

   D.10.3. The tool for determining Conversion Rates is the Purchasing Basket, composed of most of the products consumed in the world. It is identical for all countries.

D.10.4. The Weighted Price of the Purchasing Basket (WPPB), in a country, is the price to be paid to buy all of the products which constitute the Basket. It is expressed in the monetary unit of the country.

D.10.5. Weighting of the Basket price is achieved by integrating productivity advantages that result from technological and know-how improvements, as well as the availability of natural resources in the country. This ensures that the country will not be penalised, at the level of the conversion rate of its monetary unit, as a result of developing one or another of these factors of productivity advantage.

D.10.6. The bilateral Conversion Rates between two monetary units of account Mα and Mβ is equal to the inverse ratio between the Weighted Prices of the Purchasing Baskets in these two countries, i.e:

$$\frac{M\alpha}{M\beta} = \frac{WPPB\beta}{WPPB\alpha}$$

D.11. The International Monetary Auditors

D.11.1. The mission of the International Monetary Auditors is to monitor the implementation of the operating rules and procedures of the reIMS in each member country, and at the level of the IMIs.

D.11.2. To fulfill its mission, the International Monetary Auditors rely on the supervisory organs that oversee the operation of each financial institution, i.e. the Monetary Coordination Boards of each monetary unit, and their Monetary Auditing Institutes, as they are defined in paragraphs B.8 and B.9.

D.11.3. The International Monetary Auditors continuously evaluate the proper functioning of these two types of institutions.

In the event of identified dysfunction, the International Monetary Auditors send a note or a warning to the agency concerned, with a deadline for resolving the problem.

In the event of serious misconduct, or failure to resolve identified dysfunctions within the deadline, the International Monetary Auditors withdraw the accreditation license of the non-compliant institution.

D.11.4. The International Monetary Auditors may order a Monetary Coordination Board, to withdraw the license of a member monetary institution.

D.11.5. The International Monetary Auditors can ask the International Organisation of Monetary CSOs, to exclude a member country of the reIMS, in the event of repeated non-compliance of the rules of reIMS or other serious misconduct.

D.12. The Arbitration Commission

D.12.1. The mission of the Arbitration Commission is to judge and settle disputes which might arise between the member institutions and participants of the reIMS.

D.12.2. The entities that can refer a dispute to the Arbitration Commission are :

▷ In the first instance, the International Monetary Institutions.

    ▷ In the second instance, the Monetary Auditing Institutes, the Monetary Coordination Boards, the CSOs and User Associations that are active in the monetary domain.

D.12.3. The decisions of the Arbitration Commission are final and binding.

D.13. The International Organisation of Monetary CSOs

D.13.1. The International Organisation of Monetary CSOs is composed of representatives of CSOs active at the international level, in the monetary and non-profit areas.

D.13.2. The International Organisation of Monetary CSOs designates, in a general assembly, the representatives of CSOs who will sit on the supervisory boards (SB) of the IMIs.

D.13.3. The International Organisation of Monetary CSOs supervises the activity of the International Office of Conversion Rates and of the International Monetary Auditors.

D.13.4. The International Organisation of Monetary CSOs admits or excludes the countries or monetary unit jurisdictions within the reIMS.

D.13.5. The International Organisation of Monetary CSOs has an arbitration commission which deals, at first instance, with the complaints and disputes coming from CSOs or citizens and concerning the functioning of a CSO that is involved in a monetary institution.

The diagram on the following page presents a synthesis of the articulation between the different organs of the reIMS.

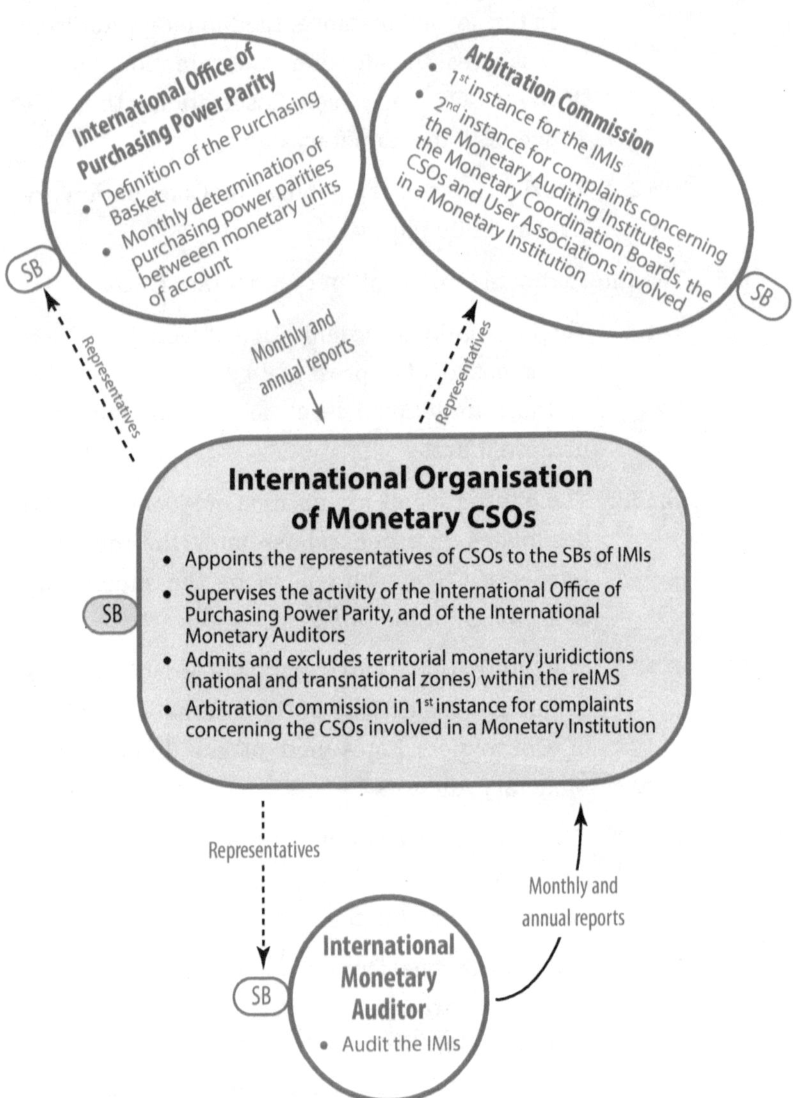

Diag. 14 - The Real Economy Monetary System (reIMS)

29

Let us not fight the wrong battle

Indignation is rising and the crises of disaster capitalism makes lucid those who aspire to greater solidarity and equity. The dysfunctions of the current system are now clearly revealed. For many people, it is bringing civilization to its knees. Many of us therefore want to replace the incumbent system. But by what?

Almost everywhere, we see initiatives and proposals blossoming. Most are aimed at an immediate and committed action, at the local level, in an associative or individual way. These initiatives seek to bring about direct change, on the ground. There are also some projects orientated towards a more extensive plan of action.

In the monetary domain, these two levels of initiative coexist. On the one hand as local and complementary money initiatives, and, on the other hand, new forms of national money.

Local money initiatives:

The Local Exchange Trading Systems (LETS), are a well known example of local initiatives. Most of them consist of an accounting of the reciprocal exchange of services rendered between LETS members, often on the basis of working time (i.e. time being the unit of account). As such, LETS represents a kind of Ledger Money. Other projects use printed notes, which are used by the members of the association that is responsible for this initiative. The membership is mostly composed of individuals, but can also include local merchants and artisans and, sometimes SMEs. The goal is to facilitate local production and exchange of goods and services, and thereby to create local jobs.

National complementary money initiatives:

Some experiments were conducted on a larger scale. The most important of them is undoubtedly that of Créditos, a parallel currency that was born in 1995 in Argentina. The country was experiencing a serious monetary crisis that paralyzed the economy. To avoid falling into poverty, some citizens in a suburb of Buenos Aires began to barter, and then to organise a network of clubs, the Nodos (Nodes), which printed their own notes, called the Créditos, in order to facilitate the exchange of goods and services between members.

In the early 2000s, the number of Nodos amounted to more than 8,000, with transactions in Créditos being the equivalent of 500 million dollars per year between millions of Argentines. The scope of this experience is impressive. It also proved its social utility. Not only did it enable a parallel economy to develop, to substitute for the paralysed economy based on the official money, but it also created a social link between the members of the Nodos.

"These exchange networks recreate the social link, and are thus opposed, de facto, to the current economic system, which exalts and develops the individualism of every man for himself " (Duboin, 2007. p.176).

" (...) parallel currencies, because they are for local use, are restricted and marginal, so at best, they can keep at bay certain effects of the general crisis, but only for those who are active as members of these associations " (Duboin, 2007. p.200).

It is a fact that complementary currencies tend to appear in times of crisis. However, what would be their usefulness if money was playing its proper economic role. With the implementation of Purchasing Money, as we have proposed, the recourse to this parallel circuit would prove to be an obstacle to economic exchange, because it would add unnecessary complication.

Why, in fact, have two kinds of notes when one is enough? Our focus should instead be on the need to establish the conditions for a healthy monetary system. Let us not fight the wrong battle!

The need for complementary currencies appears whenever there is a lack of purchasing power. Essentially, this is not linked to a monetary malfunction, but to income. It is this issue that should be addressed. Once we have rethought these matters in Volume 2, we might question the amount of effort usually devoted to the creation of complementary currencies, and wonder if it would not be better to tackle the real causes of our problems.

Again, let us not fight the wrong battle. The real error lies not in the fact of implementing an additional monetary tool, whether as the Créditos, Chiemgauer, or the Sols-Violettes, and so on. This error is not just strategic. It is more profound. It is conceptual. It gives or allows money to have an attribute that lies outside its proper field of action.

Certainly, the economy suffers from serious monetary malfunctions. We have described them in detail and from several angles. We have seen the importance of remedying these dysfunctions, and we have proposed solutions based on a whole new approach, which really considers money as an accounting system, and not as a commodity.

In the theory of the German economist Silvio Gesell, to whom many alternative economy thinkers refer, money is also considered as *"a particular commodity"*. Gesell proposed some interesting ideas, in particular what he called *"Free-Money"* (Freigeld), where instead of using interest as an incentive for recycling stagnant accumulations of money, Gesell proposed a kind of liquidity tax, known as monetary demurrage[99]. In his book *"The Natural Economic Order"*, Gesell writes:

"Money, by an inherent natural force, will steadily tend towards the limit of the velocity of circulation possible for the time being, or rather it will in all conceivable circumstances tend to overleap this limit. Just as the moon, calm and unaffected by what may be going on here below, moves in its orbit, so Free-Money, detached from the wishes of its holders, will move through the market.

---

99   See chapter 11: Monetary Demurrage.

In all conceivable circumstances, in fair weather and in foul, demand will then exactly equal: 1. the quantity of money circulated and controlled by the State. 2. the maximum velocity of circulation possible with the existing commercial organisation.

What is the effect upon economic life ? The effect is that we now dominate the fluctuations of the market; that the Currency Office, by issuing and withdrawing money, is able to tune demand to the needs of the market; that demand is no longer controlled by the holders of money, by the fears of the middle classes, the gambling of speculators or the tone of the Stock Exchange, but that its amount is determined absolutely by the Currency Office. The Currency Office now creates demand, just as the State manufactures postage stamps, or as the workers create supply.

When prices fall, the Currency Office creates money and puts it in circulation. And this money is demand, materialised demand. When prices rise the Currency Office destroys money, and what it destroys is demand." (Gesell, 1916. p.127)".

Points 1 and 2 in the above passage summarise perfectly the conception that directs local and complementary currencies, i.e:

1. money is regarded as a commodity that circulates in the market, in a quantity that is either too much, or too little;

2. the velocity of money in circulation is regarded as playing a decisive role in the magnitude of its supply.

Now, this conception of money is the same as that used in the actual economic system, the one that we intend to transform. Already, in chapter 4, we indicated that there is a deficit of economic thinking, both on the side of those who defend the existing system, and by those who advocate alternative proposals. In the succeeding chapters, we examined in detail how to free ourselves from the fallacy of this commodity-money approach, and the illusion of the velocity of money in circulation.

In the case of complementary currencies, this confusion sometimes reaches the point of believing that the money itself would create purchasing power. In the *real economy*, I have never seen purchasing power appear thanks to money, which at the most, can only measure or account for it.

The purchasing rights which an actor of the *real economy* has at their disposal always result from a series of acts within this domain. Even pensions and social benefits come by this means.

Purchasing power is earned as remuneration, in one form or another. If someone does not have sufficient purchasing power, the cause should be sought in its appropriate sphere. In our diagram of the Economic Cross[100], we placed work and money facing each other. By exploring this sphere of work, from a new perspective, we will discover how to resolve this crucial issue of remuneration, which manifests as a lack of purchasing power for an increasing number of people throughout the world.

---

100 See Diagram 1: The Economic Cross. ch.3

The Economic Cross can help to track back to the root causes of economic problems, and avoid attributing the origin of a problem to the wrong sphere.

Otherwise we make the same erroneous approach that we characterised regarding the manipulation by Central Banks of their interest rates: of acting externally on a symptom, without treating the cause, as we saw by our analogy of the pacemaker, which regulates heartbeat and thereby blood circulation. We concluded, nobody could consider the implant of a pacemaker as being characteristic of good human health.

Do we have an idea of what a healthy economy looks like, meaning what its normal state should be? We should address this point in depth before moving towards a solution. How should money be, so that the economy is healthy? A correct understanding of the nature and function of money is a prerequisite, before taking any direction towards a solution. Three other prerequisites must also be explored to correctly identify the causes for the purchasing of non-local products and of pollution: these prerequisites are located in the other three branches of the Economic Cross. By exploring these branches, we will be able to identify the core reasons for non-local purchasing and of pollution, which should be sought in the direction of financial capital, labour, and land/real estate. All three make the economy sick, by the way they are inserted into it as commodities.

For example, we should consider how the price of real estate influences the cost of local production, and also the purchasing power of local consumers. Therefore, the problem is not only doubled, it is *"squared"* and has a disproportionate influence when local production is confronted with *"delocalised production"*.

We must therefore consider how the four branches of the Economic Cross disrupt the economy and make it sick. It is about entering into these phenomena and revealing them. Only then, we can find the remedies for each of these four branches.

When goods and services are equal in terms of quality and service, but local products are neglected, it means that price comes to the fore. In the context of this issue, nothing changes, whether prices are expressed in official money, or in a complementary/local currency. Like at the time of the transition to the Euro, prices were displayed both in the old and new money units. There was no difference between paying in French Francs or Euros. This reveals a conflation between money and its physical accounting instruments.

The initiators of the WIR, which we previously exampled, did not make this conflation. If the function of WIR money had been limited to the exchange function, that is to say purchasing, it would not have lasted. The primordial reason for the establishment of the WIR was to provide credit to productive enterprises. This credit therefore comes into existence as Financing Money, which at the moment of its use enters into circulation as Purchasing Money.

Enterprises resort to WIR money for cash flow and funding needs when the provision of credit by conventional banks is either unavailable or charged at unaffordable interest rates. This scenario happens particularly in times of financial/banking crises. The use of WIR money decreases in periods of *"easy credit "*, or when the interest rate of the Swiss Central Bank is so low, that commercial bank credit denominated in Swiss Francs is cheap - which is currently the case, and so (at the time of writing), transactions in WIR money have declined.

We can therefore see that complementary money only has meaning if it is allocated as Financing Money, i.e. as the result of monetary creation that is linked to an economic activity. To make it function as Purchasing Money, by issuing it as a substitute for the existing official money, does not change the economic equation.

Some local money projects offer a purchasing power bonus of up to 5% for exchanging Euros for the local/loyalty money: e.g. for 100 official euros, you receive up to 105 localised/loyalty euros. Some might believe this to be monetary creation. But a careful observation will show that it does not have the attributes of monetary creation. So this purchasing power bonus looks more like a special offer, similar to what merchants already do to promote their merchandise. In this case, it is as if complementary money is being sold on special offer!

In some cases, complementary money schemes are also linked to microcredit programmes. Again it would be appropriate to well observe if this corresponds to a real monetary creation, in the sense of Financing Money. Because there are situations where the retired Euros, which backed the complementary currency, are used as reserves to back microcredit loans, which are also denominated in the complementary currency. In such a case, this would represent fractional reserve monetary creation, similar to that of a traditional commercial bank. Everything will be fine as long as requests to convert the complementary money back into official Euros remains low; in other words, as long as people still want to play the game. If too many members decided to leave this monetary zone, there could be some surprises.

Monetary pluralism has long existed. At the beginning of the twentieth century, in several regions of Europe, each bank issued its own money. There arose, on a daily basis, the problem of conversion from one bank note to the other, as well as the uncertainty of trust in the quantity of money issued, relative to its coverage which, at that time was in gold or trusted banknotes.

It is interesting to note that complementary currencies are going through the same evolutionary steps as those already experienced in the history of the official money. Perhaps this would be a factor that awakens our citizen awareness regarding monetary issues? But sometimes, one may wonder if we are not in the process of reinventing the wheel.

There have been times when the launch of a complementary money, as Purchasing Money, has proved useful. We have cited the case of the Crédito. It emerged because the Peso was no longer playing its role. Many banks had closed, and the Argentines had lost their money or no longer had access to it. There was no more circulation of Purchasing Money. It was defaulting.

Are we in a similar situation in Europe? It could have happened in 2008-2009. It is very likely that other crises will occur. We can even imagine that the Eurozone breaks down. Whether this happens, or we continue from crisis to crisis, to maintain the current state of affairs, the day will arrive when we shall have to face reality: we are not going to find viable solutions, which would allow a sustainable development of the life of Society and nature, as long as we do not approach the economy in a way that corresponds to what it is in essence. To achieve this, we need an all-encompassing vision.

Earlier in this chapter, we demonstrated by an example, of how the price of goods is influenced by real estate. Other factors could also have been added, including wages and environmental protection. All these price determination elements can originate thousands of kilometers from a French city or village. But they are included in the price of an imported product in a French shop, which is in competition with those produced locally. Whether the customer pays in euros or in complementary money, this does not change the question that is put to him, and which is even less easy to answer, since his purchasing power is restricted.

The question is the following: how to act on factors that are so distant and apparently beyond reach? We have a problem of price between two products. Instead of seeking an external means of intervention, we should enter into the heart of the difficulty, that is to say into the formation of prices. Now, the price is also dependent on the conversion rate between monetary units. Therefore we will have to include this element in the determination of prices, so that costs that have been externalised are reintroduced, into the price of the product during the conversion between monetary units.

In chapter 25, *"A new International Monetary System"*, we proposed a method to achieve this, while remaining within the economy. The relocalisation of economic activity definitely has a monetary component. But relocalisation is far more global than it is usually percieved.

A popular slogan of anti-globalisation is: *"think global, act local"*. If we take this slogan seriously, what is the sense of *"acting local"*, if it does not proceed from *"holistic thinking"*, that is, from an all-encompassing vision of the economy and, in particular, of money? In this area, our local action could be to work on these issues in depth, so as to develop a citizenship that is more aware, more awake, more knowledgeable, and which is able to mobilise itself in order to make progress with the most crucial challenges.

In other words, by going directly from justified indignation to strategies such as complementary currencies, are we not taking the battle into a dead end, which in turn would enable disaster capitalism to occupy even more of the field, and to exhaust, little by little, the forces of resilience which are so alive, and that we see emerging almost everywhere in the world?

In my opinion, this dilemma is most serious, and should not be treated lightly by those who aspire to change things.

Currently, we are witnessing a profusion of reflections and initiatives in the field of complementary currencies. Some economists, aware of the limits of a money which would only be local, are working on inter-operative conversion modes between these different currencies.

Others propose a national complementary money. There is a lot more to say about these projects. In the framework of this book, I will not expand on this point further. I refer the interested reader to the site of Démocratie Évolutive[101], to the heading Monnaie/Money. Everything that I have expounded upon so far, should be sufficient to show where the knot of the problem lies, and how to undo it.

We are not talking about building a parallel monetary system, as (if I may call it) an *"Off-world"*, which would leave the *"In-world"* of the official system to continue its path. We have seen that the *"In-world"* system is ill with the cancer of speculation. The tendency of this disease is to spread throughout the whole of the body, and to deplete its forces of healing. Today, the *"Off-world"* still has the possibility to exist. But we do not know for how long, or whether it could become so marginal, relative to the *"In-world"* system, so as to become insignificant. The *"In-world"* could also find ways to co-opt the impetus of the *"Off-world"* to its functioning. Has it not already begun to do so, in France for example, with the creation of a Ministry of the Social and Solidarity Economy? In this domain, the imagination of the State apparatus is without limits. By State apparatus, I am referring to a system that has its own dynamic, over which the citizen has only very little power, or only an appearance of power.

In his book *"The liberal dictatorship"* (Rufin, 1994), Jean-Christophe Rufin well described this hijacking mechanism, at the base of the functioning of what we

---

101 www.democratie-evolutive.fr

call democracy. Drawing a parallel with Adam Smith's famous invisible hand of the market, he describes the invisible hand policy which *"ensures the cohesion of the system. It is this hand that feeds the system of what opposes it "*. He then shows how the opposition or dissent are not an obstacle, and how the system will hijack them. *"The contradictions of democratic societies are not drawbacks or weaknesses: they are at the heart of the system and give it its force (...) Democratic societies can, without fear, leave all initiatives to flourish, since such initiatives do not jeopardise them. They can release human energies to the full, since they are assured that their turbulence, regardless of the heat generated, does not lead to the melting of what contains them."* (Rufin, 1994. p. 299 & 300).

A little further, the author shows the risk of fighting for causes that have a too limited focus: *"Let us ensure that the fragmentation, the insignificance of the human revolts, increasingly local, microscopic and patchy, do not lead to an excessive weakening of disruptive mechanisms."* (Rufin, 1994. p.306). And he continues by quoting Alexis de Tocqueville: *"It is believed by some that modern society will always be changing its aspect; for myself, I fear that it will ultimately be too invariably fixed in the same institutions, the same prejudices, the same manners, so that mankind will be stopped and circumscribed; that the mind will swing backwards and forwards forever without begetting fresh ideas; that man will waste his strength in bootless and solitary trifling, and, though in continual motion, that humanity will cease to advance."*[102].

---

102 Tocqueville (de), 1840), Section 3, chapter 25, Why great revolutions will become more rare.

It is therefore vital to understand the real challenges. Certain issues cannot be addressed at the local level alone, nor within a complementary circuit. By their nature, these issues are rooted in another level.

Basically, we can consider three levels: the microsocial, the mezzosocial, and the macrosocial. The microsocial concerns life at the individual level, including direct relations with other people: with members of our family, our friends, our work colleagues, our neighbors, and so on.We are on the second level of the mezzosocial, when we are working within an institution, an enterprise, an association, and so on. The concerns of macrosocial organisations are of a wider nature, whose radius of activity goes from the regional to the international, whether it be the State or international institutions, such as: the UN, the WTO, the IMF, the ECB, and so on. Macroeconomics is one of the components of the macrosocial level.

It is useful to know at what level any particular matter is rooted in. Of course, there is always an interaction between the three levels. For example, the macrosocial action of a head of State cannot be dissociated from the way he enters into relationship, at the microsocial level, with his counterparts, nor with the experience that he gained whilst functioning within the mezzosocial fabric.

Each of us participates in all three social levels. Whilst it may be easy to understand this in terms of the first two levels, it may be less obvious for the third one (the macrosocial). But everything that we do is part of the overall framework of the macrosocial level, including the macroeconomic, unless one lives in autarky and is stateless. Thus, we can ask ourselves: *"How can I become more cognizant of the macrosocial level, and how can I intervene so that it promotes life on the mezzosocial and microsocial levels? "*.

Today, we often hear the exhortations of the kind: *"transform yourself and the world will change"*. There is nothing wrong with this proposition ... to the extent where such transformation of oneself is not limited to the microsocial level. To work on one's own way of being is, of course, essential. It is a necessary condition. But it is not sufficient. In particular, for the macrosocial level, which needs competence of another kind, requiring knowledge and understanding of phenomena. These capabilities are accessible to all. But one does not acquire them without spending some time for this purpose. Herein lies part of the problem. Because someone who, in addition to personal transformation at the microsocial level, and who is also actively engaged in the mezzosocial level, often finds that all their time is fully occupied.

We are in a vicious circle. The dysfunctions of the macrosocial level generate more and more problems on the other social levels. In an attempt to resolve them, a growing number of people, in addition to their usual work, engage themselves in the activities of Civil Society Organisations (CSOs). They sometimes support several causes, informing themselves, participating in debates, signing petitions, and so on. The life of an engaged activist is time consuming. It does make things progress. At the same time, the macrosocial level, in particular the macroeconomic, generates new problems, or makes existing ones even more difficult to resolve. The complexity of these problems increases, giving the impression that it is inextricable.

To break out of this vicious circle, should we not address the root causes, and thereby give them some time and energy? If a fire continues to wreak havoc, in spite of our efforts, should we not deal with what feeds the flames? In other words, we could go from treating the symptoms to the treatment of the causes.

But the macrosocial level seems inaccessible. For example, how can we intervene in the transformation of the monetary system, in the way described in this book? We would need to change the laws. However, with the exception of Switzerland, the citizen does not have direct access to this domain.

Here we come to the first of all the battles, the one on which all the others depend. In a genuine democracy, the citizen should have the possibility to intervene directly in the domain of law, to propose new ones and to change the old ones, including those that the parliament has adopted.

It is therefore about obtaining a subsistence level of democracy: the right of citizens to legislative initiative, as well as the right of citizens to legislative referendum, which only fully exists in Switzerland. It seems to me that civil society should concentrate on this first objective which, once achieved, would open the doors to real change in the domains of money, financial capital, labour and land-real estate.

Today, societal problems are so numerous, so diverse, that everyone can be caught by the one or another of them, and devote their energy and time trying to alleviate them. This thereby leaves no availability to address the origins of the problems that each one aims to resolve.

The causes to fight for are multiple. They exert a centrifugal force on civil society, which makes it lose sight of the central issues, and allows the installation of a confused dispersion. To gather its energy on a common centre, to concentrate on one goal, is perhaps the current challenge that civil society should take up.

Some will think that this objective should be the preservation of the environment. Then they should ask themselves if the best way to achieve this is to limit ourselves to this battle, or whether it would be better to go back to the cause of all causes, that is to say, to the pollution of the economy, which determines all dysfunctions, of both nature and society.

30

Evolutive implementation

Transformation of the monetary system, such as we have described it, is so deep that it seems difficult to envision it in a single step. This is not because of technical problems that would need to be solved; for example, the reunification of the two Germany or the changeover to the euro were not less complex. Experience shows that from an organisational perspective, such operations are feasible if they are well prepared. The obstacle lies elsewhere. It resides in the resistance to change that is specific to the particular form of our democracies. This can be seen clearly in the way in which the whole system is paralysed in front of reforms that are urgently needed, such as in responding to ecosystem degradation and climate warming.

This is not the place to examine the reasons for this incapacity to change. I have done so in my previous book (Laloux, 2007), and I will deal with this question again in a forthcoming book.

We have a true systemic problem, which we will have to address at some time, by asking ourselves: what would real democracy look like?

However, we are not going to rely on a reformation of democracy, as a prerequisite to any transformation in the economic domain. Preferably, we will look at how solutions could be implemented, in a way that is evolutive, in parallel with what exists, and without having to mobilise resources that are too significant.

Before going into detail, we must introduce an indispensable element: the right to experimentation, which Lucien Pfeiffer wrote about in his book (Pfeiffer, 2006). In observing that delegation by the people to three governance powers: legislative, executive and judicial; might lead to a deadlock of society, Pfeiffer deduced that *"we lack the fourth power, the power to suspend the effect of the other three, when they prevent life to flourish. Thanks to it [the fourth power], we could invent our future, by not making the past sacred in a sclerosing conservatism. But this future must be experimented, so that its development can be observed, before generalising it, and of course in a legal way."*

Two pages later, Lucien Pfeiffer specifies how he sees the realisation of this right to experimentation: *"Imagine that an institution, let us call it for example "General Commission for Experimental Structures", receives the power to suspend the effect of a given law, given decree, given order, given circular, given decision of Justice in favor of an experimentation of new schools, new businesses, new municipalities, new prisons, etc. (...)*

What a fantastic way to invent the future in the legality we would give to ourselves! " (Pfeiffer, 2006. p. 132 & 134).

We will not look at the form proposed to achieve this idea. It proceeds from a trend, particularly in France, to create a Ministry for each social problem that arises. We have thus seen the Ministries of the city, of the family, of the elderly and dependent persons, of the rights of women, of educational success, of the social and solidarity economy and, let us not be afraid of anything, of productive recovery !!!

We believe that it is enough to institutionalise a cause to make it progress. Experience however, shows us that problems are not resolved by creating a new apparatus at the top of the pyramid. With his General Commission for Experimental Structures, Lucien Pfeiffer is trapped by this mirage. One can imagine the bureaucratisation which would result; the meandering dossiers, streaming in synchronisation through several Ministries and departmental directions; without mentioning the opportunities for the lobbies to put a spoke in the wheels.

This experimentation should not be made by a government commission, but by Civil Society Organisations (CSOs), specialized in the field concerned. We have shown in the threefold monetary system, how such a supervision can be self-organised, with guarantees superior to those offered by the centralism of the State. The design of money as a public service, managed by civil society, is perfectly suited to this experimental framework.

In practice, how to incarnate this design?

Imagine, in a given country, that a law was passed giving the possibility to create, on an experimental basis, and under certain conditions, Banks of Purchasing Money, Financing Institutes and Contribution Money Funds (we will examine the modalities for adopting such a law later on). If this law has been voted within the framework of representative democracy, it means that there has been a movement of citizens who have successfully campaigned for it. The citizens will therefore be dynamic in the creation of the above mentioned monetary institutions. They will need to find people with the necessary skills, either in banking practice, or in credit allocation, or in the auditing of such banking practice. Two actions will therefore need to be taken:

1. *Establishing the experimental banking system:*

   In a first step, two monetary institutions would be created, more or less simultaneously: a Bank of Purchasing Money, and a Financing Institute, together with an auditing agency for each one.

   The auditing agencies will be responsible for controlling several institutions of the same type if there were to be created in different regions. Each one would work according to the rules we have described previously.

   Being depositor in a Bank of Purchasing Money implies that one accepts the application of monetary demurrage, which includes the renunciation of interest based revenue on savings. In exchange, a user enjoys the guarantee that their purchasing rights (accounted for as Purchasing Money), will always be preserved, even upon of cessation of the Bank that was providing the monetary accounting service for them. In addition, a user also benefits from interest-free credit allocated by the Financing Institute. The participants in this system will also know that their money will be at the service of the real economy.

Reality will show by itself if such an experimentation corresponds to a need of society. If these monetary institutions develop and see users flock to them, and if their operation is sound, then conclusions can be drawn at the level of the whole of the monetary system. In the contrary case, it will be necessary to look at the reasons, to see if the experimentation must stop, or if it should be modified, or even if it could continue in parallel with the existing system.

The enabling law that was originally voted might determine the duration of experimentation, and the terms of evaluation, of extension or discontinuation.

2. *Funding the operation of the experimental banking system:*

One element will play a crucial role here. It is the mode of financing this experimental monetary system. In this regard, a legal principle must prevail here: granting rights only has meaning if there are the means to exercise those rights. In the domain that concerns us, it is about implementing a new public service of money. These experimental monetary institutions will therefore receive public money to assure their budget (in addition to the operating fees they will charge to users, as we have previously described).

How will this public money be allocated to the experimental monetary institutions? This represents an opportunity to experiment the third type of monetary institution: Contribution Money Funds. These funds would be created to collect the money required for operating the threefold monetary institutional framework of: the Banks of Purchasing Money, the Financing Institutes, as well as of the Contribution Money Funds themselves. The Contribution Money Funds would receive the money of the taxpayers who are in favour of this experimentation. These taxpayers would deduct their contribution to the experimental monetary institutions from their taxes, according to the terms and limits laid down in the experimentation regulations. The rules regarding the disbursement and use of these funds have been described in the Chapter 22, A third form of money: Contribution Money.

This funding by tax exemption will allow the experimentation to demonstrate, by itself, the value attributed to it by the citizens. If many citizens direct a share of their tax contribution towards the operation of these new monetary institutions, they will have the means to exist. This is a more direct way for citizens to express their choices, compared to the election of political party representatives or of a Head of State.

The experimental establishment of these new type of monetary institutions is different from existing parallel monetary systems, such as complementary currencies. The monetary unit of account, will be that of the monetary zone of the country (for example, the Euro for France, the Swiss franc for Switzerland, and so on).

When a user opens an account with a Bank of Purchasing Money, they will be able to transfer to this account, the money recorded on their account with a traditional bank. They will also be given a bank card, so that they can make electronic payments and transfers to any other account in the national or international banking system.

With Information Technology development, a Bank of Purchasing Money would not need to have a branch with bank tellers. But if a Bank of Purchasing Money decides to open a physical branch, and if it offers the possibility of cash withdrawals, then it will need a source of Cash Money instruments. In the experimental phase, it will not be necessary to create the Institute of Cash Money that we have described. The Bank of Purchasing Money will transfer Ledger Money to the Central Bank, in an amount that corresponds to its cash requirement, and will receive the counterparty in the form of banknotes and coins.[103]

Let us remember that the Bank of Purchasing Money offers a service that is limited to registering purchasing rights (deposits in conventional terms), and carry out their transfer. In addition, it does not use the funds (purchasing rights) of depositors (account users) to fund its own operating costs, nor for making investments. There is a complete separation between the Purchasing Money of the depositors (account users) and those of the Bank, which are recorded separately, in an account at another Bank of Purchasing Money. Thus, the requirements for deposit guarantee schemes, and for commercial bank reserves held as Central Bank deposits are irrelevant and redundant. The relations with the Central Bank will be limited to exchanges of Ledger Money against cash and vice versa.

---

103 Translator's note : see also Branchless banking as an alternative solution

In this sense, the Banks of Purchasing Money will not have to follow the rules of the conventional banking system, but those that are in accordance with the inherent rules that we have described in this book.

The same goes for the Financing Institutes. The Basel III accords and the rules of the so-called Liquidity coverage ratio will not apply. The Financing Institutes we propose, will only issue credit to depositors (users) who have an account with a Bank of Purchasing Money, which means that these depositors (users) have thereby chosen not to do business with the virtual economy. All credit issuance will be intended for the *real economy*. The Financing Institutes and Audit agencies will monitor the use of the funds made available.

Therefore, other prudential rules will prevail. We have described them in Chapter 19, *"Future-oriented money"*. We will complete them in Volume 2, when we will deal with Operations Insurance, which will minimise the risk of loans repayment defaults.

We have here described, in broad outline, what would be an evolutive implementation of this new monetary system. In front of the stalemate reached by the current system, in front of new crises which are already looming, in front of the damage caused to the social fabric by speculation, in front of the number of unemployed and poor generated by the pollution of the economy, do citizens have any other choice than to seize the initiative over these questions, and to impose new solutions at the political level, in particular in the monetary domain?

We have another difficulty to surmount : In most countries, citizens have relatively very little means to lobby their political representatives, and to impose the reforms they wish. Representative democracy is organised in such a way that, beyond impotent speeches and in practice, any will of the people for change is diluted, as it meanders through the political system, or is quashed by counter pressures arising within the financialised economy.

The Swiss people have the greatest means for making their voice heard, and to assert their will. They are truly sovereign, because they have the dual right to oppose laws voted by Parliament (right of referendum) and to themselves propose new laws (right of initiative). The Swiss people could therefore initiate a popular vote, to allow an experimentation of a new banking system as proposed in this book. This would be ironic if such a thing happened, in a country that has a banking system so contrary to what we propose. It would certainly pose a great challenge, because the resistance from the incumbent system would be enormous. However, the Swiss people have sometimes been able to impose their will, despite powerful lobbies and resistance within the establishment.

Other countries do not have the same rights of initiative and referendum (or to the same extent), as they exist in Switzerland; which I would endorse as the vital minimum of democracy.

France has, in appearance, such a provision. On the one hand, it is rendered impracticable, because a referendum requires more than four million signatures, plus 20% of the Members of Parliament (without mentioning other barriers). On the other hand, the right of initiative, that is to say the right of citizens directly submit a proposal of law to referendum, is not integrated in the existing provision. In other words, this provision denies the people access to a direct form of democracy.

Therefore, the first reform that the French people should impose is this vital minimum of democracy: the right of direct access to the laws.

It is unlikely that the monetary system changes that we advocate can be implemented by those who benefit from the existing system. On the contrary, it is those who are most excluded, as well as those who disagree with the dysfunctions of the existing system, who will have the will to impose the necessary changes. If we want to accomplish this in a democratic manner, and without revolution, it is essential that the People acquire the basic instruments of real democracy, namely the right of popular legislative initiative and the right of popular legislative referendum. This is the first condition for an evolutive capacity within democracy.

But there is also a second condition: democracy cannot fully exist within a dictatorship of the economy. It is therefore necessary to act on this field by transforming in depth the domain of money, as we have outlined in this first volume. In volume 2, we will also extend this to the domains of financial capital, labour and land-real estate. Once again, we will have to think the unthinkable, and to revolutionise our economic approach, regarding these other domains, so that civil society can ensure their detoxification.

Endnotes

1. (referenced from ch.22 / parag. 33)

   The Multilateral Agreement on Investment (MAI) was secretly negotiated within the twenty-nine member countries of the Organisation of Economic Cooperation and Development (OECD) between 1995 and April 1997. Offering a greater liberalisation of trade (prohibition of discrimination by nationality between investors), it led to strong protests by supporters of Cultural Exception, of environmental protection movements, and by some trade unions when it was disclosed to the public at large by American civil society movements. (Source Wikipedia/fr)

2. (referenced from ch.22 / parag.33)

   The General Agreement on Trade in Services (GATS) constitutes Annex 1B to the Marrakech Agreement establishing the World Trade Organization (WTO) in 1994. It is a multilateral agreement of the liberalisation of trade in services, which according to its proponents, aims to make a more effective use of the means of production by promoting the comparative advantage of the countries concerned, while its critics see a threat for the universality of the public services. (Source Wikipedia/fr)

3. (referenced from ch.25 / parag.27)

In this Volume 1, we only outline the principle of what should be the subject of a thorough study of the formation of prices in *real economy*. By further developing this issue in more detail, we would see the error committed by Adam Smith. His approach to the international division of labour did not integrate four key factors of price formation : wages, working conditions, social benefits, and environmental health. Therefore, he compares things which are not comparable. With these four factors being at the same level across the countries, the specialisation of any of the countries in a production only has meaning when it entails an additional advantage that the other countries cannot achieve. Price formation has to be seen from a new perspective. Here we only indicate a track of work that will be resumed in more detail in Volume 2.

Appendix

Accounting innovation for the separation
of Financing and Purchasing Moneys

A reader familiar with accounting procedures may be surprised by the recording format of accounts proposed in Table 9, which illustrate the loans operations by the Financing Institute. The reader might think that it is too simplistic, and that it could give rise to a problem when it comes to drawing up the final balance for the financial year. We will therefore consider different aspects of this question, as follows:

1. The transformation of the traditional commercial banking model into two separate entities: Banks of Purchasing Money and Financing Institutes, is a veritable monetary revolution. Thus, a transformation in accounting practice would not be extraordinary. Rather than making the accounting practice of these new institutions fit into the mold of traditional practice, it would be wiser to start from the needs of these new entities, and to innovate as necessary, in terms of reliability, readability, and simplicity of use.

2. An essential point must be borne in mind: as is the case for all new monetary institutions described in this book, the accounts of each Financing Institute are divided in two. On one side there are the accounts of Monetary Movements of users and monetary issuance to users by the Financing Institution (User Accounts); whilst on the other side, is the accounting relating to the institution itself, as a corporate entity, with its charges and products (Operating Accounts), as well as its assets and liabilities (Balance sheet). Table 9 concerns the first side (loans from Dujardin, borrowing by Lambda, etc.). The fees that the Lambda enterprise pays for this borrowing (i.e. 5% of 500,000, in total), are paid from Lambda's Current Purchasing Account (CPA), to the CPA of the Financing Institute F, which, as we remember, is located in a Bank of Purchasing Money. The invoicing and settlement of these expenses will be recorded in the Operating Accounts of the Financing Institute F. The User Accounts that record Monetary Movements and Monetary Issuance will not be affected. There is therefore a total separation between User Accounts and Operating Accounts. The User Accounts have an unusual character that makes the financial institution a simple recording chamber, which constrains money to be only an accounting instrument. This also prevents the accounts of users being affected by a possible bankruptcy of the financial institution, as the User Accounts will be transferred to another institution of the same type. So here we have a different kind of accounting, which could justify the use of other innovative techniques.

3. On the left side of Table 9 is the Ledger Money Movements account, which records the counterpart of the transactions on the accounts of lenders and borrowers, from or to a Current Purchasing Account. Its accounting operation is similar to that of the Cash in Bank account as it is recorded in the accounting of a business. It can therefore be *"overdrawn"*, and it will generally be so, since the Financing Institute will, in general, be a net lender. At the end of the financial year, the final balance will therefore be negative. The Ledger Money Movements account will therefore appear not as assets, but as liabilities. In the example of Table 10, the balance sheets for years n and n+1 will thus be as follows:

Description	Year n		Year n+1	
	Assets	Liabilities	Assets	Liabilities
Monetary issuance	480'000		384'000	
Ledger Money movements		480'000		384'000
	480'000	480'000	384'000	384'000

Table 10 - Balance sheets of a Financing Institute for years n and n+1

4. The Monetary Issuance account is an account of debtors, presented in a simplified way. In practice, it would be split into sub-accounts for each borrower, as it is done in the case of the Accounts receivable of a normal business. An extract of the sub-account of the Lambda enterprise would show immediately the situation of the loan, the repayments made, and what must still be repaid.

5. In Table 9, some informed readers will be surprised to see that the balance of the Dujardin Loan Account is zero, and is therefore not included in the balance sheet of Institute F. The Dujardin Loan Account is about the relationship between Dujardin and Lambda, in which Institute F merely serves as an intermediary. The sum of 20,000 appears in the Lambda Financing Account as a debt to Dujardin. This is what happens today if someone lends money to an enterprise, by transfer from their bank account. This operation does not directly concern the Bank. In the event of dispute, Institute F will be able to obtain an extract of Dujardin's account. All operations will have left an audit trail.

   According to the principle of Financing Money, it is normal that the Dujardin Loan Account has returned to zero at the end of the financial year. If Dujardin wanted to lend the 4,000 that Lambda reimbursed him, and if he has not been able to do so before the year-end closing of Institute F's accounts, then this sum would appear in what could be called the *"Loans Awaiting Assignment Account"*, with the balance being shown on the liabilities side.

6. Similarly the Lambda Financing Account has a nil balance, which shows that the accounts are in order. If the enterprise borrows, it means that it is in need of this money. As soon as it is recorded on its account with Institute F, the loaned money is transferred to the Current Purchasing Account of its own bank. In the event of Institute F allocating the loan in several installments, only the amounts actually paid

would be shown in the Lambda Financing Account. However, for the purpose of transparency, Institute F will without doubt resort to an off balance sheet account, which will record the entire loan granted and the installments that have been paid. Once again, we present a principle. The technical details will need to be adapted to the needs of reliability, traceability, transparency and simplicity.

Postscript by the translator

A phenomenological approach
to analysing the economy

Reading this book provides us with *"the opportunity to train ourselves to think about [economic] phenomena, with much more precision than is done usually. We [are] thereby [enabled] to delve into the facts (...)"*, so that *"we will sharpen our ability to look with rigorous attention, at their evolution and their consequences on the overall economy and life of Society."*. (Chapter 4, parag. 9, 20, 21).

The author, Michel Laloux defines this phenomenological approach to analysing the economy, as one where we: *"(...) dive into economic phenomena, enlightening them from the inside, and deducing the operational laws of an Economy of Human Added Value"*.

He advocates that a phenomenological approach to analysing the economy will help us overcome *"the primary cause of the crises we are facing: a deficit of economic thinking, which renders us helpless in front of the steamroller of finance."*. Michel Laloux further states that "*our eyes should become habituated to monitor economic phenomena in a much more precise way, and not to be fooled by (...) a smokescreen*" of unquestioned received and shared conceptualisations, for example conflating tangible monetary accounting instruments (e.g. cash), with money, which he argues is an intangible accounting of purchasing rights (credit), as a claim on past production, to enable discharge in the present, of obligations of production, within a certain future timeframe (debt).

For example, at chapter 18, parag. 29, in dealing with the orthodox concept of "the velocity of money in circulation", the author explains that: "*Economists have their eyes fixed on the circulation of physical money instruments (coins and banknotes). In our example, they would track visually the 1,000 [cash units] transferred from enterprise A, to enterprise B, and then from B to C, and so on. But in terms of velocity of circulation, what counts is not the Cash Money, but the purchases. Our economist eyes should focus on observing the purchasing circuit between enterprises A, B, C, D, E and F. There we can observe a velocity of real circulation, which is a function of the needs of these companies, relative to the offers of available goods and services. It is therefore obvious that our economist eyes should follow the real phenomena of the real economy.*".

Further on at chapter 9, parag. 3-5, and 26-7, the author writes that: "*if we deviate from what is inherent in the real economy, then the economy becomes unbalanced, dysfunctional and diseased. Through its crises, it [the economy] shows us what we have to rectify. One has just to be attentive and to learn to read within the social and economic phenomena what needs to be corrected.". " I would even say that the economy carries its health within itself. Its normal state is to be balanced. If it is not, it means that some foreign elements have been introduced into it, which always prove to be speculative.". " But the disease caused by speculation, which itself becomes included as part of the economy is, with the passage of time, getting more and more costly. The economy always ends up presenting us with the bill. When it is high enough, we decide to take action.". " If we better understand this, we will cease to put moralising but ineffective exhortations, in substitution of our need for a clear approach to economic phenomena. Because, in practice, this so-called ethical vision distracts us from the real issues.". " Wanting to create ethical circuits in parallel to what exists, is not addressing the real causes. It would be more useful and more directly effective to recognize how the economy carries, within itself, fraternity and solidarity. Today it seems to me urgent that we do not fight the wrong battle.".*

At chapter 14, parag. 4, Michel Laloux warns that: "*It will always be possible to say that all evil comes from the incompetence of experts serving the voracious appetite of unscrupulous financiers. Unfortunately, such remarks only show that we are mired in second-tier phenomena. We need to go back a notch and see that the problem is first of all monetary, and that it concerns all countries. We will describe this monetary problem in broad outline, and then see how it would be resolved in the Economy of Human Added Value.".*

And finally at chapter 18, he concludes that: "*It is about entering into these phenomena and revealing them.*". "*Anyone who would address what we have just presented without linking it to concrete facts, that is to say to the real economy, could say we "quibble" on questions of detail. But that is what is precisely lacking in the actual theories that led to the present state of disaster capitalism. What is required now is this ability to track economic phenomena in their reality, in detail, and to follow them through to their economic, social, environmental and cultural consequences.*".

Raymond Aitken

Translator's Glossary

Cash Money

Cash Money is a physical monetary instrument, comprising banknotes and coins, which circulates counter-wise to the circulation of goods and services in the economy. Cash Money (otherwise known as "*cash*"), is not in itself money, but a monetary instrument, which carries information about the monetised purchasing rights that have been transferred to it from the centralised ledger money account, so that these purchasing rights can circulate "off-ledger", to account for the exchange of goods and services in a decentralised way. It therefore represents a complementary accounting function to ledger money transfers between bank accounts.

See this Glossary: Currency vs Money; Foreign Currency; Ledger Money.

See chapter 13: *The Institute of Cash Money.*

Circulation of money

In chapter 18, parag. 43; the author makes a very important statement concerning "circulation": **"It is**

not money that circulates. In the real economy it is goods and services that are circulating.". And at chapter 7, parag. 15, the author confirms that: **"In reality, only commodities are circulated. Money's function is to enable the circulation of commodities**, *through an exchange process based on a disconnection between the sale and the purchase; in space, in time, and between people.*".

Again in chapter 18, parag. 29, the author observes that: *"Economists have their eyes fixed on the circulation of physical money instruments (coins and banknotes). In our example, they would track visually the 1,000 [cash units] transferred from enterprise A, to enterprise B, and then from B to C, and so on. But in terms of velocity of circulation, what counts is not the Cash Money, but the purchases. Our economist eyes should focus on observing the purchasing circuit between enterprises A, B, C, D, E and F. There we can observe a velocity of real circulation, which is a function of the needs of these companies, relative to the offers of available goods and services. It is therefore obvious that our economist eyes should follow the real phenomena of the real economy.*".

It is important for the reader to bear in mind these important statements by the author regarding the use and meaning of the word "circulation". Especially so when this same word is used elsewhere in this book, in terms of the "circulation of money" (not goods). With advances in information technology, payments can be made today in real time electronically, so that *"there is no room for misunderstanding the nature of money,* because **there is no thing to be held and handed over to someone else as a means of payment.".** That is to say there is **nothing to "circulate"**. *"There are only accounts inside the (imagined) digital social balance sheet.* **Any change in one account must have its exact balancing changes in one or more other accounts**. *All that occurs is transfer of rights."* (Moini 2001).

See: Currency.

See also: Postscript by the translator: A phenomenological approach to analysing the economy.

Commercial and noncommercial circuits of the economy

The commercial circuit of the economy, is the circuit that generates the economic surplus, through private sector agents, whose output in terms of goods and services are exchanged on a for-profit basis (i.e. above the direct costs of production). This activity by private sector producers within the commercial circuit, can only exist posterior to the anterior existence of the commonwealth of natural and cultural factors of production (i.e. the resources that pre-existed these private sector producers, or which they did not themselves create).

The noncommercial circuit of the economy, is the circuit that regenerates the pre-existing commonwealth of natural and cultural factors of production, upon which the surplus generating activities of the commercial circuit depend. The original French book used the terms "merchant" and "non-merchant" circuits of the economy.

Commonwealth goods and services are produced and exchanged on a not-for-profit basis, by public sector agents, comprising two main categories: (1) the State, and (2) Civil Society Organisations (CSOs); also known as the "Third Sector". With regard to the provision of public services in the tertiary sector of the economy, two noncommercial sub-circuits have also been defined: (i) the sub-circuit of Law and (ii) the sub-circuit of Culture (ch.22, parag. 23).

In order to transcend the inherently mutually corruptive bilateral relationship between the State (in the domain of governance), and financial agents (in the domain of economy); this book proposes that public services provided by the State be limited to the noncommercial sub-circuit of convening and upholding the Law, especially through the monopolistic provision of human rights protection, both internally (police service), and externally (the military). All other commonwealth goods and services being produced in the noncommercial circuit by Civil Society Organisations (CSOs); including in the noncommercial sub-circuit of Culture, for example: education, research and development, cultural development and activities, healthcare, social welfare; in addition to non-cultural goods and services such as: the construction and operation of infrastructures for: transportation and communication, waste treatment and recycling, water supply, and so on.

Taxation has been the traditional means of transferring purchasing power from the surplus generating commercial circuit in order to fund the noncommercial circuit on which its existence and continuance depends. This is one of the reasons and justifications for private sector producers in the commercial circuit to exchange their output on a for-profit basis. The evidence of experience, both past and present, shows that the traditional mechanism of taxation has been thoroughly circumvented and discredited by economically powerful agents, to the detriment of the institutional integrity of the State, including the systemic corruption of the process of democracy.

Therefore this book advocates for the vital transfer of purchasing power, from the commercial circuit to the noncommercial circuit, to be embedded within the proposed architecture of a threefold monetary accounting system. It is proposed that excess economic surplus in the commercial circuit, represented by accumulated purchasing power in the Purchasing Money Bank accounts of commercial circuit producers, be transferred via monetary demurrage (and other means), to Contribution Money Funds. It is envisaged that this will maintain the liquidity function of the monetary system, remove the flow of accumulated purchasing power towards speculative purposes, and assure the funding for the vital production of commonwealth goods and services.

Conversion rate vs. exchange rate

Regarding the often used term of an *"exchange rates between currencies"*, we have chosen to use the alternative form of a *"conversion rate between monetary units"*. From the perspective of money, not as a commodity to be exchanged in the financial market, but as a purchasing right that is accounted for on the basis of a unit of account, there cannot be *"exchange"* between different monetary units, only *"conversion"* (as is the case with other units of measurement).

See: Monetary units vs. currency; Currency.

Currency

The use of the term *"currency"* or *"currencies"*, especially in the context of international trade, is highly problematic. It creates a veil of obfuscation over the fallacious fusion between the two conflicting paradigms of money: (i) the paradigm of money as a fungible commodity, which can be traded for other commodities, and (ii) the paradigm of money as a unit of account, inscribed as a ledger entry, for the accounting of monetary rights and obligations. The word *"currency"* is derived from *"current"*, meaning to flow, which alludes to physical coins and banknotes, which flow counterwise to the circulation of goods and services during the exchange process.

See: Monetary units vs. currency; Conversion vs. exchange; Ledger money.

Currency vs Money

The terms *"currency"* and *"money"* are usually used as if they were synonyms of one another. They actually refer to two co-existing forms of economic accountancy: by physical circulating tokens (currency, cash, coins, banknotes, vault money etc); or by bookkeeping (bank deposits, ledger money, scriptural money, credit etc). Monetary units of account can be transferred between these two economic accounting systems, one being a centralised ledger (bank accounts), and the other being a decentralised *"off-ledger"* P2P analogue-computing device (currency). For clarity, we will preferably use the term *"money"*, in the sense of a unit of account that measures purchasing power, whether in the form of physical tokens (currency), or ledger entries (monetised credit).

See: Ledger money.

Demurrage

Monetary Demurrage is usually considered to be a "liquidity tax", or "negative interest" that penalises the accumulation of money. In this book it is proposed, not so much as a penalty, but as a necessary mechanism to ensure that the economic surplus, represented by accumulated Purchasing Money, is transferred for spending in the noncommercial circuit of the economy, in order to regenerate the commonwealth factors of production, including the environment (waste treatment and recycling), human culture (through education and research), as well as for humane solidarity purposes.

See chapter 11: *Monetary Demurrage*; and chapter 22: *A third form of money: Contribution Money.*

Deposits

The term bank *"deposits"* and its derivatives are problematic, because it is rooted in the commodity money paradigm, where a monetary commodity is *"deposited"*, by *"depositors"*, for safekeeping in the vault of a bank. Deposits can therefore be redefined as "registered purchasing rights", which is coherent with the advocated paradigm of money being the accounting of purchasing rights backed by production obligations; therefore monetary rights (as purchasing power) are "registered" in bank accounts, not "deposited".

Ledger money or bank money, scriptural money, or demand deposits; are synonymous terms for funds held in demand deposit accounts in commercial banks.

See: Depositors vs. Users; Ledger money.

Depositors vs. Users

We use the term *"Users"* instead of the usual anachronistic one of *"Depositors"*, which is rooted in the paradigm of money being a physical commodity that was deposited with a bank, instead of the correct paradigm of money being an accounting entry representing purchasing rights. Therefore in the paradigm of money as purchasing rights conditional to real production obligations, depositors can be redefined as "users" of the public service of a social accounting system, which underlies the function of banking (See: Additional Bibliography; Bezemer, 2009) and (Additional Bibliography; Stiglitz and Weiss, 1988). This concept of "banks as social accountants" is in line with the author's assertion that "money becomes accountancy, which, if maintained with rigor, is as reliable as the bookkeeping of a firm." (ch.13, parag. 5).

See: Deposits; Ledger money.

Economy of Human Added Value

This means an economy where economic value is created, as a result of human activity that adds value to existing natural and cultural resources. Unlike in the *unreal economy* of financial markets, speculative practice does not exist in an *Economy of Human Added Value*. ch.8, parag. 3, 4.

"... an economy designed and organized for the human being" ch.3, parag. 10.

"... an economy based on the production, distribution and consumption of real goods and services." ch.28, parag. A1.

See: Speculation, *unreal economy.*

See chapter 8: The creation of value.

Hot money

In economics, hot money is the flow of funds (or capital) from one country to another in order to earn a short-term profit on interest rate differences and/or anticipated exchange rate shifts. These speculative capital flows are called 'hot money' because they can move very quickly in and out of markets, potentially leading to market instability. Source: https://en.wikipedia.org/wiki/Hot_money.

Ledger Money

The original French text uses the term "monnaie scripturale", meaning "written money". Although the term "scriptural money" exists in English, it is so little used that the English connotation of the "sacred or religious" dominates. We have therefore chosen the more frequently used term of "ledger money", which provides the additional connotation of money as an instrument of economic accountancy.

See: Cash Money; Monetary units vs. currency; Foreign Currency.

Monetary units vs. currency

Currency is derived from Latin and Middle English words for "current" and "circulation"; which was used to describe the circulation of monetary instruments (coins) as an off-ledger decentralised P2P accounting device. Currency belongs to the paradigm of money as a fungible commodity with intrinsic value, which is negotiable (variable) in money/financial markets (e.g. FOREX), and thereby untenable as an objective independent measure of value, to facilitate the exchange of real goods and services, across the boundaries of time, place and person.

Monetary units mean the agreed objective unit of account to measure economic value, for the purpose of reciprocity, in the extension of credit as purchasing rights backed by production obligations, thereby functioning as a means of intermediate settlement, between holders of past produced commodities, and those presently engaged in the production of new commodities.

See: Currency; Conversion vs. exchange.

Speculation

Speculation is the buying of something, and the selling of it at a higher price, without having added any value to it through one's own activity.

See: ch.7, parag. 18; ch.8, parag.14 and *unreal economy.*

Unreal economy

The translation of original French "économie *virtuelle*" or "*sphère virtuelle*" would be translated into English as the "virtual economy", which in English is predominantly associated with *"an emergent economy existing in a virtual persistent world, usually exchanging virtual goods in the context of an Internet game."* (Source: Wikipedia). In the French version of the book, "économie *virtuelle"* refers to the practice of financialization. Therefore we had to coin the term *"unreal economy"* for the French term "économie *virtuelle"*, especially in distinction to the *"Real economy"*.

See: Speculation.

Users   See: Depositors vs users.

Value of money

The concept of money having value, as in the expression "value of the Euro", belongs to the fallacious paradigm of money as a commodity, wherein the unit of measure is itself a commodity, measured by itself, so that the monetary unit of account (the Euro), erroneously gains an intrinsic value, independent of the real economic goods and services that it is supposed to measure, which thereby renders its function as a unit of account untenable, since its supposed intrinsic value is negotiable (variable), as a commodity within financial markets.

In the paradigm of money as a means of intermediate settlement, which accounts for production obligations and the exchange of real commodities in the *real economy*, money has no intrinsic value, but is merely an accounting device that registers the allocation and transfer of purchasing rights backed by production obligations, which are discharged and cancelled upon final settlement in real goods and services.

References

▷ Blanton, T. and Kornbluh, P. (no date) *Prisoner abuse: Patterns from the past*. Available at: http://nsarchive. gwu.edu/NSAEBB/NSAEBB122/ (Accessed: 22 February 2016).

▷ CIA interrogation manual: KUBARK Counterintelligence Interrogation - July 1963

▷ Creutz, H. (2010) *The money syndrome*. Upfront Publishing.

▷ Derudder, P. (2005) *Rendre la création monétaire à la société civile: Vers une économie au service de l'homme et de la planète*. France: Editions Yves Michel.

▷ *Discontinuance of M3* (2005) Federal Reserve Statistical Release, H.6 Money Stock Measures. Available at: http://www.federalreserve.gov/releases/h6/discm3. htm (Accessed: 13 March 2016).

▷ Duboin, M.-L. (2007) *Mais où va l'argent ?*. France: Editions du Sextant.

▷ Frankel, J. (1999) 'Soros' split personality: Scanty proposals from the financial wizard', *Foreign Affairs*, 78(2).

▷ Gesell, S. (1916) *The natural economic order*. Available at: https://archive.org/details/TheNaturalEconomicOrder (Accessed: 8 March 2016).

▷ *Give our States some room to breathe* (2012) Available at: http://roosevelt2012.com/public/proposal1-Roosevelt2012_en.pdf (Accessed: 12 March 2016).

▷ Halimi, S. (2008) Penser l'impensable. *Le Monde diplomatique*. Available at: https://www.monde-diplomatique.fr/2008/11/HALIMI/16446 (Accessed: 26 February 2016).

▷ Hessel, S. (2011) *Time for outrage: Indignez-vous!*. Quartet Books.

▷ Holbecq, A.-J. and Derudder, P. (2008) *La dette publique, une affaire rentable*. Editions Yves Michel.

▷ Kalinowski, W. (2011) *Currency pluralism and economic stability: The Swiss experience*. Available at: http://www.veblen-institute.org/IMG/pdf/currency_pluralism_and_economic_stability_eng_oct_2011_.pdf (Accessed: 14 March 2016).

▷ Kireyev, A. (2017) *The Macroeconomics of De-Cashing, IMF Working Paper*. Available at : https://www.imf.org/en/Publications/WP/Issues/2017/03/27/The-Macroeconomics-of-De-Cashing-44768 (Accessed: 5 January 2018)

▷ Klein, N. (2008) *The shock doctrine: The rise of disaster capitalism*. Picador.

▷ Laloux, M. (2007) *La démocratie évolutive : Restituer la démocratie à la société civile*. Editions Yves Michel.

▷ Matherat, S. and Mongars, P. (eds.) (2010) *FINANCIAL CRISIS, ECONOMIC CRISIS*.

▷ Banque de France, Documents and Debates, No.3, January 2010. Available at: https://www.banque-france.fr/fileadmin/user_upload/banque_de_france/publications/financial-crisis-economic-crisis-documents-and-debates-n3.pdf (Accessed: 12 March 2016).

▷ Narassiguin, P. (1993) *L'unification monétaire européenne*. Economica.

▷ Pfeiffer, L. (2006) *La fin du capitalisme… Et après ?*. Editions Yves Michel.

▷ Rocard, M. and Larrouturou, P. (2012) *Pourquoi faut-il que les Etats payent 600 fois plus que les banques ?*. Available at: http://www.lemonde.fr/idees/article/2012/01/02/pourquoi-faut-il-que-les-etats-payent-600-fois-plus-que-les-banques_1624815_3232.html (Accessed: 12 March 2016).

▷ Rufin, J.-C. (1994) *La Dictature libérale*. Jean-Claude Lattès.

▷ Sankara, T. (1987) 'Speech of Burkina Faso President Thomas Sankara', English translation published by CADTM (2011): http://www.cadtm.org/A-United-Front-Against-the-Debt (Accessed: 15 may 2017)

▷ Soros, G. (1998a) *The crisis of global capitalism: Open society endangered*. PublicAffairs.

▷ Soros, G. (1998b) *Toward a global open society*. Available at: http://www.theatlantic.com/past/docs/issues/98jan/opensoc.htm (Accessed: 28 February 2016).

▷ Steiner, R. (2013) *Rethinking economics: Lectures and seminars on world economics (collected works of Rudolf Steiner)*. Steiner Books.

▷ Stern, N. (2006) *Stern Review on the Economics of Climate Change*. Available at: http://mudancasclimaticas.cptec.inpe.br/~rmclima/pdfs/destaques/stern-review_report_complete.pdf (Accessed: 29 February 2016).

▷ Tocqueville (de), A. (1840) *De La Démocratie en Amérique (Democracy in America)*. Available at: http://xroads.virginia.edu/~hyper/detoc/toc_indx.html (Accessed: 16 March 2016).

▷ Toussaint, E. (2005) *Your money or your life: The tyranny of global finance*. Haymarket Books.

▷ Toussaint, E. and Millet, D. (2010) *Debt, the IMF, and the world bank: Sixty questions, Sixty answers*. Available at: http://monthlyreview.org/product/debt_the_imf_and_the_world_bank/ (Accessed: 12 March 2016).

▷ *Treaty of Lisbon* amending the Treaty on European Union and the Treaty establishing the European Community, (2007), signed at Lisbon, 13 December 2007. Official Journal of the European Union, 50(C 306). Available at: http://eur-lex.europa.eu/legal-content/EN/TXT/PDF/?uri=OJ:C:2007:306:FULL&from=EN (Accessed: 15 March 2016).

▷ *Treaty of Maastricht on European Union* (1993). Signed in Maastricht on 7 February 1992, entered into force on 1 November 1993. Available at: http://eur-lex.europa.eu/legal-content/EN/TXT/HTML/?uri=URISERV:xy0026&from=EN (Accessed: 15 March 2016).

Additional bibliography
by the translator

▷ Bendell, J. and Slater, M. (2015) *Money and Society MOOC: Lesson 1 - Introduction to money: functions, forms and fallacies*. Available at: www.iflas.info .

▷ Bezemer, D.J. (2009) *Banks As Social Accountants: Credit and Crisis Through an Accounting Lens*. Available at: https://mpra.ub.uni-muenchen.de/15766/1/MPRA_paper_15766.pdf (Accessed: 22 March 2016).

▷ Brown, E. (2013) *It can happen here: The bank confiscation scheme for US and UK depositors*. Available at: http://www.washingtonsblog.com/2013/03/it-can-happen-here-the-bank-confiscation-scheme-for-us-and-uk-depositors.html (Accessed: 11 March 2016).

▷ Flomenhoft, G. (2016) 'Escaping the Polanyi matrix: The impact of fictitious commodities: Money, land, and labor on consumer welfare', *real-world economics review*, (74). Available at: http://www.paecon.net/PAEReview/issue74/Flomenhoft74.pdf.

▷ Graeber, D. (2011) *Debt: The First 5000 Years*. Melville House. Chapter Two, "The Myth of Barter", p. 40.

▷ Häring, N. (2013) 'The veil of deception over money: How central bankers and textbooks distort the nature of banking and central banking', *real-world economics review*, (63). Available at: http://www.paecon.net/PAEReview/issue63/Haring63.pdf.

▷ Henderson, D. (2012) *An answer to a monetary riddle*. Available at: http://econlog.econlib.org/archives/2012/01/an_answer_to_a.html (Accessed: 26 February 2016). Library of economics and liberty.

▷ Hossein-Zadeh, I. (2014) *Financial bubble Implosions. Asset price inflation and social inequality*. Available at: http://www.globalresearch.ca/financial-bubble-implosions-asset-price-inflation-and-social-inequality/5389535 (Accessed: 8 April 2016).

▷ *How central banks create money* (no date). Positive Money Available at: http://positivemoney.org/how-money-works/advanced/how-central-banks-create-money/ (Accessed: 12 March 2016).

▷ Hudson, M (2013) *The Insider's Economic Dictionary* Available at: http://michael-hudson.com/2013/07/the-insiders-economicdictionary-part-a/ (Accessed: 14 March 2016).

▷ King, M. (1999) 'Challenges for monetary policy: New and old - speech by Mervyn King, deputy governor', *Bank of England*. pp. 25-26. Available at: http://www.bankofengland.co.uk/archive/Documents/historic-pubs/speeches/1999/speech51.pdf.

▷ Kocherlakota, N. (1998) 'The technological role of fiat money', *Federal reserve bank of Minneapolis Quarterly Review*, 22(3), p. 10, concluding paragraph. Available at: https://www.minneapolisfed.org/research/qr/qr2231.pdf.

▷ Kuttner, R. (1992) *The end of Laissez-Faire: National purpose and the global economy after the cold war.* University of Pennsylvania Press.

▷ Leftly, M. (2011) *Banks to separate savings and investments in system overhaul.* Available at: http://www.independent.co.uk/news/business/news/banks-to-separate-savings-and-investments-in-system-overhaul-2265866.html (Accessed: 27 February 2016).

▷ Thomas Robert Malthus, (1827), *Definitions in Political Economy.* Available at: https://archive.org/details/definitionsinpo02maltgoog (Accessed: 22 March 2016).

▷ Moini, M. (2001) *Toward a general theory of credit and money.* Available at: https://is.muni.cz/el/1456/podzim2007/PETMI/Moini__2001_.pdf (Accessed: 6 April 2016).

▷ Preparata, G.G. (2003) *Perishable money in a threefold commonwealth: Rudolf Steiner and the economics of German Anarchism.* Available at: http://www.tripartizione.it/articoli/GGPreparata_Perishable_Money_in_a_Threefold_Commonwealth.pdf (Accessed: 8 March 2016). Presented at the World Conference of The International Confederation of Associations for Pluralism in Economics (ICAPE) by The Future of Heterodox Economics, University of Missouri at Kansas City, USA, 5 - 7 June 2003.

▷ Smaghi, L.B. (2009) *Conventional and unconventional monetary policy.* Available at: https://www.ecb.europa.eu/press/key/date/2009/html/sp090428.en.html (Accessed: 19 March 2016). Member of the Executive

Board of the European Central Bank, keynote lecture at the International Center for Monetary and Banking Studies (ICMB). Published by the European Central Bank (ECB).

▷ Stiglitz, J.E. and Weiss, A. (1988) *Banks as social accountants and screening devices for the allocation of credit*. Available at: http://www.nber.org/papers/w2710.pdf (Accessed: 22 March 2016).

Index of Diagrams and Tables

DIAGRAMS

TABLES

Abbreviations, acronyms & symbols used

1. Standard acronyms and abbreviations

B2B   Business to Business

CSO   Civil Society Organisation

ECB   European Central Bank

EU   European Union

Fed   Federal Reserve System (the central banking system of the United States)

GATS   General Agreement on Trade in Services

GDP   Gross Domestic Product

GMO   Genetically Modified Organism

IMF   International Monetary Fund

IMS   International Monetary System

MAI   Multilateral Agreement on Investment

OECD   Organisation for Economic Co-operation and Development

QE   Quantitative Easing

QMS   Quality Management System

SAPs   Structural Adjustment Programmes

SDR   Special Drawing Right

TNC   Transnational corporation

VAT   Value-added tax

WTO   World Trade Organization

2. Created acronyms and abbreviations for this book

CP Account / CPA   Current Purchasing Account

DP Account / DPA   Deferred Purchasing Account

reIMS   *Real Economy International Monetary System*

Acknowledgements

In an invisible way, a book is a collective work, even though the only name shown on its cover might be that of one author. If I would say to a student or seminar participant: "Your question has put me on the right track", they would certainly be astonished. However, most of the concepts developed in this book emerged from questions raised by participants in my courses, many of whom may not be aware of their great service. Certainly I had to reflect at length, in order to develop new concepts spurred by their questions. But the point of departure was always born from this living exchange within a group. Therefore, I firstly want to acknowledge all those students and seminar participants, who without knowing it, have been my real trainers in the subject of economy.

I also want to acknowledge Raymond Aitken for his work of extreme precision, in always seeking the best word, turn of phrase or idiom in English, to express the essential meaning of my original French text. In many other ways, his contribution to this English edition of my book, went well beyond what is usually required of a translator.

I warmly thank him as well as his wife, Hermine Aitken, who not only did a tremendous job in preparing a first draft translation for Raymond to work on, but simultaneously performed a rigorous proof reading of my original French, never letting go of any imperfections of language that still remained in the original. Hermine died of a terminal illness before this book was published. However, even though she lacked her usual energy, and was in pain, she made an excellent pre-publication proofreading of this book. Hermine made this effort because she felt it was very important that the ideas in this book should be disseminated in English. I am deeply grateful for her generous contribution.

This work of translation has also been made possible thanks to donations by Françoise G., Christine and Stéphane L., Marie-Pierre L., Elizabeth and Georges Q., Vincent M. and Stéphane D. I heartily thank each one for their sponsorship of this translation, which by auspicious coincidence resembles one of the key concepts of this book: "Contribution money"!